HISTORICAL ATLAS OF THE CLASSICAL WORLD

500 BC
AD 600

JOHN HAYWOOD

with

CHARLES FREEMAN
PAUL GARWOOD
JUDITH TOMS

BARNES
&NOBLE
BOOKS
NEW YORK

Project director	Peter Furtado
Cartographic manager	Richard Watts
Advisory editors	Jeremy Black

Advisory editors Jeremy Black
Professor of History, University of Exeter, UK

K.M. Chaudhuri
Vasco da Gama Professor of European Exploration, European University Institute, Florence, Italy

Barry Cunliffe
Professor of European Archaeology, University of Oxford, UK

Brian M. Fagan
Professor of Anthropology, University of California, Santa Barbara, USA

J.E. Spence
Associate Fellow, Royal Institute of International Affairs, UK

Academic advisors J.I. Catto
Oriel College, University of Oxford, UK

Professor Robin Cohen
University of Warwick, UK

Professor J.H. Elliott
Regius Professor of Modern History, University of Oxford, UK

Professor Harold James
Princeton University, New Jersey, USA

Professor Maldwyn A. Jones
University of London, UK

Dr Stuart Kewley
University of Cambridge, UK

Dr Stewart Lone
Australian Defence Force Academy

Dr Oswyn Murray
Balliol College, University of Oxford, UK

Professor A.J.S. Reid
The Australian National University

Professor Francis Robinson
Royal Holloway, University of London, UK

Professor John K. Thornton
Millersville University, Pennsylvania, USA

This page:
Silver coins from Athens, c.450 BC

Opposite above left:
Roman merchant ship, c.100 AD

Opposite right :
Mosaic of the emperor Justinian, c.550 AD

Opposite below left:
Chinese bronze horseman, c.100 AD

Following page:
Sasanian silver bowl with hunt scene, c.480 AD

Art director	Ayala Kingsley
Art editor	Martin Anderson
Cartographic editor	Tim Williams
Editors	Susan Kennedy
	Peter Lewis
(Encyclopedic dictionary)	BCS Publishing
Cartographer	Nathalie Johns
Picture research	Claire Turner
Production	Clive Sparling
Editorial assistance	Marian Dreier
Typesetter	Brian Blackmore
Illustrations	Charles Raymond
Proof reader	Lynne Elson
Index	Ann Barrett

AN ANDROMEDA BOOK

Produced and prepared by
Andromeda Oxford Ltd
11–15 The Vineyard
Abingdon
Oxfordshire OX14 3PX

© 1998 Andromeda Oxford Ltd

This edition published by Barnes & Noble, Inc.,
by arrangement with Andromeda Oxford Ltd

2002 Barnes & Noble Books

ISBN 0-7607-1973-X *casebound*
ISBN 0-7607-1974-8 *trade paperback*

Printed and bound in Spain by
Graficromo S.A., Córdoba

00 01 02 03 04 MC 9 8 7 6 5 4 3 2
00 01 02 03 04 MT 9 8 7 6 5 4 3 2

Contents

INTRODUCTION

In the thirty generations between 500 BC and AD 600, populations increased across the globe; states with complex systems of social and economic control emerged; food production intensified, allowing artists, architects, poets and thinkers to develop their skills. All the major religions, with the exception of Islam, took root.

Amidst the vivid mass of detail, certain themes recur. In certain areas, favored by their access to natural resources and their position astride trade routes, centers of social or economic innovation sprang up. Powerful chiefs often commanded discrete territories. They copied and competed with one another, often acquiring prestige goods for display, in life and on death, for others to wonder at. Conspicuous consumption and ritual destruction of luxuries by burying them with chieftains meant that ever more prestige goods were needed. This gave momentum to trade and, sometimes, to warfare.

In some areas chiefdoms were transformed into states through a complex phase of warfare and social reordering. Thus the Mycenaean chiefdoms of the late second millennium BC became the young city-states of Greece two centuries later. On the other side of the world in about 500 BC, in the Oaxaca valley of Mesoamerica, three competing chiefdoms came together to found a new political capital on the mountain-top of Monte Albán; it remained preeminent for over one thousand years. The unification of rival polities under a single authority was seen throughout the world. In 408 BC, a century after the foundation of Monte Albán, three rival Greek cities on the island of Rhodes agreed to found the city of Rhodes.

A dynamic relationship arose between these innovating centers and the peripheries around them. A complex state needed raw materials and human power to maintain it. A regular supply of rare metals, exotic stones and woods, furs and fabrics was essential to support the structure of the social hierarchy, while human power, in the form of slaves or a supply of food for a free workforce, was needed to support the state's bureaucrats, soldiers, priests or scholars. The demands of centralizing powers thus encouraged trade with the surrounding peripheries. African and Indian communities were drawn into the economic sphere of the Roman empire, despite knowing little of the state that gave them pottery, coins and trinkets in return for raw materials and slaves. Communities closer to the centers were in a better position to learn from their neighbors and imitate them.

There was a continual drift of creative energy from the center to the periphery, as the seeds of innovation took root in the fertile periphery while the core decayed. The early core of Europe developed in the Greek cities around the Aegean; later, the focus for innovation was on the Greek mainland. Power then shifted to the central Mediterranean, where Rome emerged preeminent. Six centuries later, power moved to the peripheral Black Sea region, with the rise of Constantinople and the Byzantine empire. In Mesoamerica the same pattern can be seen, in the spread of power from the Oaxaca Valley to the Valley of Mexico and then the Maya area of the Yucatán.

The cycle of growth and decay and the inexorable shift of centers of power were accelerated by warfare and invasion. The Celtic tribes who attacked the Greco-Roman world in the fourth and third centuries BC confronted energetic states well able to defend themselves; but the Germanic peoples who attacked around AD 400 found the Roman empire in a state of decay. They rapidly overran Rome and set up a number of new kingdoms within the carcass of the old empire.

The collapse of empires is a common theme in this period, and a fascinating subject. Each case is different and the reasons are always complex: natural catastrophy, population decline, economic over-extension, invasion, disease. In prehistoric Mesoamerica, archeologists speculate about "ecological over-shoot" and the destructive role of parasitic elites; whereas in China, detailed written records show what caused the collapse of the Han empire – foreign wars, internal power struggles and peasant revolts as the empire split into rival warlords' factions.

Yet it is possible to turn the notions of center and periphery inside out and to see the states and empires of Europe, India and China not as centers but as developments on the periphery of the huge, central landmass of Asia – an unending steppe land, home of horse-riding nomads who for centuries moved out to strike terror into the hearts of their sedentary, civilized neighbors. In Europe the first recorded invaders were the Cimmerians, around 700 BC. Then followed the Scythians, the Sarmatians, the Alans and the Huns, the last contributing to the chaos at the end of the Roman era. Other groups moved into India, while the northern borders of China were constantly at risk – a threat which the Great Wall was eventually designed to avert. The history of Old World civilization was intimately bound up with population pressures on the Eurasian steppes.

During the millennium 500 BC–AD 600, many foundations of the modern world were laid. Pyrotechnical skills developed, bronze and iron became widely available throughout the Old World, and steel was made in Han China. The powers of wind and water were harnessed; horse-riding was transformed by the development of the stirrup; and science, astronomy and mathematics made enormous strides in the Hellenistic world, India, China and Mesoamerica. By AD 600 a plateau had been reached. There was to be little further advance until the fifteenth century, when the arts of navigation and seamanship opened up the world ▪

USING THIS ATLAS

This atlas is part of a six-volume chronological set covering the Ancient (1), Classical (2), Medieval (3), Early Modern (4), 19th Century (5), and Modern (6) worlds. To help the user pinpoint straight away which era any particular map relates to, pages are numbered first by volume, and then by 2-page spread within that volume. Thus, map spread 14 in volume 2 is identified by the page number 2.14.

World map spreads outline global history on the date shown. Different typographical categories (see table opposite) denote different kinds of political or social entity. The text on these spreads includes many cross-references to other relevant spreads. The timelines here are organized by region.

Regional map spreads cover a part of the world over a specific period. Maps for a continent or major region are grouped in a section, named in the heading on the right-hand side of the spread. These sections also appear in the Contents page.

Maps are shown in true cartographic projections. North is generally at the top of the page. Some distortion is evident in those maps that cover huge areas of the world (e.g. Asia). Where necessary location maps have been included.

Each regional map has certain standard features: thick grey lines denote major borders, thin grey lines internal borders. Campaigns or journeys are shown by lines with arrowheads; thicker grey arrows are used for mass movements of people. Trade routes are thinner lines, with arrowheads when the trade is one-way. All map-key items are referred to in text. The main text explains and amplifies the information on the map.

The timelines on regional maps are arranged in geographical or thematic sections. Civilizations, cultures, and dynasties are shown with colored bands; broad historical phases (such as "Bronze Age") are indicated with grey bands. Every regional map also has several numbered "pointers", whose captions offer further historical detail on the places marked. Finally, the panel bottom right cross-refers to other spreads with related information, listing their numbers and themes.

A substantial encyclopedic section at the end of the book contains an A–Z guide to the people, places, and events of the period. It is cross-referenced both within the section and to the information that appears on the map spreads.

The index provides detailed references to the text, timelines, pointer captions and map keys. Space constraints have precluded indexing every location on the maps themselves.

TYPOGRAPHICAL CONVENTIONS	
World maps	
FRANCE	state or empire
Belgian Congo	dependency or territory
Mongols	tribe, chiefdom or people
Anasazi culture	cultural group
Regional maps	
HUNGARY	state or empire
Bohemia	dependency or territory
Slavs	tribe, chiefdom or people
ANATOLIA	geographical region
✗	battle
•	site or town

In 500 BC the world's most impressive state was the Achemenid empire of Persia, extending from Libya to the Indus. The empire's first setback occurred when Xerxes I invaded Greece (▷2.07). The quarrelsome Greek city-states united in the face of the common enemy and defeated the Persians at sea at Salamis and on land at Plataea. The Greeks went back to their quarrels and did little to follow up their victory: Persia lost its foothold in Europe but continued to dominate the Middle East for eighty years (▷2.11). Then, in 404, Egypt rebelled and Persian control was not restored until 343. In 380 Persia's Indian provinces were lost.

Late 5th-century Greece was dominated by rivalry between Sparta and Athens, culminating in the Peloponnesian war which engulfed most of the Greek world but settled nothing. Further indecisive wars between shifting alliances ensued. Meanwhile, the Balkan kingdom of Macedon rose unopposed under Philip II and in 338 all the Greek city-states were forcibly enrolled in the Macedonian-dominated Hellenic league. Philip planned to invade Persia but his assassination in 336 left it to his son Alexander to carry out his plans. In only six years he conquered almost all the Persian empire, opening the whole Middle East to Greek influence (▷2.09).

By the 4th century the old south Arabian kingdom of Saba had been joined by the new states of Qataban and Hadramaut, driven by a demand from the Mediterranean for the precious gums, frankincense and myrrh, which were produced in the region. By the same period Sabean influence was seen in Damot on the African Red Sea coast.

Through most of the 5th and 4th centuries the main power in the western Mediterranean was Carthage. Carthage was more interested in commerce than conquest and its empire grew little between 500 and 323. Most of central and western Europe was now dominated by Celtic peoples. Around 400, Celts crossed the Alps and invaded Italy, breaking the power of the Etruscans and settling the Po valley. Though still insignificant on the map, by 323 Rome was a major power in Italy, having conquered its Latin and Etruscan neighbors earlier in the century (▷2.12).

The strongest state in India in 500 was Magadha in the lower Ganges plain. From 364 it brought most of northern India under its control (▷2.22). Southern India was a mosaic of minor states and chiefdoms with little urban development. The Zhou kingdom of China, which had broken up into a dozen competing states in the 8th century, was still disunited, although many of the smaller states had been absorbed by the bigger players (▷2.24). The continual warfare

c.450 Beginning of the La Tène phase of Celtic Iron Age culture

500–400 Mesoamerican state formation occurs in the Oaxaca valley (Monte Albán and Zapotec civilization)

450–400 Domestication of the reindeer in the Sayan Mountains of central Asia

c.400 Olmec civilization in steep decline

431–404 The Peloponnesian war takes place, between Athens and Sparta

509–507 Foundation of democracy in Athens

480–479 The Greeks defeat the Persian invasion

c.400 The Celts settle northern Italy; decline of Etruscan civilization

TIMELINE		500		450		400
The Americas						
Europe						
Middle East						
Africa						
East and South Asia						

525 Egypt comes under Achemenid Persian control

483 Death of Siddhartha Gautama, the Buddha, in India

400–300 Iron working is practiced in east Africa

c.515 The Achemenid Persian empire is at its height

480–221 China breaks into competing kingdoms in the "Warring States" period

399 Death of Socrates, Greek philosopher, in Athens

479 Death of Confucius, Chinese philosopher

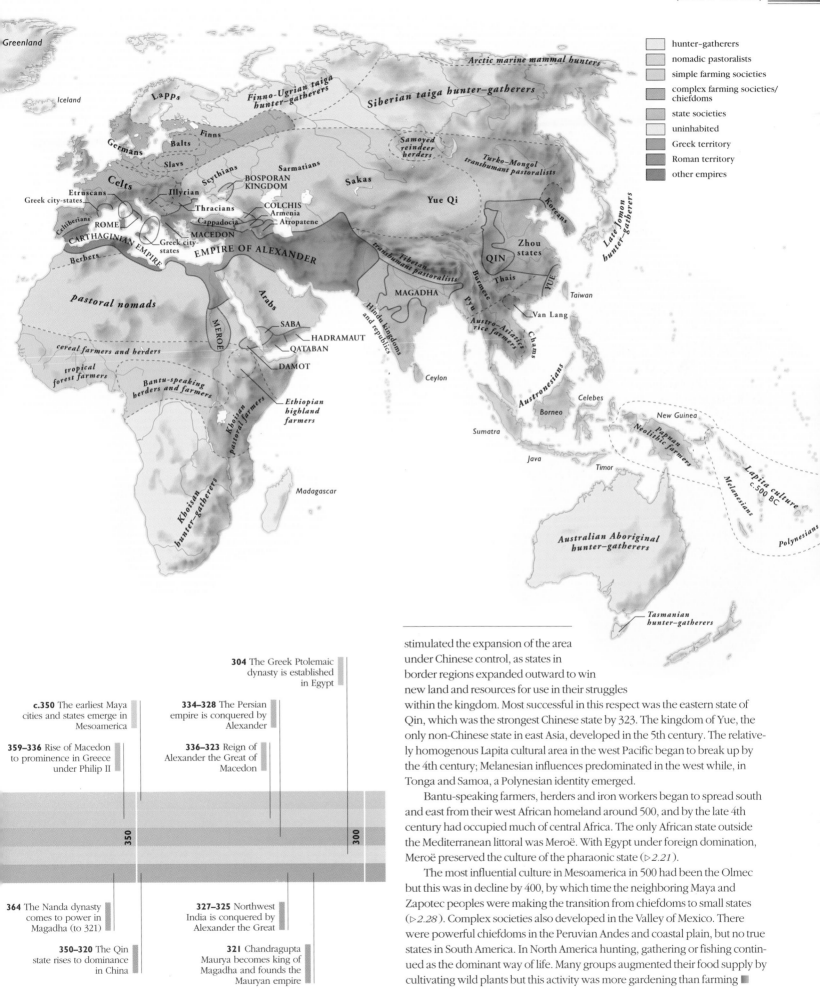

Greenland

Iceland

Lapps

Finno-Ugrian taiga hunter-gatherers

Siberian taiga hunter-gatherers

Arctic marine mammal hunters

hunter-gatherers
nomadic pastoralists
simple farming societies
complex farming societies/chiefdoms
state societies
uninhabited
Greek territory
Roman territory
other empires

Finns

Germans

Balts

Slavs

Celts

Etruscans

Greek city-states

Celtiberians

ROME

CARTHAGINIAN EMPIRE

Berbers

Illyrian

Scythians

Thracians

Cappadocia

MACEDON

Greek city-states

EMPIRE OF ALEXANDER

Sarmatians

BOSPORAN KINGDOM

COLCHIS

Armenia

Atropatene

Sakas

Samoyed reindeer herders

Turko-Mongol transhumant pastoralists

Yue Qi

Koreans

Zhou states

QIN

Late Jomon hunter-gatherers

Tibetan transhumant pastoralists

Burmese

Thais

YUE

Taiwan

Arabs

pastoral nomads

MEROE

SABA

HADRAMAUT

QATABAN

DAMOT

Hindu kingdoms and republics

MAGADHA

Pyu

Austro-Asiatic rice farmers

Chams

Van Lang

cereal farmers and herders

tropical forest farmers

Bantu-speaking herders and farmers

Khoisan pastoral farmers

Ethiopian highland farmers

Ceylon

Austronesians

Celebes

Sumatra

Borneo

Java

Timor

New Guinea

Papuan Neolithic farmers

Lapita culture c.500 BC

Melanesians

Polynesians

Madagascar

Khoisan hunter-gatherers

Australian Aboriginal hunter-gatherers

Tasmanian hunter-gatherers

stimulated the expansion of the area under Chinese control, as states in border regions expanded outward to win new land and resources for use in their struggles within the kingdom. Most successful in this respect was the eastern state of Qin, which was the strongest Chinese state by 323. The kingdom of Yue, the only non-Chinese state in east Asia, developed in the 5th century. The relatively homogenous Lapita cultural area in the west Pacific began to break up by the 4th century; Melanesian influences predominated in the west while, in Tonga and Samoa, a Polynesian identity emerged.

Bantu-speaking farmers, herders and iron workers began to spread south and east from their west African homeland around 500, and by the late 4th century had occupied much of central Africa. The only African state outside the Mediterranean littoral was Meroë. With Egypt under foreign domination, Meroë preserved the culture of the pharaonic state (▷2.21).

The most influential culture in Mesoamerica in 500 had been the Olmec but this was in decline by 400, by which time the neighboring Maya and Zapotec peoples were making the transition from chiefdoms to small states (▷2.28). Complex societies also developed in the Valley of Mexico. There were powerful chiefdoms in the Peruvian Andes and coastal plain, but no true states in South America. In North America hunting, gathering or fishing continued as the dominant way of life. Many groups augmented their food supply by cultivating wild plants but this activity was more gardening than farming ▪

304 The Greek Ptolemaic dynasty is established in Egypt

c.350 The earliest Maya cities and states emerge in Mesoamerica

334–328 The Persian empire is conquered by Alexander

359–336 Rise of Macedon to prominence in Greece under Philip II

336–323 Reign of Alexander the Great of Macedon

350

300

364 The Nanda dynasty comes to power in Magadha (to 321)

327–325 Northwest India is conquered by Alexander the Great

350–320 The Qin state rises to dominance in China

321 Chandragupta Maurya becomes king of Magadha and founds the Mauryan empire

Alexander's empire did not survive his death in 323 – the immediate cause of its breakup being his failure to provide an heir – and within a few years his generals had become the rulers of independent kingdoms (▷2.10). Seleucos built a state which incorporated most of Anatolia, Mesopotamia, and Iran and extended into central Asia; despite successful rebellions by the Bactrian Greeks in 239 and the Parthians in 238, the Seleucid kingdom was still the largest of the successor states in 200. Ptolemy seized Egypt and founded a dynasty which was to last until 31 BC, ending only with Cleopatra's suicide after the battle of Actium. Macedon itself fell to Antipater, who reasserted Macedonian supremacy in Greece in the face of an Athenian-led rebellion. Macedon was still the leading power in Greece in 200.

The leading power in the western Mediterranean by 200 was Rome. The Romans had completed the conquest of peninsular Italy in 272, and in 264 were drawn into a war with Carthage over Sicily. This, the First Punic War, dragged on for over twenty years until the Romans had wrested control of Sicily, Sardinia and Corsica. Carthaginian expansion in Spain, arousing Roman hostility once again, led in 218 to the outbreak of the Second Punic War. The Carthaginian general Hannibal surprised the Romans by attacking Italy from the north, but counterattacks in Spain and north Africa brought Rome crushing victory, and Carthage was shorn of its empire (▷2.12).

Several centuries of stability on the Eurasian steppes came to an end in the 3rd century as the Sarmatians began to push westward against the Scythians. On the far eastern steppes the Turko-Mongol pastoralists made the transition to a horse-mounted fully nomadic way of life around 300, and by 200 they were united in the powerful Xiong-nu confederation. Their use of the composite bow gave the Xiongnu a decided military advantage over their nomadic Iranian neighbors to the west and made them a formidable adversary for the newly united Chinese (▷2.20).

In 321 Chandragupta Maurya (321–c. 293) seized the throne of the kingdom of Magadha, overthrowing the Nanda dynasty. Chandragupta spent most of his reign building a strong central administration, but he defeated a Seleucid invasion, adding all of northwest India to his domains (▷2.22). His son Bindusara also conquered much of southern India. Under Ashoka the Mauryan empire reached its greatest extent. Appalled by his bloody conquest of the east coast kingdom of Kalinga in 261, Ashoka abjured further warfare and, becoming a Buddhist, tried to impose Buddhist standards of behavior on his people. Little is known

323–280 Wars of the Diadochi: Alexander's generals split up his empire

323 Alexander the Great dies without naming a successor

264 Roman–Carthaginian rivalry in Sicily sets off the First Punic War

272 Rome completes its conquest of peninsular Italy

239 The Bactrian Greeks break away from the Seleucid kingdom

241 A Roman naval victory off Lilybaeum ends the First Punic war

	325		300		275		250
The Americas							
Europe							
Middle East							
Africa							
East and South Asia							

TIMELINE

321 Chandragupta Maurya, founder of the Mauryan empire, becomes king of Magadha

c.300 The Turko-Mongol tribes of the eastern steppes adopt a fully nomadic way of life

268–233 Reign of Ashoka: Buddhism spreads through the Mauryan empire

c.300 Beginning of rice farming in Japan

Arctic marine mammal hunters

Aleuts

sub-Arctic forest hunter-gatherers

west coast foraging hunting and fishing peoples

Plateau fishers and hunter gatherers

desert hunter-gatherers

plains bison hunters

eastern woodlands hunter-gatherers

Adena complex

maize farmers

Bahamas

Teotihuacán

Cuba

Hispaniola

Puerto Rico

Monte Albán

Caribbean hunter-gatherers

Olmec culture

Maya chiefdoms and states

maize farmers

manioc farmers

Hawaiian Islands

Andean chiefdoms

Nazca culture

Pukara culture

savanna hunter-gatherers

Polynesians

shellfish gatherers

South Andean hunter-gatherers

pampas hunter-gatherers

shellfish gatherers and marine mammal hunters

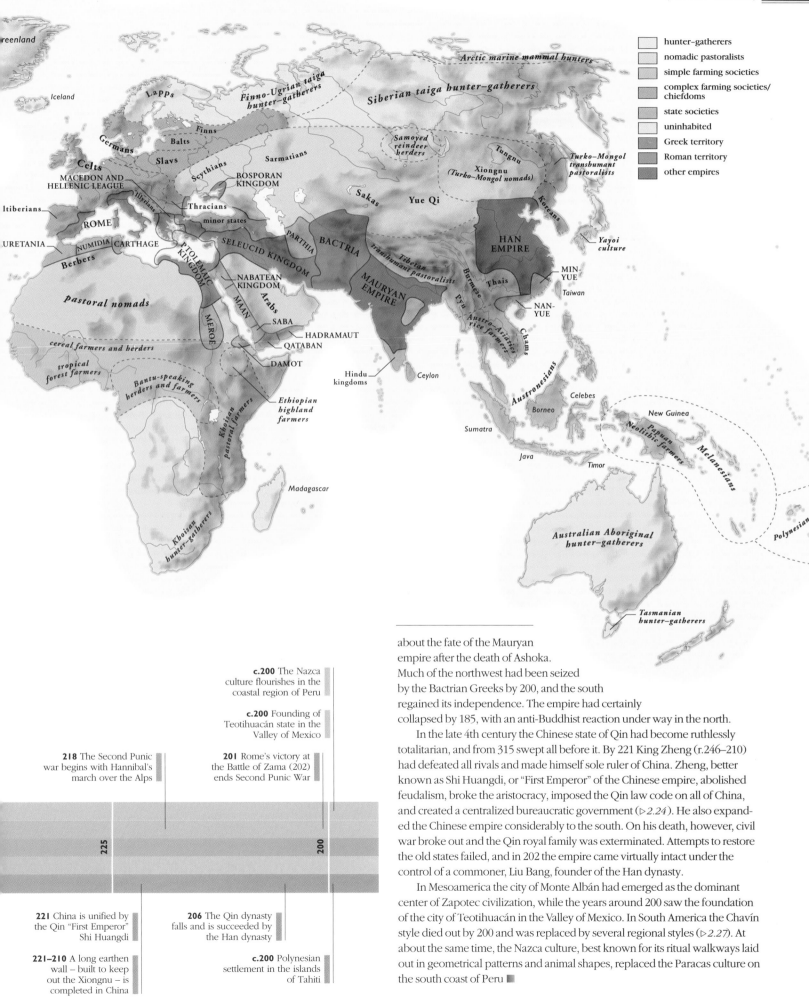

Legend:
- hunter-gatherers
- nomadic pastoralists
- simple farming societies
- complex farming societies/chiefdoms
- state societies
- uninhabited
- Greek territory
- Roman territory
- other empires

Map labels:

Greenland · Iceland · Lapps · Finno-Ugrian taiga hunter-gatherers · Arctic marine mammal hunters · Siberian taiga hunter-gatherers · Finns · Balts · Germans · Slavs · Celts · MACEDON AND HELLENIC LEAGUE · Scythians · Sarmatians · Samoyed reindeer herders · Tungnu · Turko–Mongol transhumant pastoralists · Koreans · Itiberians · ROME · Illyrians · Thracians · BOSPORAN KINGDOM · minor states · Xiongnu (Turko–Mongol nomads) · Yue Qi · Sakas · Yayoi culture · URETANIA · NUMIDIA · CARTHAGE · Berbers · PTOLEMAIC KINGDOM · SELEUCID KINGDOM · PARTHIA · BACTRIA · Tibetan transhumant pastoralists · HAN EMPIRE · NABATEAN KINGDOM · Arabs · MAAN · MAURYAN EMPIRE · Burmese · Thais · MIN-YUE · Taiwan · pastoral nomads · MEROË · SABA · HADRAMAUT · QATABAN · DAMOT · Pyu · Austro-Asiatic rice farmers · NAN-YUE · Chams · cereal farmers and herders · Hindu kingdoms · Ceylon · Austronesians · tropical forest farmers · Bantu-speaking herders and farmers · Khoisan pastoral farmers · Ethiopian highland farmers · Celebes · Borneo · New Guinea · Papuan Neolithic farmers · Melanesians · Sumatra · Java · Timor · Madagascar · Khoisan hunter-gatherers · Australian Aboriginal hunter-gatherers · Polynesians · Tasmanian hunter-gatherers

---

c.200 The Nazca culture flourishes in the coastal region of Peru

c.200 Founding of Teotihuacán state in the Valley of Mexico

218 The Second Punic war begins with Hannibal's march over the Alps

201 Rome's victory at the Battle of Zama (202) ends Second Punic War

225 · 200

221 China is unified by the Qin "First Emperor" Shi Huangdi

206 The Qin dynasty falls and is succeeded by the Han dynasty

221–210 A long earthen wall – built to keep out the Xiongnu – is completed in China

c.200 Polynesian settlement in the islands of Tahiti

---

about the fate of the Mauryan empire after the death of Ashoka. Much of the northwest had been seized by the Bactrian Greeks by 200, and the south regained its independence. The empire had certainly collapsed by 185, with an anti-Buddhist reaction under way in the north.

In the late 4th century the Chinese state of Qin had become ruthlessly totalitarian, and from 315 swept all before it. By 221 King Zheng (r.246–210) had defeated all rivals and made himself sole ruler of China. Zheng, better known as Shi Huangdi, or "First Emperor" of the Chinese empire, abolished feudalism, broke the aristocracy, imposed the Qin law code on all of China, and created a centralized bureaucratic government (▷2.24). He also expanded the Chinese empire considerably to the south. On his death, however, civil war broke out and the Qin royal family was exterminated. Attempts to restore the old states failed, and in 202 the empire came virtually intact under the control of a commoner, Liu Bang, founder of the Han dynasty.

In Mesoamerica the city of Monte Albán had emerged as the dominant center of Zapotec civilization, while the years around 200 saw the foundation of the city of Teotihuacán in the Valley of Mexico. In South America the Chavín style died out by 200 and was replaced by several regional styles (▷2.27). At about the same time, the Nazca culture, best known for its ritual walkways laid out in geometrical patterns and animal shapes, replaced the Paracas culture on the south coast of Peru ∎

A decisive Roman victory at the battle of Cynoscephalae in 197 BC had broken the power of Macedon, who had supported Carthage in the Second Punic War. This victory opened the way for Roman domination of Greece. In 146 Rome brought the whole of Greece under direct control; and in the same year ruthlessly destroyed Carthage, though it had long ceased to be a threat (▷2.12). The Hellenistic kingdoms of the east were also powerless to prevent Roman expansion. By 64 BC most of Anatolia and the Levant were under Roman rule and Egypt had been made a protectorate. Direct rule was imposed on Egypt in 30 BC (▷2.13).

Rome's successes put its republican system of government – designed for a city-state, not a world empire – under increasing strain: and a succession of civil wars between 50 and 31 BC brought about the collapse of the Roman republic. The eventual victor, Octavian, created a new form of government – in effect, an absolute monarchy. King in all but name, he took the titles *princeps* (first citizen) and Augustus. His successors used the title *imperator* (commander or emperor).

In northern Europe, the Celts found themselves caught between the Romans, who were expanding northward, and the Germans, who were pushing south: by 1 BC the only remaining independent Celts were in the British Isles (▷2.18).

In Africa, the Sabean colonies had developed into the kingdom of Axum around 100 BC. At about the same time the dromedary camel was introduced to the northern Sahara, transforming the lives of the desert nomads much as horse riding had earlier changed the steppe pastoralist way of life, enabling them to range widely and raid settled peoples almost at will. By 1 BC pastoralism had spread among the Khoisan-speaking peoples as far south as the Transvaal region and Bantu-speaking peoples had begun to settle on the east African plateau (▷2.21).

Following his victory in the civil war in China (202), Liu Bang restored prosperity by introducing a series of agricultural and administrative reforms but, despite heroic efforts, failed to stop damaging raids by the nomadic Xiongnu who continued to be a serious threat to China until 38 BC. The Han period saw Chinese expansion in the south (▷2.24), where the non-Chinese kingdoms of Min-yue and Nan-yue were conquered, and in Korea. Small kingdoms had begun to develop in parts of Korea not under Chinese occupation by 50 BC.

The rise of the Xiongnu had a destabilizing effect on the Iranian nomads to the west (▷2.20). In 170 the Xiongnu inflicted a crushing defeat on the Yue Qi, who fled westward, unsettling the Sakas, before overrunning the Bactrian kingdom around 135. The Sakas headed south, first invading the Parthian

TIMELINE

	200		150		100
The Americas					
Europe					
Middle East					
Africa					
East and South Asia					

c.135 The westward-driven Yue Qi overrun the Bactrian kingdom

170–141 The Parthians conquer the Seleucid kingdom

146 Roman control is extended throughout Greece

c.100 Foundation of the Moche state in the region of Peru

c.185 Fall of the Mauryan dynasty after Bactrians invade the Punjab

149–146 The Third Punic War: Rome levels the city of Carthage to the ground

101 China under the Han dynasty conquers Van Lang

170 The Hsiung-nu defeat the Yue Qi and dominate the eastern steppes

c.141 The Sakas invade the Parthian empire and northern India

c.100 The beginning of camel nomadism in the Sahara desert

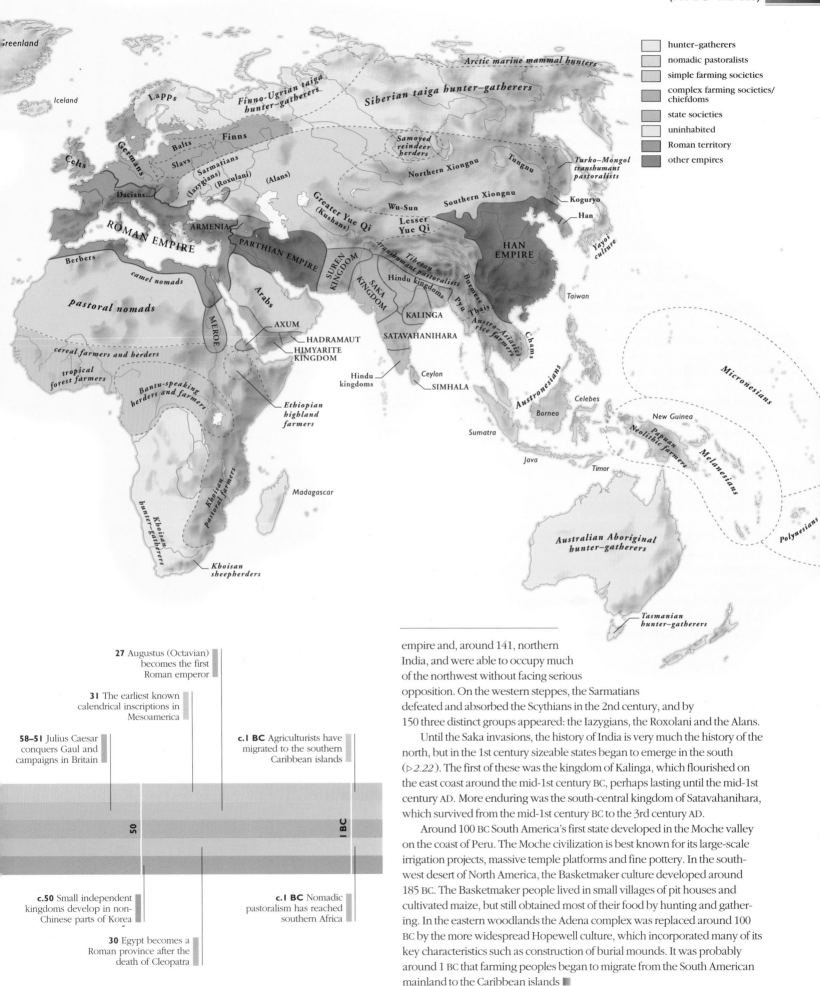

hunter-gatherers
nomadic pastoralists
simple farming societies
complex farming societies/
chiefdoms
state societies
uninhabited
Roman territory
other empires

27 Augustus (Octavian) becomes the first Roman emperor

31 The earliest known calendrical inscriptions in Mesoamerica

58–51 BC Julius Caesar conquers Gaul and campaigns in Britain

c.1 BC Agriculturists have migrated to the southern Caribbean islands

c.50 Small independent kingdoms develop in non-Chinese parts of Korea

c.1 BC Nomadic pastoralism has reached southern Africa

30 Egypt becomes a Roman province after the death of Cleopatra

empire and, around 141, northern India, and were able to occupy much of the northwest without facing serious opposition. On the western steppes, the Sarmatians defeated and absorbed the Scythians in the 2nd century, and by 150 three distinct groups appeared: the Iazygians, the Roxolani and the Alans.

Until the Saka invasions, the history of India is very much the history of the north, but in the 1st century sizeable states began to emerge in the south (▷2.22). The first of these was the kingdom of Kalinga, which flourished on the east coast around the mid-1st century BC, perhaps lasting until the mid-1st century AD. More enduring was the south-central kingdom of Satavahanihara, which survived from the mid-1st century BC to the 3rd century AD.

Around 100 BC South America's first state developed in the Moche valley on the coast of Peru. The Moche civilization is best known for its large-scale irrigation projects, massive temple platforms and fine pottery. In the south-west desert of North America, the Basketmaker culture developed around 185 BC. The Basketmaker people lived in small villages of pit houses and cultivated maize, but still obtained most of their food by hunting and gathering. In the eastern woodlands the Adena complex was replaced around 100 BC by the more widespread Hopewell culture, which incorporated many of its key characteristics such as construction of burial mounds. It was probably around 1 BC that farming peoples began to migrate from the South American mainland to the Caribbean islands ■

The area of the – now Christian – Roman empire in AD 400, though slightly greater than in 1 BC, disguises Rome's true position. Although the emperor Diocletian (r.284–305) had given the empire a new lease of life by dividing it into eastern and western halves and completely reforming the administration and army, Rome was a state under siege. Pressure on the empire's borders was constant and the cost of maintaining defenses ruinous, especially in the poorer west. When the Huns, a Turkic-dominated nomad confederation from somewhere in central Asia, arrived in eastern Europe around 372, destabilizing the Germanic tribes, the empire was plunged back into crisis (▷2.15). To the east, the Sasanians, who had overthrown the Parthian empire in 226, were also posing a threat.

From around AD 50 the Kushan clan, which had become dominant among the Yue Qi, established an empire extending from the Aral Sea to the Indian Ocean and into northwest India. The empire had fallen by the late 4th century. Northern India continued to be divided into small states, until around 350, when Samudragupta (d.c.380) founded the Gupta empire (▷2.23), which by 410 had reached its greatest extent under Chandragupta II (r.380–414).

Farther east, the authority of the Han dynasty, which had reached the summit of its power in the 1st century, began to decline. In 189 the empire collapsed in chaos as army and court factions struggled to control an isolated and powerless emperor. The dynasty was overthrown in 220, when the empire split into three kingdoms (▷2.25). In 280 unity was briefly restored, but civil war again broke out, giving the Xiongnu the opportunity to conquer the north of the country. A second wave of nomads – the Turkic Toba tribes – arrived in 386 and won control of the north. The Toba Wei state itself was threatened by the Juan-juan, a Mongol-dominated nomad confederation which arose in the late 4th century and controlled the eastern steppes by 400.

Small states sprang up in southern Japan in the 2nd or 3rd centuries, though most of these had been incorporated into the Yamato kingdom of Honshu by 400. The first southeast Asian states – the trading kingdom of Funan and the Cham kingdom of Champa – had developed by the 2nd century. Madagascar had been discovered and settled by Austronesian peoples from Indonesia in the 1st century AD, a voyaging feat to be matched by the Polynesians, who by 400 had colonized Hawaii and Easter Island.

In Africa the kingdom of Meroë collapsed around 350 as a result of nomad

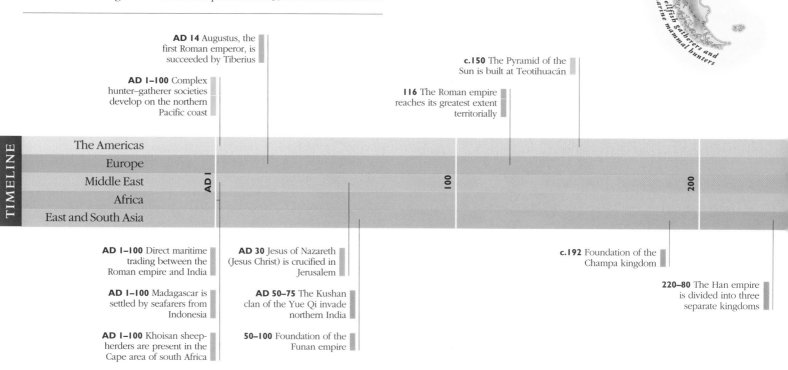

AD 14 Augustus, the first Roman emperor, is succeeded by Tiberius

AD 1–100 Complex hunter–gatherer societies develop on the northern Pacific coast

c.150 The Pyramid of the Sun is built at Teotihuacán

116 The Roman empire reaches its greatest extent territorially

TIMELINE					
The Americas					
Europe					
Middle East	AD 1		100		200
Africa					
East and South Asia					

AD 1–100 Direct maritime trading between the Roman empire and India

AD 30 Jesus of Nazareth (Jesus Christ) is crucified in Jerusalem

c.192 Foundation of the Champa kingdom

AD 1–100 Madagascar is settled by seafarers from Indonesia

AD 50–75 The Kushan clan of the Yue Qi invade northern India

220–80 The Han empire is divided into three separate kingdoms

AD 1–100 Khoisan sheep-herders are present in the Cape area of south Africa

50–100 Foundation of the Funan empire

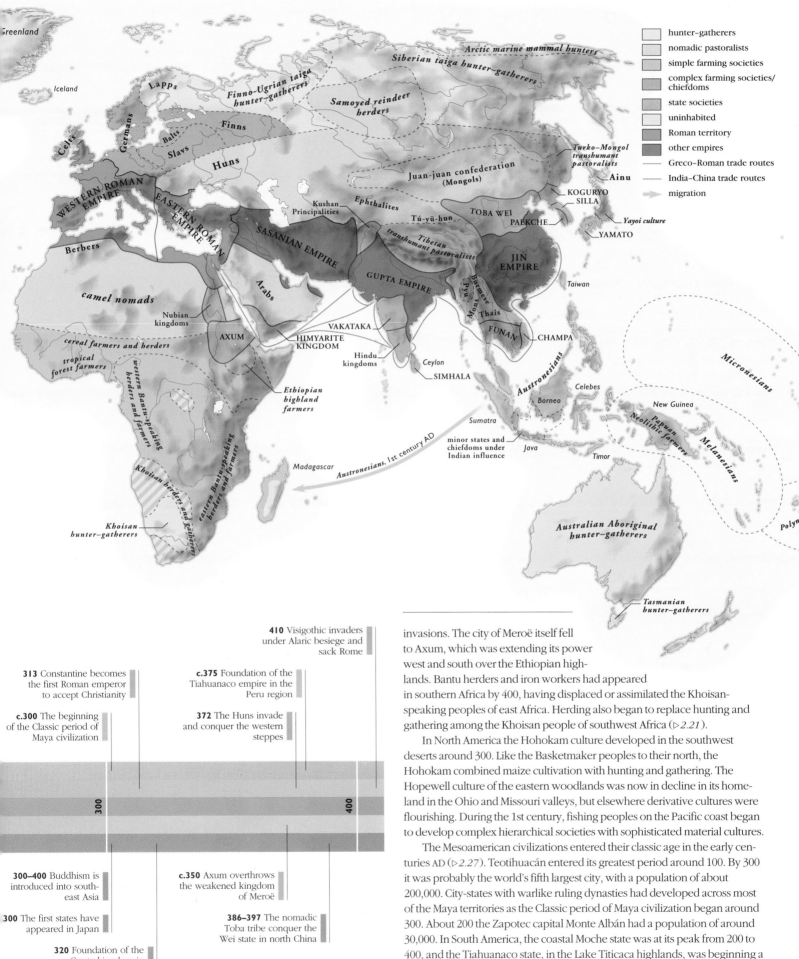

Legend:
- hunter-gatherers
- nomadic pastoralists
- simple farming societies
- complex farming societies/chiefdoms
- state societies
- uninhabited
- Roman territory
- other empires
- Greco-Roman trade routes
- India-China trade routes
- migration

313 Constantine becomes the first Roman emperor to accept Christianity

c.300 The beginning of the Classic period of Maya civilization

410 Visigothic invaders under Alaric besiege and sack Rome

c.375 Foundation of the Tiahuanaco empire in the Peru region

372 The Huns invade and conquer the western steppes

300

400

300–400 Buddhism is introduced into south-east Asia

300 The first states have appeared in Japan

320 Foundation of the Gupta kingdom in northern India

c.350 Axum overthrows the weakened kingdom of Meroë

386–397 The nomadic Toba tribe conquer the Wei state in north China

invasions. The city of Meroë itself fell to Axum, which was extending its power west and south over the Ethiopian highlands. Bantu herders and iron workers had appeared in southern Africa by 400, having displaced or assimilated the Khoisan-speaking peoples of east Africa. Herding also began to replace hunting and gathering among the Khoisan people of southwest Africa (▷2.21).

In North America the Hohokam culture developed in the southwest deserts around 300. Like the Basketmaker peoples to their north, the Hohokam combined maize cultivation with hunting and gathering. The Hopewell culture of the eastern woodlands was now in decline in its homeland in the Ohio and Missouri valleys, but elsewhere derivative cultures were flourishing. During the 1st century, fishing peoples on the Pacific coast began to develop complex hierarchical societies with sophisticated material cultures.

The Mesoamerican civilizations entered their classic age in the early centuries AD (▷2.27). Teotihuacán entered its greatest period around 100. By 300 it was probably the world's fifth largest city, with a population of about 200,000. City-states with warlike ruling dynasties had developed across most of the Maya territories as the Classic period of Maya civilization began around 300. About 200 the Zapotec capital Monte Albán had a population of around 30,000. In South America, the coastal Moche state was at its peak from 200 to 400, and the Tiahuanaco state, in the Lake Titicaca highlands, was beginning a period of imperial expansion (▷2.28) ∎

The western half of the Roman empire, altogether poorer and less populated than the east, was also more exposed to Germanic barbarian attack. In 406 German tribes – Goths, Franks, Vandals and others – overran the Rhine frontier and by 476 the western Roman empire was almost entirely under their control. The wealthy eastern half of the Roman empire survived more or less unscathed and its emperor Justinian counter-attacked against the barbarians in the 530s, restoring Roman rule in Italy, north Africa and southern Spain (▷2.17). However, the empire was put back on the defensive after Justinian's death; much of Italy fell to the Lombards and most of southern Spain to the Visigoths by 600. The most successful of the Germanic invaders were the Franks, who had settled northern Gaul in the early 5th century. From 486 they were united by Clovis, who extended his kingdom into southern Gaul and east into Germany. By 600 the Frankish kingdom stretched from the Pyrenees almost to the Elbe. The end of Roman rule in Britain saw a revival of Celtic culture but in about 450 Angles and Saxons from north Germany began to settle the fertile east of Britain, driving the Celts to the hillier west.

Fear of the Huns drove the Germanic peoples to invade the Roman empire. The Huns extended their control as far west as the Rhine – further west than any steppe nomads in history – and raided both halves of the Roman empire under Attila (r. 433–453). However, after his death the Hun confederation broke up and returned to the steppes. Between 460 and 515 the Ephthalite (or "White") Huns destroyed the last Kushan principalities of central Asia, raided the Sasanian empire and conquered northwest India, only to be driven out in 528 (▷2.20). On the eastern steppes, the Mongol-dominated Juan-juan confederacy was broken by a rebellion of the Turks in 552. By 600 the Turks had destroyed the Ephthalites and dominated the steppes as far west as the Aral Sea. The Khazars, another Turkic people, were established on the Caspian steppes. A part of the Juan-juan, the Avars, fled from the Turks and arrived on the European steppes in about 562 where they mopped up the remnants of the Huns and raided the Balkans. North of the Caucasus the Alans – the sole remnant of the Iranian peoples who had once dominated the steppes – re-emerged from Hunnic dominance in the 450s.

In Africa, Christianity had spread to Nubia and Axum by the 6th century, strengthening cultural and political links with the eastern Roman empire (▷2.21). With Roman encouragement, the Axumites conquered southwest Arabia in 528 but were expelled by the Sasanians in 574, ending Christian influence in Arabia just four years after the birth of Muhammad at Mecca. In west Africa intensive dry-rice farming led to a rising population on the upper Niger and the foundation of large villages in the 3rd and 4th centuries. One of these, Jenne-jeno, became the center of a wideranging network of west

c.500 Foundation of the Huari empire in the highlands of Peru

481–511 Reign of Clovis, undisputed Frankish king of Gaul from 486

476 Fall of the western Roman empire when the the emperor Romulus is deposed

c.450 The Angles and Saxons begin to settle eastern Britain

410 The Visigoths, led by Alaric, sack Rome

533–54 Roman emperor Justinian reconquers most of north Africa and Italy

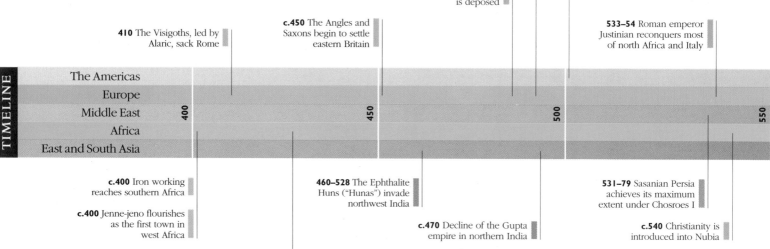

TIMELINE

	400	450	500	550
The Americas				
Europe				
Middle East				
Africa				
East and South Asia				

c.400 Iron working reaches southern Africa

c.400 Jenne-jeno flourishes as the first town in west Africa

429 A wealthy Vandal kingdom is set up in north Africa

460–528 The Ephthalite Huns ("Hunas") invade northwest India

c.470 Decline of the Gupta empire in northern India

531–79 Sasanian Persia achieves its maximum extent under Chosroes I

c.540 Christianity is introduced into Nubia

c.550 The Turkish khanates are dominant throughout central Asia

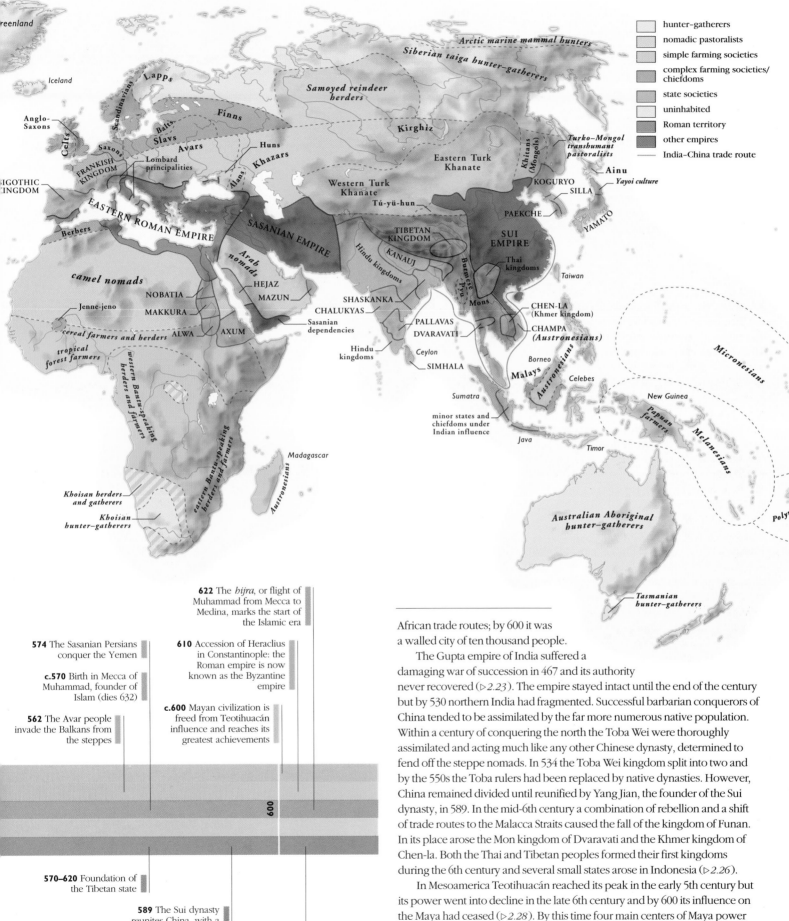

hunter-gatherers
nomadic pastoralists
simple farming societies
complex farming societies/
chiefdoms
state societies
uninhabited
Roman territory
other empires
India–China trade route

622 The *hijra*, or flight of
Muhammad from Mecca to
Medina, marks the start of
the Islamic era

574 The Sasanian Persians
conquer the Yemen

610 Accession of Heraclius
in Constantinople: the
Roman empire is now
known as the Byzantine
empire

c.570 Birth in Mecca of
Muhammad, founder of
Islam (dies 632)

562 The Avar people
invade the Balkans from
the steppes

c.600 Mayan civilization is
freed from Teotihuacán
influence and reaches its
greatest achievements

600

570–620 Foundation of
the Tibetan state

589 The Sui dynasty
reunites China, with a
capital at Chang'an

618 The Tang dynasty
replaces the Sui in China

African trade routes; by 600 it was
a walled city of ten thousand people.

The Gupta empire of India suffered a
damaging war of succession in 467 and its authority
never recovered (▷2.23). The empire stayed intact until the end of the century
but by 530 northern India had fragmented. Successful barbarian conquerors of
China tended to be assimilated by the far more numerous native population.
Within a century of conquering the north the Toba Wei were thoroughly
assimilated and acting much like any other Chinese dynasty, determined to
fend off the steppe nomads. In 534 the Toba Wei kingdom split into two and
by the 550s the Toba rulers had been replaced by native dynasties. However,
China remained divided until reunified by Yang Jian, the founder of the Sui
dynasty, in 589. In the mid-6th century a combination of rebellion and a shift
of trade routes to the Malacca Straits caused the fall of the kingdom of Funan.
In its place arose the Mon kingdom of Dvaravati and the Khmer kingdom of
Chen-la. Both the Thai and Tibetan peoples formed their first kingdoms
during the 6th century and several small states arose in Indonesia (▷2.26).

In Mesoamerica Teotihuacán reached its peak in the early 5th century but
its power went into decline in the late 6th century and by 600 its influence on
the Maya had ceased (▷2.28). By this time four main centers of Maya power
had emerged. In Peru, climatic instability in the 6th century caused the decline
of the coastal Moche state and power shifted to the highlands where the cities
of Tiahuanaco and Huari had built considerable empires by 600 (▷2.27) ■

The years 1000 BC–AD 600 saw the emergence of every major world religion except Islam (a world religion is one that has endured and influenced diverse civilizations). Hinduism and Judaism had earlier roots but assumed their present form at this time; Christianity, Buddhism, Zoroastrianism, Daoism and Confucianism all arose 600 BC–AD 600.

Early Hinduism was based on the Vedas, hymns of the Aryans who invaded India around 1500 BC, but was also influenced by indigenous Dravidian traditions. Vedic Hinduism looked forward to a future existence in heaven; it was not until the 6th century BC that the belief in *karma* and rebirth, central to modern Hinduism, developed. The complex rituals of early Hinduism gave rise to a distinctive feature of Indian civilization, the caste system – the priestly Brahmins forming the highest caste. By 500 BC Hinduism dominated the Indian subcontinent, but discontent with Brahminical traditions grew on the Gangetic plain, where urbanization created a more materialistic society. New sects developed there, the most successful of them being Buddhism.

The founder of Buddhism was Siddhartha Gautama, known as the Buddha, or "Enlightened One." Many legends have become associated with the Buddha and little is known for certain of his life: even his original teachings are a matter of debate as the canon of Buddhist scripture was not written down until four centuries after his death. Buddhism remained a minor sect until the Mauryan emperor Ashoka converted in 260 BC. Under his patronage Buddhist missionaries spread the religion throughout India and to Ceylon and the Iranian nomads in central Asia. In northern India Buddhism supplanted Hinduism as the majority religion. It then spread from central Asia along the Silk Route, reaching China in the 1st century AD; Indian seafarers took it to southeast Asia in the 4th century. By the 3rd century AD Buddhism had divided into two schools: Theravada (Doctrine of the Elders), which adhered strictly to the established Buddhist canon, and Mahayana (Great Vehicle), a more liberal, eclectic

THE MENORAH symbolizes the survival of the Jewish people through the vicissitudes of history, including the Diaspora of the 1st century AD.

tradition. Hinduism responded to the rise of Buddhism by becoming more flexible and tolerant, and by AD 400 it was beginning to recover in India. In the 5th century Hinduism spread to southeast Asia.

The central influence on Chinese thought was the ethical teaching of Confucius. Its emphasis on respect for legitimate authority and moral education made this the official orthodoxy under the Han dynasty (206 BC–AD 220). In the disorder following the fall of the Han, Confucianism declined and Buddhism became a stronger influence in China. Buddhism was itself influenced by Chinese philosophies, particularly Daoism, a system inspired by the teachings of Lao Zi, a philosopher of the 6th century BC. The traditional Chinese practice of ancestor worship remained strong throughout these changes.

Although it was the religion of a minor and relatively unimportant people, the Hebrews, Judaism was the most influential religion of the Middle East. It was the first major monotheistic religion and its

TIMELINE

Middle East and Europe

600 BC	AD 1	AD 600
c.630–553 The life of Zoroaster, founder of Zoroastrianism	**c.6 BC–AD 30** The life of Jesus of Nazareth	**313** The Roman empire under Constantine officially tolerates Christianity
587 The Jews are deported to Babylonia by Nebuchadnezzar. This marks the beginning of the Diaspora	**AD 1–100** Mithraism spreads to the Roman empire	**c. 405** St Jerome completes the Vulgate Latin translation of the Bible
	AD 42–62 St Paul undertakes his missionary journeys throughout Asia Minor, Greece and to Rome	**c. 570** The birth of the prophet Muhammad
	AD 70–100 The Christian Gospels are written	**596** The English conversion to Christianity begins
	220–40 Zoroastrianism is the Persian state religion	

South and east Asia

600 BC	AD 1	AD 600
800–400 The *Upanishads* of Hinduism are composed	**260** The Mauryan emperor Ashoka becomes a Buddhist and sends Buddhist missions to Ceylon and central Asia	**253–333** The life of Ko Hung, founder of religious Daoism
6th century The life of Lao Zi, the inspirer of Daoism		**259** Chinese Buddhists begin pilgrimages to India
c.563–483 Life of Siddhartha Gautama, the Buddha	**c.240 BC** The *Dao De Jing*, the basic text of Daoism, is composed	**300–500** The Hindu epics the *Ramayana* and the *Mahabharata* are written down in their final form
551–479 The life of the Chinese sage Confucius	**AD 1–100** Mahayana Buddhism develops	
600 BC	AD 1	AD 600

Map labels:

5th century AD Clonard AD 520 · Iona AD 563 · 6th century AD Whithorn AD 360–432 · ATLANTIC OCEAN · 4th century AD · Canterbury AD 596 · Marmoutier AD 372 · Massilia AD 415 · Vercelli AD 360 · Danube · CARPATHIAN MTS · Goths c.AD 350 · Dniepr · Nursia AD 480 · Rome · Mediterranean Sea · Monte Cassino AD 529 · Nola AD 394 · Black Sea · CAUCASUS MTS · Volga · Caspian Sea · Thagaste AD 388 · Carthage · Constantinople · Chalcedon AD 400 · ROMAN EMPIRE Christianity tolerated AD 313, Official religion AD 391 · Athens · Ephesus · Caesarea AD 360 · Armenia c.300 AD · Antiochia · Nisibis AD 325 · Gushnasp · Salamis AD 335 · Sidon · Hamadan · Alexandria · Wadi Natrun AD 320 · Jerusalem · Ctesiphon · Tigris · Susa · Scetis AD 330 · Bethlehem AD 386–420 · Euphrates · PERSIA · Bishapur · Firuzabad · Nile · NOBATIA c.AD 550 · MAKKURA c.AD 550 · Red Sea · ALWA c.AD 580 · ARABIA · AXUM c.AD 350

1 Although Hinduism is an ancient religion, few physical traces survive before the medieval period.

2 Ellora is the site of rock-cut temples of Buddhist, Hindu and Jain origin, dating from the 6th–8th centuries AD.

3 Southern Britain became Christian by the 4th century but reverted to paganism following the settlements of the Anglo-Saxons in the 5th century.

4 Christian monasticism originated on the edges of the Sahara desert, which developed from communities of hermits in the early 4th century.

5 Mithraism was popular in the Roman army: several Mithraic sites have been discovered on the strongly garrisoned Rhine frontier.

6 Armenia became the first state to adopt Christianity as its official religion, in about 300.

7 A major early Buddhist center developed around *stupas* (mounds) built by Ashoka to house relics of the Buddha and his followers.

8 Sacred Fire, believed to be a manifestation of Ahura Mazda, was the focus of ritual in Zoroastrian temples.

9 The influence of Daoism led Chinese Buddhists to found monasteries on mountains such as at Lingjiu (Vulture Peak).

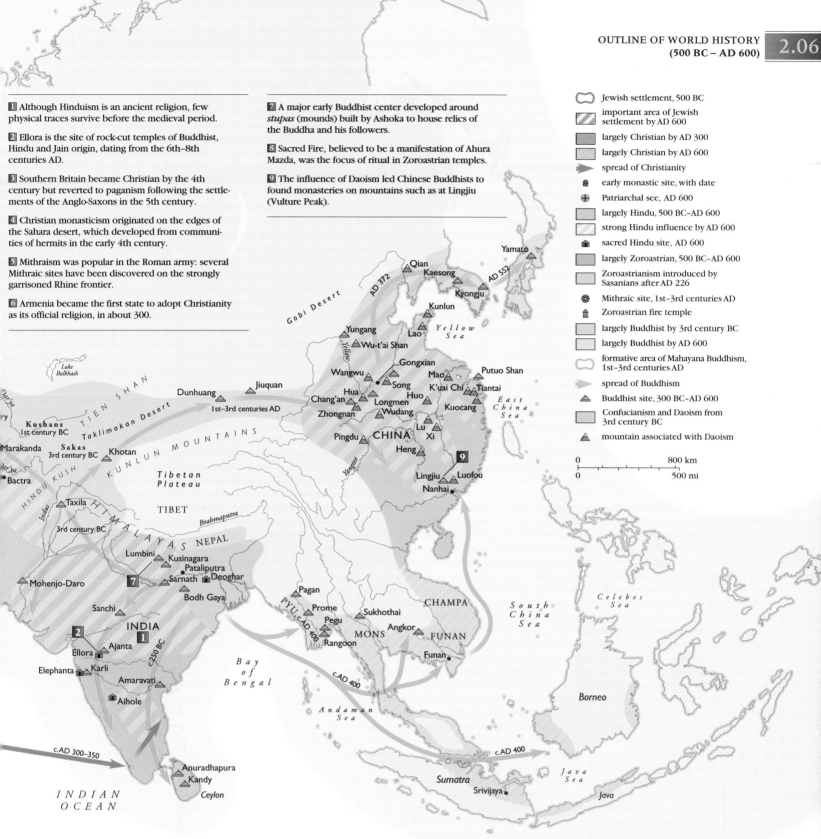

Key:
- Jewish settlement, 500 BC
- important area of Jewish settlement by AD 600
- largely Christian by AD 300
- largely Christian by AD 600
- spread of Christianity
- early monastic site, with date
- Patriarchal see, AD 600
- largely Hindu, 500 BC–AD 600
- strong Hindu influence by AD 600
- sacred Hindu site, AD 600
- largely Zoroastrian, 500 BC–AD 600
- Zoroastrianism introduced by Sasanians after AD 226
- Mithraic site, 1st–3rd centuries AD
- Zoroastrian fire temple
- largely Buddhist by 3rd century BC
- largely Buddhist by AD 600
- formative area of Mahayana Buddhism, 1st–3rd centuries AD
- spread of Buddhism
- Buddhist site, 300 BC–AD 600
- Confucianism and Daoism from 3rd century BC
- mountain associated with Daoism

0   800 km
0   500 mi

teachings provided the basis of Christianity and Islam. Judaism was a national religion and did not actively seek converts among non-Jews; yet the Hebrews' turbulent history meant that it became very widespread in the Mediterranean and Middle East by AD 600. The Diaspora, or dispersal of the Jews, began in the 6th century BC when communities of exiles from Palestine were established in Egypt and Mesopotamia. The greatest dispersal of Jews occurred in the 1st and 2nd centuries AD, following rebellions in Palestine against Roman rule.

Christianity originated in the teachings of a Jew, Jesus of Nazareth, who rejected the current practice of Judaism. Christianity developed initially as a Jewish sect, but the influence of St Paul and others made the religion more attractive to non-Jews, and by AD 70 its separation from Judaism was complete. Because of their refusal to pay formal homage to the state gods, Christians often faced persecution by the Roman emperors. Despite this Christianity was well established, especially in the eastern empire, by 312 when the emperor Constantine converted, introducing formal toleration the following year. Christianity made rapid progress after this, and in 391 it became the Roman empire's official religion. Christians came to believe that God had created the Roman empire specifically for the purpose of spreading Christianity.

An early rival to Christianity in the Roman empire was Mithraism, a derivative of the Persian Zoroastrian religion. Zoroaster, the religion's founder, reformed the ancient Iranian religion, dividing the pantheon into good and evil deities. It developed into a dualist religion which taught that the chief god Ahura Mazda, aided by Mithra, was locked in combat to protect the world from his evil rival Ahriman. Zoroastrianism became the religion of the Achemenid rulers of Persia and flourished under the Parthians and Sasanians. Although in its pure form it won few converts outside Persia, its teaching on the nature of good and evil had an important influence on Hellenistic, Jewish, Christian and Islamic thought.

See also 2.15 (the Christian empire)

After Cyrus, founder of the Persian empire, conquered Lydia in 546 BC, his generals mopped up the relatively insignificant Greek cities of Ionia, but in 499 they rebelled again under the leadership of Aristagoras of Miletos and introduced democratic rule. The rebels received aid from Athens and this provoked the Persian king Darius (r.521–486) to plan a punitive invasion of Greece after the revolt had been crushed in 494.

Darius' first invasion, in 492, was defeated by the weather when the fleet supporting his army was destroyed in a storm rounding Mount Athos. After a second expedition was humiliatingly defeated by the Athenians at Marathon in 490, Darius decided that the conquest of the whole of Greece was needed to secure the Persian position in Ionia. He died before his preparations were complete and it was left to his son Xerxes to carry out his plans. Meanwhile the Greeks prepared for an invasion, with Themistocles persuading Athens – by far the largest and wealthiest *polis* or city-state – to invest in an urgent naval building program.

The history of this invasion was memorably recorded by the Ionian-born Herodotos, the first major Greek prose writer and historian, later in the 5th century. Xerxes' army, said to have been 200,000 strong, was one of the largest forces ever assembled in antiquity and was supported by a fleet of perhaps a thousand ships. Faced with this vast force, most of the northern Greek states opted for neutrality or (in a few cases) alliance with Persia. The southern Greek states, however, united under the leadership of Athens and Sparta and prepared to resist the Persians. The resulting struggle was less uneven than expected. The very size of the Persian army proved a serious handicap; it was difficult to supply and impossible to control effectively on a battlefield; the quality of its troops varied enormously and only around 10,000 were elite troops. In contrast the Greeks, though greatly outnumbered, were heavily armed, experienced, disciplined and highly motivated: they were citizens defending their states, homes and families.

The Greeks, led by Sparta, attempted to halt the Persian invasion at Thermopylae but were defeated after heroic resistance. The Persians went on to occupy Athens, although its population had been evacuated to Salamis. The Persian fleet, which was needed to outflank Spartan defenses on the Isthmus of Corinth, was now ambushed and destroyed by the Athenian navy at Salamis. Since it was clear that Greece could not now be conquered in a single campaign, Xerxes returned to Asia with half of the army: the remainder wintered in Greece only to be defeated decisively by a Spartan-led army at Plataea in the following year. The threat to Greece ended, the old rivalries of the Greek world resurfaced and Sparta and most of the other states withdrew from the war against Persia. Athens and its allies continued hostilities, destroying the last Persian garrisons in Europe, re-opening the Bosporus to Greek shipping by 475, and freeing the Ionian Greeks from

Persian rule in 468. The Athenians also intervened unsuccessfully against the Persians in Egypt in 454 and captured Cyprus in 450. Hostilities came to a formal end in 448 when the Persians recognized Ionian independence.

To pursue its war aims, Athens created the anti-Persian Delian league of Aegean cities, with a common treasury on the island of Delos to which all members contributed. As its richest member and greatest naval power, Athens dominated the league and came increasingly to regard it as its empire. Some states, such as Aegina, were forcibly enrolled, and if a dissatisfied member tried to withhold contributions, the Athenian fleet was sent to enforce obedience. When the Athenians moved the treasury to Athens in 454 its domination became even more apparent. Despite this, many members remained loyal, being grateful to Athens for its role in the Persian wars and for introducing democracy. After the end of the war with Persia the league became as much a commercial as a military organization, although still serving Athenian interests. Athenian coinage, weights and measures were introduced throughout the league.

Under the leadership of the highly nationalistic Pericles, Athens also extended its power on the mainland and by 460 had achieved a dominant position in central Greece. Sparta – unusual in still having a monarchical constitution – had the strongest army in Greece and was unwilling to surrender its primacy to the increasingly arrogant Athenians. Throughout the 460s the Spartans were preoccupied with a *helot* (serf) revolt, but moves to increase the influence of Athens within the Peloponnese led to the outbreak of war between the two rivals in 457.

Athens was unable to sustain a war against Persia and Sparta at the same time, but the peace treaty with Persia in 448 in some ways weakened the Athenian position. Without the fear of a return to Persian rule, many members of the Delian league felt less closely bound to Athens. Sparta, which had no navy, concentrated its attack on the Athenian position on the mainland of central Greece while attempting to foment rebellion in the league. The Athenians successfully put down rebellions in

Legend

Persian wars, 499–448

- Greek states allied against Persia
- Greek states remaining neutral
- Greek vassals and allies of Persia
- Persian empire on accession of Xerxes, 486
- Persian empire after peace of Kallias, 448
- → Persian campaign under Darius, 492
- → Persian fleet (Marathon campaign), 490
- → Persian campaign under Xerxes, 480
- — border, 448

Athenian empire, 477–431

- Athens and the Delian league
- Athenian allies and conquests
- Spartan league
- *Skyros* Athenian military colony
- ✳ rebellion against Athens, with date

```
0                    200 km
0                    150 mi
```

ATHENS had a strong coinage based on its local silver mines; the owl was the universally known symbol of the city.

TIMELINE

Political change

500	475	450
509–507 Kleisthenes introduces a democratic constitution in Athens	**478** Sparta withdraws from the alliance against Persia	**447** Athens begins to establish military settlements in the Aegean
499–494 The Ionian cities rebel against Persian rule	**478** The Delian league is set up, with Athens at its head	
492 Darius of Persia launches an expedition against Greece; it is defeated by the Athenians at Marathon in 490	**462–458** Democratic institutions are completed in Athens, with Pericles as the dominant political figure	
	457–445 The first Peloponnesian war between Athens and Sparta	
480 Xerxes' invasion of Greece is stopped on sea at Salamis, and on land at Plataea (479)	**448** The peace of Kallias secures Ionian independence from Persia	

Cultural change

500	475	450
c.500 The black-figure style of vase painting flourishes in Athens	**c.460** The temple of Zeus at Olympia is built	
		449 Pericles begins to rebuild Athens, and starts work on the Parthenon (447–432)
484 The playwright Aeschylos wins the Athenian tragedy prize for the first time		

Illyrians

Thracians

Black Sea

Apollonia

Epidamnos

Apollonia

Lake Ohrid

Lake Prespa

Bosporus

Byzantium 440

MACEDON
Persian vassal, 492

Pella

Amphipolis Eion

Abdera

465 *Thasos*

9

Akanthos

7

Cyzicus

Methone
Poteidaia 432

2

Mt Athos

Chersonesos 3
Abydos

Hellespont

Imbros

Troy

EPIRUS

Lemnos

orcyra

Ambracia

Larissa Kosthanaia

THESSALY

Pinios

Northern Sporades

Skyros

Aegean Sea

Mytilene

Lesbos

LYDIA

Anaktorion

Artemisium 480

Thermopylae 480

Oreos

Euboea

Phokaia

Sardis

Kephallenia

Delphi

LOKRIS

PHOCIS

EUBOEA
Chalcis 447
Eretria

Erythraia

Plataea 479

Thebes

Chios

BOEOTIA

Marathon 490

Zakynthos

ACHAEA

Megara

ATTICA

Athens

Andros

Ephesos

6

Buyuk Menderes

Elis

ARCADIA

Corinth

Salamis 480

Laurion

Ikaria

Samos *Samos*
440

ELIS

Argos

Aegina

Mycale 479

Tegea

Troizen

8

1

Miletos

Sparta

Delos

Halikarnassos

SPARTA

469 *Naxos*

Kos

Mediterranean Sea

Rhodes

Carpathos

Crete

Euboea and Thasos, but by 445 they had lost control in central Greece and agreed to peace terms which recognized Spartan dominance in the Peloponnese.

Despite being almost constantly at war, Athens flourished economically in the 5th century as a result of its dominance of eastern Mediterranean and Black Sea trade and its own rich silver mines – worked by more than 20,000 slaves – at Laurion in Attica. Athenian democratic institutions continued to be developed and by 458 all citizens (excluding slaves, women and foreigners) were eligible to vote for and (except for the poorest) to serve in the highest offices of the government and the judiciary. The triumph in the war with Persia led to an exceptional outburst of cultural confidence in Greece as a whole, and especially in Athens, where vase-painting, sculpture and drama all reached new heights. The

city, and notably its Acropolis, were rebuilt and the "classical" style of art and architecture matured. No other Greek city-state saw such a program of public building at this time.

1 The Greek cities of Ionia, led by Miletos, rebelled against Persian rule in 499 and sacked Sardis.

2 A Persian fleet was destroyed rounding Mt Athos in 492. To avoid the same thing happening in 480, the Persians dug a canal across the peninsula neck.

3 A bridge of boats was built across the Hellespont for Xerxes' expedition in 480.

4 At Thermopylae, the Greeks under Leonidas of Sparta were outflanked; most withdrew, but the Spartans' heroic stand inspired later Greek defense.

5 At the comprehensive Greek victory of Plataea, the Persian general Mardonios was killed and the leading Theban allies of the Persians were executed.

6 The last of the Persian fleet was destroyed at Mycale in 479.

7 Eion, the last important Persian stronghold in Europe, was captured by the Athenians in 475.

8 The common treasury of the Delian league was kept on Delos, but was removed to Athens in 454.

9 Delian league member Thasos rebelled in 465, but the Athenians invaded and tore down the city walls.

See also 2.08 (Peloponnesian war)

The first Peloponnesian War had been indecisive and a second, much larger, war broke out in 431. Although the war eventually broke the power of Athens, it did not leave Sparta, the victor, strong enough to achieve the undisputed dominance in Greece. The war confirmed that no Greek city-state could achieve permanent dominance.

In the 430s, Athens was entering its most exceptional age, with the Parthenon completed in 432, and with values embodied in Periclean rhetoric and the plays of Sophocles and Euripides. In 430 Socrates began his career as teacher and philosopher. The 4th century brought philosophers such as Plato and Aristotle (who was to be the tutor of Alexander of Macedon). And the Peloponnesian War found in Thucydides a great Athenian historian able to record the complex chain of events.

In 435 a minor war broke out between the Corcyreans and Corinth, an ally of Sparta. Anxious that Corinth would seek revenge, the victorious Corcyreans allied with Athens in 433 but this only led the Spartans to fear that the Athenians once again had expansionist ambitions. When Athens attacked the northern city of Poteidaia for defecting from the Delian league, the Spartans demanded that Athens free all members of the league.

Sparta's strength was its army, Athens' its navy: when war broke out between the two in 431, they pursued very different strategies. Sparta's hope was that Athens could be starved into surrender by ravaging its agricultural hinterland in Attica. However, the Athenians had planned for this contingency. Attica was abandoned – its population taken within the city walls – while the city's wealth and command of the sea was harnessed to supply Athens from overseas and to raid the Peloponnese. However this overcrowding led to a plague (430–426) in which a third of the city's population died. By 421 neither side had achieved a decisive advantage and a peace was negotiated but on terms which alienated Sparta's allies Corinth, Elis, Mantineia and Argos, which then allied with Athens in 419. War broke out again unofficially but after a Spartan victory at Mantineia in 418 this new alliance broke up. The war

entered a decisive phase in 416 when the Athenians, to deprive their enemies of Sicilian food exports, agreed to send an expedition to besiege Syracuse. The expedition of the following year was a disaster from which Athens failed to recover. Sparta re-entered the war officially in 414 and sent help to Syracuse. The Athenians were catastrophically defeated in Sicily the following year, losing most of their 45,000-strong force. In the same year, Sparta garrisoned Dekeleia in Attica, forcing the closure of Athens' silver mines.

In 412 Persia, in return for a free hand in Ionia, paid for the construction of a Spartan fleet, tipping the balance of power decisively away from Athens.

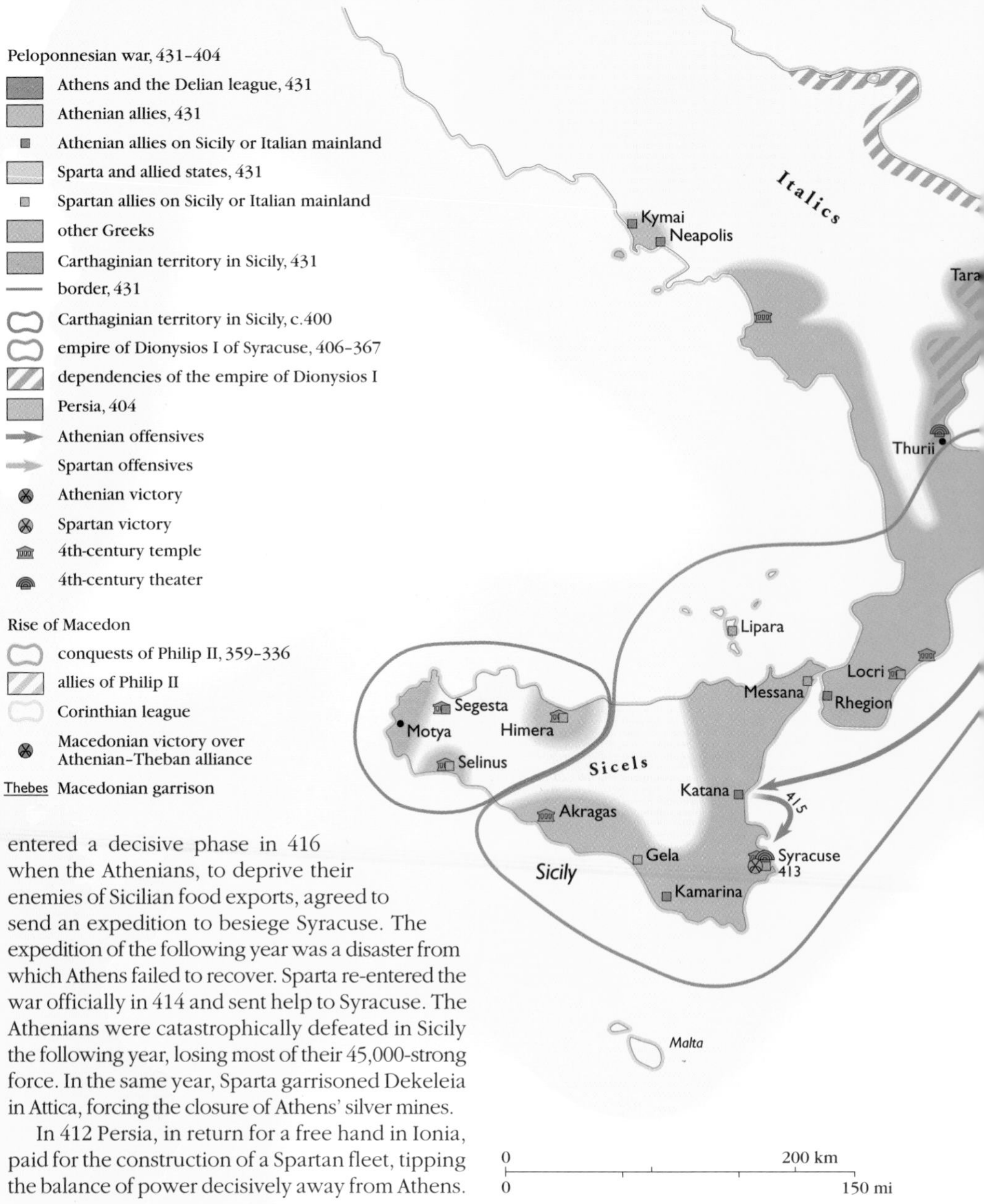

Peloponnesian war, 431–404

- Athens and the Delian league, 431
- Athenian allies, 431
- Athenian allies on Sicily or Italian mainland
- Sparta and allied states, 431
- Spartan allies on Sicily or Italian mainland
- other Greeks
- Carthaginian territory in Sicily, 431
- border, 431
- Carthaginian territory in Sicily, c.400
- empire of Dionysios I of Syracuse, 406–367
- dependencies of the empire of Dionysios I
- Persia, 404
- Athenian offensives
- Spartan offensives
- Athenian victory
- Spartan victory
- 4th-century temple
- 4th-century theater

Rise of Macedon

- conquests of Philip II, 359–336
- allies of Philip II
- Corinthian league
- Macedonian victory over Athenian–Theban alliance
- Thebes Macedonian garrison

Map labels: Kymai, Neapolis, Italics, Tara, Thurii, Lipara, Locri, Messana, Rhegion, Segesta, Himera, Motya, Selinus, Sicels, Katana, Akragas, Gela, Syracuse 413, Kamarina, Sicily, Malta

0 — 200 km
0 — 150 mi

TIMELINE

Political change

425	400	375	350	325
433 A Corcyrean alliance with Athens arouses Spartan fears	412 Sparta enters an alliance with Persia, which then takes much of Ionia	387 Dionysios I of Syracuse captures Rhegion		340 The Hellenic league of Greek states is set up
431 Outbreak of war between Sparta and Athens		379–362 Thebes becomes the leading city-state in Greece		338 Philip defeats Thebes and Athens at Chaeronea
421 Peace terms are agreed between Sparta and Athens	405 The Spartans defeat the Athenian fleet at Aegospotami; Athens itself falls the following year	371 Spartan decline begins with a defeat at the hands of Thebes		337 Macedon sets up the Corinthian league
415–413 An Athenian expedition to Syracuse ends in disaster	401–399 Expedition of the "Ten Thousand" Greek soldiers in Persia		359 Accession of Philip II of Macedon	336 Assassination of Philip and accession of Alexander
				334 Alexander invades the Persian empire

Cultural change

425	400	375	350	325
430 Herodotos completes his *History*	c.404–396 Thucydides writes the *History of the Peloponnesian War*	c.365 The Athenian Praxiteles makes his sculptures of Hermes and Aphrodite		335 Aristotle founds the peripatetic school of philosophy in Athens
c.425 The sculptors Pheidias and Polyclitos bring their art to new heights in Athens	399 Socrates is condemned to death for atheism	351 The Athenian orator Demosthenes warns of the threat posed by Macedon		
c.420 Democritos develops an atomic theory of matter	c.385 Plato founds the Academy, a school for philosophy		343 Aristotle becomes tutor to Alexander of Macedon	

| 425 | 400 | 375 | 350 | 325 |

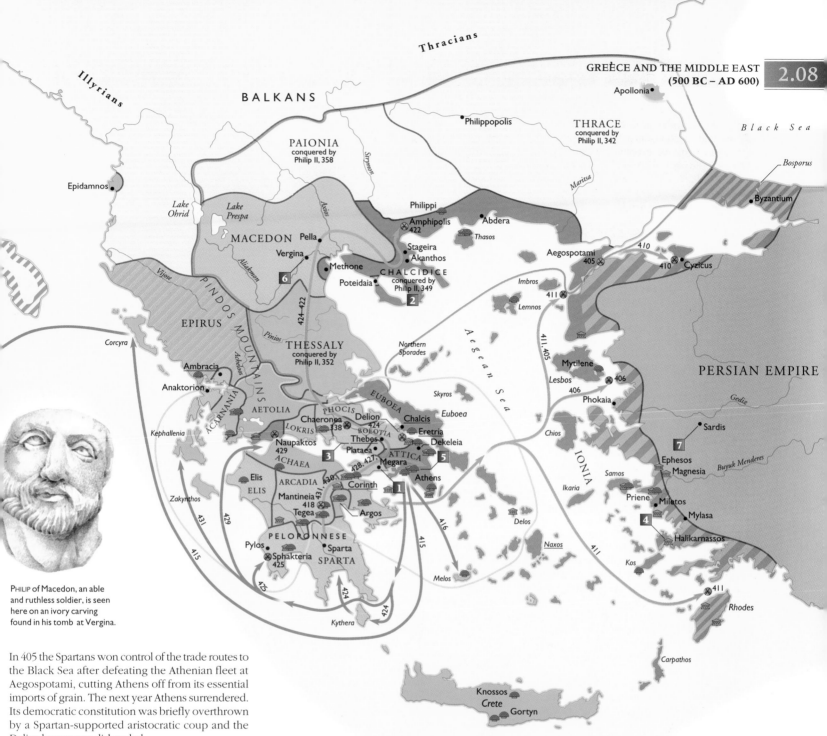

PHILIP of Macedon, an able and ruthless soldier, is seen here on an ivory carving found in his tomb at Vergina.

In 405 the Spartans won control of the trade routes to the Black Sea after defeating the Athenian fleet at Aegospotami, cutting Athens off from its essential imports of grain. The next year Athens surrendered. Its democratic constitution was briefly overthrown by a Spartan-supported aristocratic coup and the Delian league was disbanded.

Sparta was now the strongest Greek state but its victory had been paid for by Persian gold. When Sparta went to war against Persia in 400, the Persians simply switched their subsidies to Athens and the increasingly powerful Thebes, and Spartan ambitions faded. The Greek states continued to struggle fruitlessly for another fifty years until unity was imposed on them by Philip II (r.359–336) of Macedon.

Macedon had a mixed population of Greeks, Illyrians and Thracians but, even though the Athenians liked to regard it as a barbarian kingdom, it was a thoroughly hellenized state by Philip's accession. Macedon was now transformed from a backwater into a superpower. Philip ignored the convention of Greek warfare that restricted campaigning to specific times of the year and introduced siege engines to take cities quickly by storm rather than by long blockade. Philip's first conquest, Paionia in the Balkans, paid with its rich mineral resources for the expansion of the Macedonian army and thereafter his progress was inexorable. In 340 Athens made a last-ditch effort to halt Philip's expansion, forming the anti-Macedonian Hellenic league. Philip crushed this alliance at Chaeronea in 338, after which all the major Greek states, except Sparta, were forced to join the Macedonian-controlled Corinthian league.

Philip now announced a war of all Greece against Persia. The military weakness of Persia had been exposed in 401 when the rebel Persian governor of Sardis recruited an army of 10,000 Greek mercenaries to support his bid for the throne. The "Ten Thousand" marched into the heart of the Persian empire and, when their employer was killed in Babylonia, fought their way home again, demonstrating the military superiority of the Greeks. Philip's confidence was well placed but he was assassinated before his expedition was ready.

In the late 5th century the Greeks came close to being expelled from Sicily after Segesta called on the support of its ally Carthage during a boundary dispute with the aggressive Greek city of Selinus in 410. The Carthaginians went on to occupy the western half of Sicily by 405. The Greeks were united by Dionysios (r.406–367), tyrant of Syracuse, who recovered much of the territory lost to Carthage. Dionysios later extended his power to the Italian mainland where the Greek cities accepted him as their protector against the Italic peoples.

1 Megara was a neighbor and rival of Athens; when Athens blockaded it in the 430s, Sparta found an excuse for war.

2 Athens lost control of Chalcidice as a result of a campaign by the Spartan general Brasidas in 424–422.

3 The war-weariness of Sparta and Athens allowed Thebes to become dominant in Greece 379–362.

4 Halikarnassos was the site of the monument (Mausoleum) to Mausolos, a Lydian king who ruled from Mylasa and tried to build an empire in the 350s.

5 In Athens, Demosthenes spoke passionately about the Macedonian threat but failed to stem it.

6 The opulently furnished tomb of Philip II at Vergina was discovered in 1977. It contained his cremated body, his bronze armor and elegant grave goods.

7 Cyrus, governor of Sardis, recruited 10,000 Greek mercenaries to support his bid for the Persian throne in 401. Their progress was described by Xenophon.

See also 2.07 (5th-century Greece); 2.09 (Alexander); 2.12 (Sicily, Carthage and Rome)

In only eight years of tireless campaigning, Alexander of Macedon (r. 336–323) conquered the Persian empire and the Indus valley. Although his empire broke up on his death, Alexander's conquests determined that Hellenism would be the dominant cultural influence in the Middle East well into the Christian era.

Alexander was eighteen years old when his father, Philip II, was assassinated. He was bold, imaginative, well educated – Aristotle had been his tutor – and a promising soldier. In the first two years of his reign Alexander proved his abilities by securing Macedon's northern borders and subduing the rebellious Greeks. In 334, his home base now stable, Alexander launched his father's planned invasion of Persia, routing the army sent to stop him at the river Granicus. He then marched down the Anatolian coast, liberating and restoring the Greek cities of Ionia. Only Miletos and Halikarnassos, where the garrisons had been supplied by the Persian fleet, offered serious resistance. To prevent further naval interference, Alexander proceeded to conquer Phoenicia and Egypt, after first crushing a large Persian army, commanded personally by Darius III, at the river Issus in 333. With Persian naval power eliminated, Alexander marched into the heart of the Persian empire in 331, and at Gaugamela inflicted another humiliating defeat on Darius. Persian resistance crumbled, and Babylon and the Persian treasury at Susa were captured.

The following year, at the Persian Gates pass, Alexander destroyed the last sizeable Persian army and swept on to loot and burn the Persian capital, Persepolis. It took Alexander three more years of tough campaigning in Bactria and Sogdiana to complete his conquest of the Persian empire, before invading the Indus valley in 327. There, in 326, Alexander won his last major battle, over King Porus at the river Hydaspes. Alexander wanted to press on and invade the Ganges plain, but his soldiers, after marching 25,000 kilometers (15,000 miles), had had enough and they refused. Instead Alexander marched down the Indus to the sea and turned west, reaching Babylon in 324, where, the following year, aged only 32, he died, an overweight alcoholic.

Shortly before his death his adoption of the styles of oriental kingship had lost him the loyalty of some of his original Macedonian followers.

The most important factor in Alexander's success was his military genius, but he was also aided by the centuries-long tradition of imperial rule in the Middle East, which had weakened local identities and loyalties. The provincial populations of the Persian empire were used to foreign rule and, as Alexander respected local customs and did not make unreasonable demands for tribute, a change from Persian to Macedonian rule was a matter of indifference to them. Alexander's empire broke

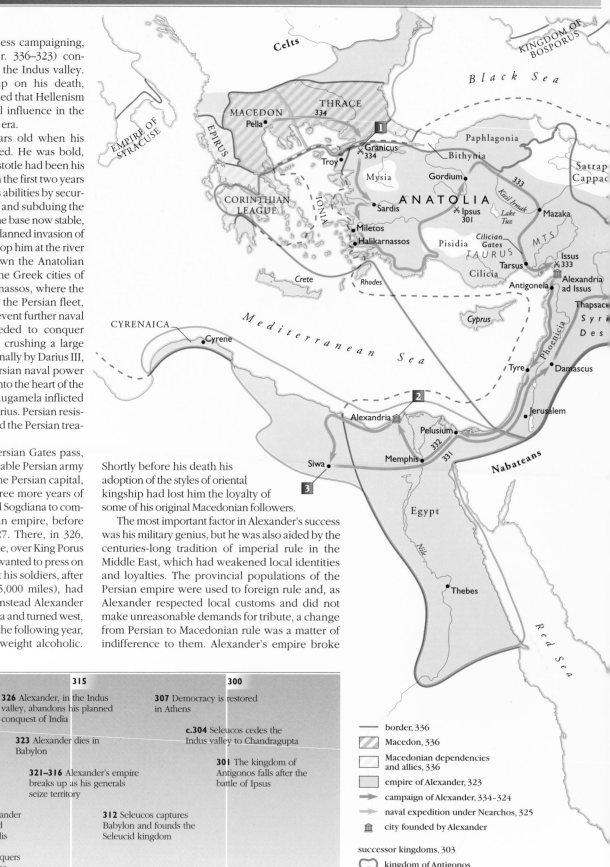

TIMELINE

	330	315	300
Political change	**334** Alexander invades Anatolia, repulsing a Persian army at the Granicus river	**326** Alexander, in the Indus valley, abandons his planned conquest of India	**307** Democracy is restored in Athens
	333 Darius III is defeated at the Battle of Issus	**323** Alexander dies in Babylon	**c.304** Seleucos cedes the Indus valley to Chandragupta
	332 Alexander conquers Egypt and founds the city of Alexandria	**321–316** Alexander's empire breaks up as his generals seize territory	**301** The kingdom of Antigonos falls after the battle of Ipsus
	331 At Gaugamela, Alexander defeats Darius again, and goes on to sack Persepolis	**312** Seleucos captures Babylon and founds the Seleucid kingdom	
	329 Alexander conquers Bactria and Sogdiana		
Cultural change	**335** Aristotle founds his school of philosophy in Athens	**312** Zeno, the first Stoic philosopher, arrives in Athens	**300** Ptolemy I founds the Museum of Alexandria
		306 The philosopher Epicuros establishes his school in Athens	
	c.325–300 Pytheas of Massilia circumnavigates Britain		
	330	315	300

— border, 336

▨ Macedon, 336

▢ Macedonian dependencies and allies, 336

▢ empire of Alexander, 323

⟶ campaign of Alexander, 334–324

⟶ naval expedition under Nearchos, 325

🏛 city founded by Alexander

successor kingdoms, 303

⬭ kingdom of Antigonos

⬭ kingdom of Cassander

⬭ kingdom of Ptolemy

⬭ kingdom of Seleucos

⬭ kingdom of Lysimachos

— modern coastline and drainage where altered

0		600 km
0		400 mi

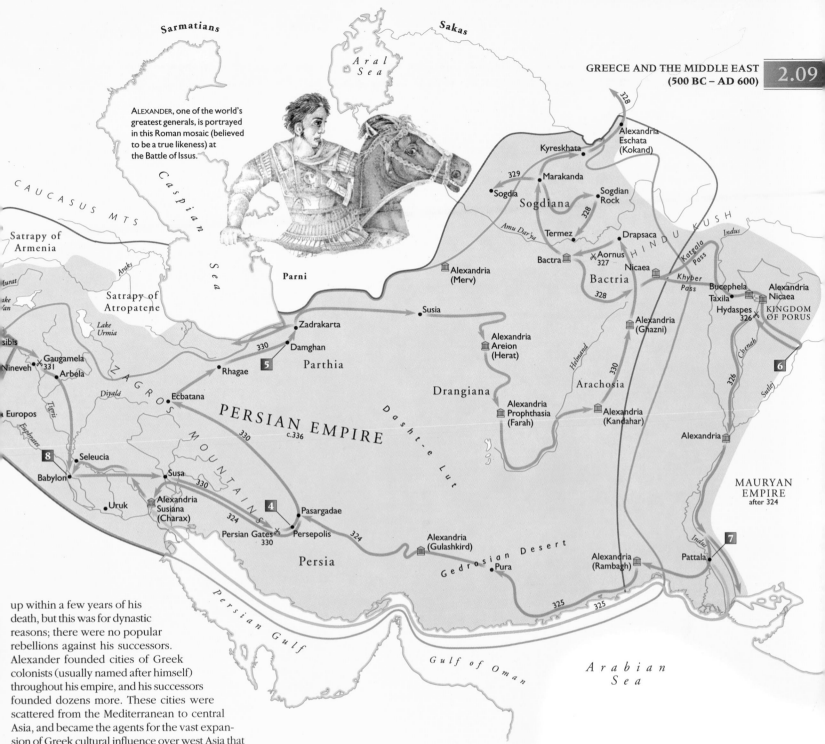

ALEXANDER, one of the world's greatest generals, is portrayed in this Roman mosaic (believed to be a true likeness) at the Battle of Issus.

up within a few years of his death, but this was for dynastic reasons; there were no popular rebellions against his successors. Alexander founded cities of Greek colonists (usually named after himself) throughout his empire, and his successors founded dozens more. These cities were scattered from the Mediterranean to central Asia, and became the agents for the vast expansion of Greek cultural influence over west Asia that was perhaps the most important consequence of Alexander's conquests.

Alexander left as his heirs a posthumous son and a mentally ill brother, neither of whom was capable of ruling in his own right. The regent Perdiccas maintained the central administration until his murder in 321, but under his successor, Antipater (d.319), the governor of Macedon, power in the provinces was seized by the generals and the empire fragmented in a series of conflicts known as the Wars of the Diadochi ("successors"). By 304 five successor kingdoms had arisen. Cassander, Antipater's son, ruled in Macedon; Lysimachos in Thrace; Antigonos had seized power in Anatolia; Seleucos in Mesopotamia and the east; and Ptolemy in Egypt. Of the five, only Antigonos aspired to recreate Alexander's empire, but this simply united the other Diadochi against him. When Antigonos was killed in battle against the combined armies of Seleucos, Lysimachos and Cassander at Ipsus in 301, his kingdom was divided up among the victors: Lysimachos taking Anatolia, Seleucus Syria and Cilicia, and Ptolemy, who had been campaigning separately, Palestine and Cyprus. Although the battle

of Ipsus did not bring an end to the struggles of the Diadochi, it did set the seal on the break-up of Alexander's empire.

During the chaos that followed his death, Alexander's empire had also begun to fray at the edges. His conquests had been rapid and the rulers of the northern satrapies of Bithynia, Paphlagonia, Cappadocia, Armenia and Atropatene had been allowed to retain their provinces after making only token submission. Alexander's early death prevented these provinces being brought into full submission, and during the Diadochan wars they became fully independent kingdoms. The Indus valley was also lost by the Greeks after Alexander's death. Preoccupied with the war against Antigonos, Seleucos ceded the Indian provinces to the Mauryan empire in 304 in return for a herd of war elephants (which he used to good effect at Ipsus). In Greece, now only a small part of the Hellenistic world, the cities of the Corinthian league rebelled unsuccessfully against Macedonian control in 323 and then defected to Antigonos in 307. However, after the defeat of Antigonos at Ipsus, Macedonian control was restored.

1 Alexander won control of Anatolia after defeating an army sent to intercept him at the river Granicus.

2 Founded in 332, Alexandria was to become the largest and richest Greek city in the 3rd century.

3 The oracle of Amun at Siwa claimed Alexander to be son of the god and heir to the Egyptian throne.

4 The burning of the palace of Xerxes at Persepolis in 330 marked the end of the Panhellenic war of revenge but not of Alexander's personal desire for conquest.

5 Darius III was murdered at Damghan by his courtiers as he fled, seeking refuge in Bactria.

6 Only when Alexander's exhausted and homesick army refused to follow him into the Ganges valley did he at last relent and turn back.

7 Nearchos built a fleet of more than 100 ships at Pattala to explore and control the Gulf coast.

8 Alexander died in Babylon in 323, having caught a fever after several days of heavy drinking.

See also 2.08 (rise of Macedon);
2.10 (Hellenistic world)

The struggles of the Diadochi continued for twenty years after the battle of Ipsus (301), during which time Lysimachos's Thracian kingdom was eliminated. Lysimachos himself was killed at the battle of Corupedion in 281, after which Seleucos took control of western Anatolia. Two years later Thrace was overrun by a Gaulish (Celtic) invasion. Some of these Gauls crossed into Anatolia, eventually establishing themselves in the region known subsequently as Galatia, from where they plundered the surrounding countryside for the next fifty years. The spate of Greek colonization of the east begun by Alexander continued until about 250. Dozens of new cities were founded and many established ones were hellenized: Greek became the common tongue from the Mediterranean to central Asia and the Indus valley.

Macedon gradually strengthened its hold on the Greek city-states during the 3rd century, but made an enemy of Rome by supporting Carthage during the Second Punic War (221–201). When Pergamon and Rhodes appealed to the Romans for protection against Macedon, Rome was happy to oblige, and at the battle of Cynoscephalae in 197 broke the kingdom's power and freed the Greek city-states. When Macedon attempted to reassert its position in Greece it was again defeated and annexation followed in 148. By this time the Romans had tired of the constant disputes of the Greek city-states and these were brought under direct Roman rule in 146.

The largest of the Hellenistic kingdoms at the end of the Diadochian wars was the Seleucid, but by the mid-3rd century it had begun a long slow decline. The first loss was the city of Pergamon in 262 BC. In 239 the Bactrian Greeks rebelled and founded an independent kingdom. The history of the Bactrian Greeks is little known, but they won back control of the Indus valley from the ailing Mauryan empire by the early 2nd century. In the 180s Greco-Bactrian rulers campaigned as far east as the Mauryan capital

at Pataliputra on the lower Ganges and won temporary control of much of central India. The Greco-Bactrians prospered from their control of the major trans-Asian trade routes and despite their isolation remained in contact with the mainstream of Greek culture. However, Bactria was exposed to attacks by the steppe nomads and around 135 BC most of the kingdom was overrun. Some independent Greek principalities survived in the upper Indus valley but were extinguished by the end of the 1st century BC.

The Seleucid kingdom suffered a further territorial loss in 238 when Parthia became independent

TIMELINE

Map legend:

— border, c.270
Macedon, c.270
Ptolemaic kingdom, c.270
Roman empire, c.270
Seleucid kingdom, c.270
Greco-Bactrians, c.185
Parthian empire, c.185
Seleucid kingdom, c.185
Parthian empire, c.90
Roman empire, c.90
Seleucid kingdom, c.90

— trans-Asia trade route
➤ migration, with date
▪ cities with Hellenistic foundations
— modern coastline and drainage where altered

0   600 km
0   400 mi

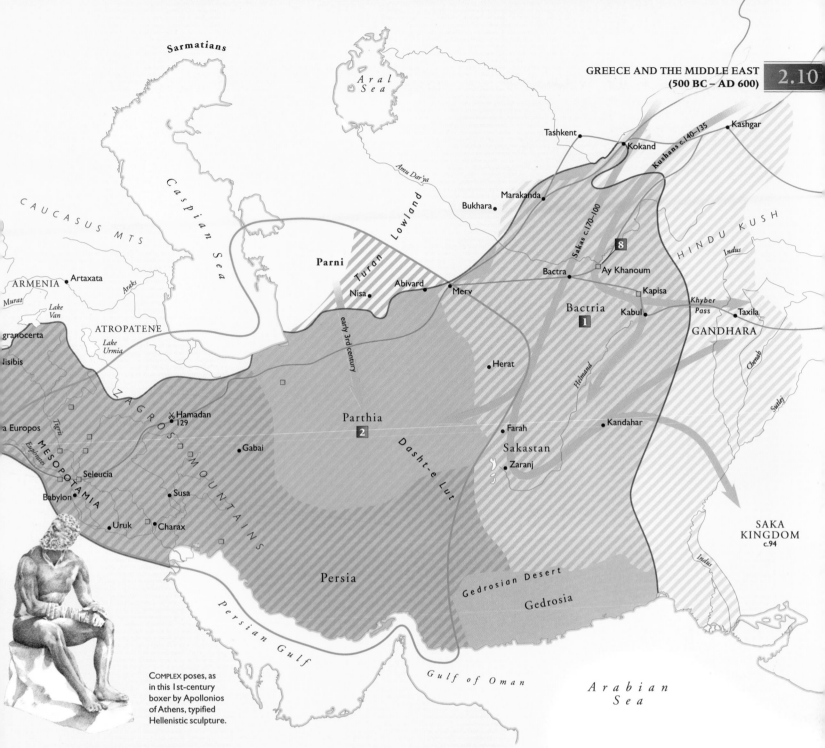

COMPLEX poses, as in this 1st-century boxer by Apollonios of Athens, typified Hellenistic sculpture.

under the Arsacid dynasty. The Arsacids were descendants of the ruling house of the Parni, Iranian nomads who had settled in Parthia earlier in the century. Under Antiochus III (223–187) the Seleucid kingdom conquered Armenia, Atropatene and Palestine and contained the expansion of Parthia and Bactria. Unfortunately, Antiochus's success alarmed the Romans, who declared war on him in 192 and two years later inflicted a crushing defeat on him at Magnesia. Armenia and Atropatene quickly regained their independence, while the Romans awarded western Anatolia to their ally Pergamon. Then in 166 Antiochus IV (r.174–163) faced a serious Jewish revolt. Around the middle of the century the Parthians conquered Persia and overran Mesopotamia, reducing the Seleucid kingdom to little more than Syria. However, the Parthians were prevented from completing the conquest of the Seleucid kingdom by the invasion of their eastern provinces by the Sakas in the 130s. The Sakas were contained by 90 BC and their main settlements, later known as Sakastan, came under the control of the Parthian Suren family, who founded a semi-independent kingdom that lasted over a century.

The most enduring of the Hellenistic kingdoms was the Ptolemaic kingdom of Egypt. Egypt had the strongest and most recent traditions of independence – it had successfully thrown off Persian rule from 404 to 341– and its population was resentful of the Greeks and Macedonians who now dominated the government and army. To placate the native Egyptians the Ptolemies adopted many of the trappings of the pharaohs and became patrons of the traditional religious cults. By the 2nd century some Egyptians had become hellenized; and some Egyptian cults, such as that of the goddess Isis, had found favor with the Greeks. Egyptians began to play an important role in the army. However, there was no real assimilation of the populations. Alexandria became the largest and richest Greek city in the world and even overshadowed Athens as a cultural center. The Ptolemaic kingdom was the major naval power of the eastern Mediterranean for most of the 3rd century but began to decline during a period of dynastic instability after the death of Ptolemy IV in 203. When, in 168, Antiochus IV conquered Egypt, only the intervention of the Romans secured the restoration of the Ptolemaic dynasty.

1 The Bactrian kingdom, independent from 239 and at its peak c.180, was destroyed by the Kushans c.135.

2 The Parthian kingdom, founded by Arsaces in 238, had conquered Persia and Mesopotamia by 141.

3 The Jewish Maccabean revolt against the Seleucids in 166–160 led to Judean independence in 142–141.

4 Ptolemaic Egypt, though ruled from the Greek city of Alexandria, saw its cultural traditions preserved.

5 The Romans broke the power of Macedon at Pydna in 168, and formally annexed the kingdom in 148.

6 The final remnant of the Seleucid kingdom was conquered in 83 BC by the Armenian king Tigranes I.

7 Under the Attalids, Pergamon was an important cultural center with a vast library, and spectacular architecture.

8 Hellenistic settlers spread Greek institutions across Asia. Gymnasia - centers of athletics and debating - have been discovered as far east as Ay Khanoum.

See also 2.09 (Alexander); 2.11 (Parthians and Sasanians); 2.13 (growth of the Roman empire)

In the chaos that followed the death of Alexander the Great, the Parni, an Iranian nomadic people, migrated from the Caspian steppes into Parthia. There they adopted Parthian language and customs, and their dominant family, the Arsacids, became the local rulers as vassals of the Seleucid kingdom. Arsaces I (r.c.247–c.211) declared his independence in 238, founding the independent Parthian state. The Seleucids contained Parthian expansion until the reign of Mithradates I (170–138), who turned Parthia into a major power by conquering Iran and Mesopotamia. Further expansion was prevented by invasions from the east by the Sakas and the Kushans and by dynastic problems. By 90–80 BC the eastern border was stabilized and the Sakas were settled in a vassal kingdom under the Parthian Suren family. Around the beginning of the Christian era this kingdom extended its control into the Indus valley. After 66 BC the Parthians had an opportunity to expand into Atropatene and seize northern Mesopotamia, where they established a common frontier with the Romans on the Euphrates.

The Romans initially regarded the Parthians as barbarians but learned to respect them when a major Roman army was destroyed at Carrhae by their horse archers almost as soon as it crossed the frontier in 53 BC. Internal troubles in Parthia saved the Romans from paying an even heavier price for their unprovoked attack. The Romans itched to avenge the humiliation, and wars between the two powers were frequent. The Roman infantry never got the measure of the Parthian horse archers and they made little headway until the 2nd century AD when the emperor Trajan took Armenia and Mesopotamia in 115–17. However, Trajan's successor Hadrian gave them up on his accession in 117. The Parthians had previously lost the Suren sub-kingdom to the Kushans, around AD 50–75.

The early Parthian kings adopted the Hellenistic traditions and governmental institutions of the Seleucid kingdom and continued to use Greek as an official language and on coinage. By the 1st century BC, however, the Parthian kingdom had developed into a decentralized feudal state made up of directly ruled provinces, vassal sub-kingdoms under local dynasties, and the fiefs of semi-independent nobles. Hellenistic cultural influence, strong at first, had also begun to decline by this time in the face of a resurgence of Persian traditions.

The frequent wars with Rome sapped the strength of the Parthian dynasty and in AD 224–26 it was overthrown following the rebellion of Ardashir I (r.c.220–40), the sub-king of Persia, who founded the Sasanian dynasty (named for Ardashir's grandfather, Sasan). The Sasanians saw themselves as the successors of the Achemenids and pursued far more aggressive and expansionist policies than the Parthians. Shapur I (r. 240–72) attempted to take Syria from the Romans but despite some spectacular victories, including the capture of the emperor Valerian at Edessa in 260, the Romans held on grimly. Shapur gained some territory from the Armenians and enjoyed spectacular success in the

Map Legend

- Suren kingdom, AD 1
- Kushan empire, c.AD 50–240
- Parthia, c.AD 114
- Roman empire, AD 114
- temporary Roman conquest, AD 114–17
- Sasanian empire, c.AD 260
- temporary Sasanian conquest, AD 607–28
- ▪ important city of the Parthian period
- ◉ rock relief of the Parthian period
- ▪ important city of the Sasanian period
- ⬢ rock relief of the Sasanian period
- ⊗ Parthian or Sasanian victory
- ⊗ Parthian or Sasanian defeat
- ᴜᴜᴜ Sasanian defensive earthworks
- —— border, c.AD 114
- —— trans–Asian trade route
- →→ campaign of Heraclius, AD 622–27
- ▶ major migration
- ----- modern coastline and drainage where altered

| 0 | 600 km |
| 0 | 400 mi |

Black Sea
AD 623
Byzantium (Constantinople after AD 330)
Aegean Sea
ANATOLIA
AD 622
Lake Tuz
Kizil Ir
TAURUS
Ginda
Crete
Rhodes
AD 622
Antioch
Cyprus
Mediterranean Sea
Damascus
Tyre
Palestine
Jerusa
Alexandria
Petra
Egypt
Nile
Red Sea

TIMELINE

	IBC	AD 300	AD 600
Political change	**238 BC** Parthia becomes independent under Arsaces I	**AD 115–17** The Romans occupy Mesopotamia	**484** King Peroz is killed by Ephthalite Huns
	c.165–140 BC The Sakas invade Parthia	**c.220–40** Ardashir I makes Zoroastrianism the state religion	**574** The Sasanians mount an expedition to Yemen
	141 BC The Parthians conquer Mesopotamia	**224–26** The Sasanians overthrow the Parthian dynasty	**616** Khosru II conquers Egypt
	c.100 BC Ctesiphon becomes the Parthian capital	**240–72** Shapur I brings the Sasanian empire to its greatest extent	**627** The Byzantine emperor Heraclius defeats Khosru II at Nineveh
	80 BC The Suren kingdom is established in Sakastan	**260** Shapur I captures the Roman emperor Valerian at Edessa	**634–51** The Sasanian empire is conquered by the Arabs
	53 BC The Parthians defeat a Roman army at the battle of Carrhae		
	c.AD 50–75 The Kushans destroy the Suren kingdom	**c.300** Armenia is the first state to adopt Christianity as its official religion	
Culture		**276** Mani, the founder of Manichaeism, is executed for heresy	**633** The recorded revelations of Muhammad (c.570–632) are published as the *Koran*
	IBC	AD 300	AD 600

1 The capital of Arsaces I, founder of the Parthian state, was Abivard. The royal necropolis was at Nisa.

2 A former Parthian winter capital, Ctesiphon was the Sasanian capital from AD 226 until 637.

3 The Kushans were conquered by Shapur I (r.240–72) but briefly regained most of their territory during the minority of Shapur II (r.309–79).

4 At Naqsh-i Rustam a monumental relief carved on a cliff face commemorates the capture of the Roman emperor Valerian by Shapur I in AD 260.

5 "Alexander's Barrier" was actually a Sasanian earthwork built as a defense against steppe nomads.

6 The fire-temples complex at Gushnasp was the holiest site of the Sasanians' Zoroastrian state church.

7 The Sasanian state collapsed after defeats by the Arabs at Al Qadisiya (637) and Nehavend (642).

8 Dura Europos was a major Parthian border fortress city, captured by the Romans in AD 165 and abandoned after it was taken by the Sasanians in 256.

Aral Sea

Caspian Sea

ABASGIA
LAZICA
IBERIA

CAUCASUS MTS

AD 626

ARMENIA

AD 623

Artaxata

Murat

Lake Van

2, AD 625

Tigranocerta

Amida
AD 260 · AD 360

D 260

Carrhae

53BC

Nisibis

Barbalissus
AD 253

8

ayra

ra Europos

Meshik
AD 244

MESOPOTAMIA

Mosul

Nineveh
AD 627

Hatra

Ashur

Arbela

Kharkha

Kangavar

Qal'eh-i
Yazdigerd

Dastagird

Al Anba

Artemita · AD 266

Seleucia

Ctesiphon

Vologesias

Babylon

Nippur

Susa

Uruk

El Mais

Ahvaz

Charax

Ubira

Al Qadisiya
AD 637

AD 637

7

Arabs

Kazerun

Bishapur

Rishahr

Firuzabad

Darabgird

Siraf

Persian Gulf

Atropatene

36 BC

Praaspa

Lake Urmia

Adhur Gushnasp
(Takht-i Sulaiman)

Nehavend
AD 642

Hamadan

Qom

Ray

5

ZAGROS

AD 624

Hecatompylos
(Shahr i-Qumis)

Nisa

Abivard

Merv

1

Turan Lowland

Turan

Nishapur

Herat

Parthia

MOUNTAINS

Naqsh-i Rustam

Istakhr

Persia

Yazd

Karmania

Veh Ardashir
(Kerman)

4

Dasht-e Lut

Farah

Nia

Sakastan

Zaranj

Gedrosian Desert

Makuran

Turan

Kashgar

Kustana

Tashkent

Kokand

*Ephthalites
c.AD 350–500*

Marakanda

Bukhara

Sogdiana

Amu Dar'ia

HINDU KUSH

Bactra

Bactria

Kabul

Kapisa

3

Indus

Gandhara

Taxila

Chenab

Helmand

Kandahar

Indus

Gulf of Oman

MAZUN

Arabian Sea

· Medina

· Mecca

AXUM

YEMEN
Sasanian dependency
AD 574–628

SASANIAN King Peroz indulges
in the favorite royal pastime of
hunting gazelle, on this silver
bowl of the 5th century AD.

east against the Kushans, conquering Sogdiana, Bactria and the Indus valley. The Kushans regained these territories during the minority of Shapur II (r.309–79), but lost them again when he took personal control. Shapur also enjoyed success against the Romans, Armenians and Arabs. Later in the 4th century the eastern provinces came under attack from the Ephthalites, or "White" Huns, who finally conquered them late in the 5th century. The kingdom also suffered severe internal problems at this time as a result of an attempted revolution by the Mazdakites, a radical religious movement. The Sasanians recovered under Khosru (Chosroes) I Anushirvan "of immortal soul" (r.531–79), who reconquered Sogdiana and Bactria, temporarily occupied Antioch in 540 and drove the Christian Axumites out of Yemen in 574. The long-running feud between the Sasanians and the Roman empire reached its climax in the reign of Khosru II (r.591–628) who took advantage of the empire's internal troubles to launch an all-out war in 607. Initially outstandingly successful – Syria, Palestine and Egypt were quickly overcome and a Persian army reached the Bosporus – the war ended in defeat at Nineveh

in 627 and Khosru's assassination. Civil war broke out and the Sasanian kingdom was left so exhausted that when the newly Islamized Arabs poured out of the desert in 637 it quickly collapsed. The last claimant to the Sasanian throne was killed in 651.

In contrast to the Parthian kingdom, the Sasanian kingdom was a highly centralized state with the provinces kept under close control. Society was rigidly organized into a caste system of priests, soldiers, scribes and commoners and Zoroastrianism was established as the state religion. Devotees of other religions were actively persecuted. Persian cultural traditions revived strongly under the Sasanians, though hellenism still retained some influence in the 3rd century. Sasanian Persian culture exerted a profound influence on early Islamic civilization, but its art styles also influenced early Christian art. The example of the Zoroastrian state church probably also influenced the 4th-century Roman emperors in promoting Christianity as a state religion.

See also 2.10 (Hellenistic world);
2.15; 2.16 (Roman empire)

Founded probably around 800 BC, Rome had by about 600 BC fallen under the control of an Etruscan dynasty. Rome benefited from its strategic position on the lowest crossing point of the Tiber but remained a minor city. In 509 the monarchy was overthrown by an aristocratic coup and a republic was founded. The first century of its history was dominated by a struggle between the lower classes (the plebeians) and the leading families (the patricians). By the end of the 5th century the senate had codified the law and granted the plebeians their own representatives: the tribunes. In the 4th century the plebeians also won the right to run for the major offices of state – though voting in the popular assembly was structured to favor the richer classes. The extension of rights to the plebeians helped build a community of interest between the classes that sustained the republic through many crises.

Roman expansion began as a series of minor wars against its immediate neighbors. There was no imperial masterplan at this stage: these wars were intended primarily to make Rome more secure from attack. Around 400 BC, Gauls crossed the Alps and made extensive settlements in the Po valley, which became known as Cisalpine Gaul (Gaul "this side of the Alps") to distinguish it from the Gaulish homeland to the north. The Gauls raided widely, even sacking Rome in 390, but mainly they weakened the Etruscans. In 354 the Romans allied against the Gauls with the Samnites, a powerful tribal confederation, but the alliance did not last. The Romans and Samnites had competing interests in central Italy, which led to the inconclusive First Samnite War (343–341). Rome conquered the Latins (340–338), before renewing its conflict with the Samnites in the Second (327–304) and Third (298–290) Samnite wars. A Roman victory at Sentinum in 295 was followed by the collapse of Samnite power and by 290 Rome dominated central Italy. The Romans planted colonies of Roman citizens in subdued territories

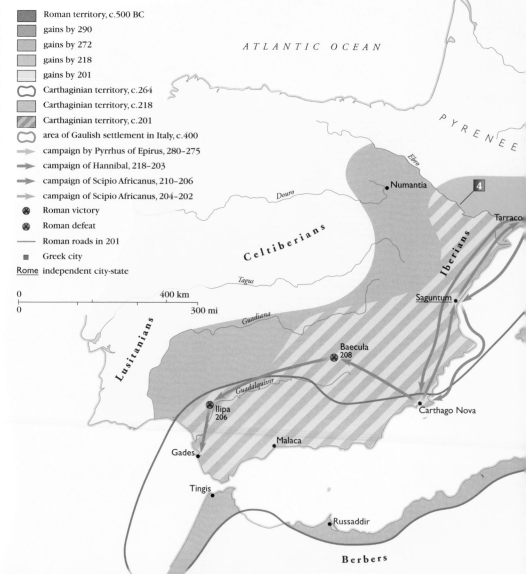

Roman territory, c.500 BC
gains by 290
gains by 272
gains by 218
gains by 201
Carthaginian territory, c.264
Carthaginian territory, c.218
Carthaginian territory, c.201
area of Gaulish settlement in Italy, c.400
campaign by Pyrrhus of Epirus, 280–275
campaign of Hannibal, 218–203
campaign of Scipio Africanus, 210–206
campaign of Scipio Africanus, 204–202
⊗ Roman victory
⊗ Roman defeat
── Roman roads in 201
■ Greek city
Rome independent city-state

0 ___ 400 km
0 ___ 300 mi

ATLANTIC OCEAN
PYRENEE[S]
Ebro
Numantia
Douro
Tarraco
Celtiberians
Iberians
Tagus
Saguntum
Guadiana
Baecula 208
Lusitanians
Guadalquivir
Ilipa 206
Carthago Nova
Gades
Malaca
Tingis
Russaddir
Berbers

and awarded their allies half-citizenship rights which could, if loyalty was proved, eventually be increased to full Roman citizenship.

The Romans began to bring the Greek cities of southern Italy under their sway. The Greeks appealed for protection to King Pyrrhus of Epirus. In 280 Pyrrhus invaded Italy after a hard-fought battle at Heraclea. The king's losses were so great that he remarked after the battle that a few more victories like this and he would lose the war. This is what in fact happened: the Romans resisted doggedly and in 275 Pyrrhus withdrew. Three years later the Romans took Tarentum, completing their conquest of peninsular Italy. Rome was now a Mediterranean power.

In 264 Rome went to war with Carthage, the major naval power of the western Mediterranean, over a dispute about spheres of influence in Sicily. The Romans called the Carthaginians "Poeni" (Phoenicians) – and the wars with Carthage came to be known as the Punic wars. Rome had no tradition of naval warfare but learned quickly, and in 260 its newly built fleet won its first victory over the Carthaginians at Mylae. In 255 the Romans tried to bring the war to a quick conclusion by invading north Africa but were repulsed. The war dragged on until 241, when the Carthaginians were vanquished at sea off Lilybaeum. Sicily became a Roman province; and in 238 the Romans also occupied Corsica

TIMELINE

Rome and Italy

400

509 The foundation of the Roman republic

c.450 The Laws of the Twelve Tables, the basis of Roman law, are laid down

c.400 Gauls settle Po valley and Etruscan power declines

396 Roman expansion begins with the capture of Veii

390 A wandering tribe of Gauls sacks Rome

c.380 City walls are built around Rome

300

343–290 The Samnite wars leave the Romans as the dominant power in Italy

280–275 Pyrrhus invades Italy but eventually withdraws

272 The Romans take Tarentum, completing the unification of peninsular Italy

c.222 The Romans conquer Cisalpine Gaul

216 At Cannae, Rome suffers its worst ever defeat, at the hands of Hannibal

200

201 End of the Second Punic War

Carthage

264–241 The First Punic War between Rome and Carthage

237–218 Carthaginian expansion occurs in Spain

218 Hannibal launches the Second Punic War

202 Rome defeats Carthage at the Battle of Zama

400   300   200

ALPS

Gauls (Celts)

Ticinus River 218 ⊗ · Mediolanum · Aquileia

CISALPINE GAUL

Trebia River 218 ⊗

Ligurians · Genua

Venetians

Po

GAUL

· Arausio

Massilia

· Narbo

Emporiae (Ampurias)

Aleria · Corsica

Sardinia

Carales

Balearic Islands

Mediterranean Sea

Drepanum 249 ⊗
Lilybaeum 241 ⊗

Hippo Regius ·

Utica · ⊗ Carthage

Bagradas 255

Cirta 203 ⊗

NUMIDIA 8

Kingdom of Syphax

Kingdom of Massinissa

Zama 202 ⊗ · Hadrumetum

Rhône

6

· Pisa

Ariminum

Metaurus River 207 ⊗

Ancona

Sentinum 295 ⊗

Lake Trasimenus 217 ⊗

Umbrians

Saturnia ·

Cosa ·

Etruscans

Veii ·

Ostia ·

Sabines

Rome

Latins

Corfinium

Samnites

Castrum Novum

Cannae 216 ⊗

Capua ·

Neapolis ·

Beneventum ·
Caudine Forks 321 ⊗

Paestum ·

Lucanians

Tarentum

Messapians

Heraclea 280

7

Croton ·

Mylae 260 ⊗

Panormus ·

Messana

Rhegium

Bruttians

MAGNA GRAECIA

Drepanum 249 ⊗

Agrigentum 262 ⊗

3 *Sicily*

Catana ·

Syracusae

Ecnomus 256 ⊗

Malta

Leptis Magna ·

Illyrians

Sava

Danube

MACEDON

Epidamnus ·

Apollonia ·

Brundisium

EPIRUS

Ambracia ·

Adriatic Sea

1

2

5

4

ELEPHANTS carried soldiers to battle, but were used to scare the enemy rather than as cavalry. This Roman plate shows one carrying a fort.

and Sardinia. In the 230s Carthage began to recoup its losses by expansion in Spain; and in the 220s Rome conquered Cisalpine Gaul. In 226 Rome and Carthage agreed on respective spheres of influence, but when Hannibal, Carthage's foremost general, attacked Saguntum, a city within Carthage's sphere but friendly to Rome, the Second Punic War broke out. Roman naval power compelled Hannibal to invade Italy by marching overland and crossing the Alps. In Italy Hannibal found ready allies in the newly conquered Gauls in the north and the Greek cities in the south – and also in the kingdom of Macedon, which viewed with concern the expansion of Roman power into Greece in the 220s. Hannibal was a brilliant general but lacked the strength to take Rome itself and so win the war. The Romans, after a catastrophic defeat at Cannae, did their best to avoid facing Hannibal in open battle, trying simply to contain him in southern Italy. The main Roman counterattack was aimed at Carthage's Spanish possessions. The decisive campaign began in 210 under Scipio Africanus, and by 206 the Carthaginians had been driven out of Spain. Then in 204 Scipio launched an invasion of north Africa and persuaded the Numidian king Massinissa to side with Rome. Hannibal was recalled from Italy to face Scipio, and in 202 the two generals met in battle at Zama. The result was a crushing defeat for Hannibal and

Carthage surrendered on harsh terms. Rome annexed Spain and the Balearic Islands, and the Numidians were given most of Carthage's north African territory. Carthage itself was reduced to a heartland in modern Tunisia: it had to disband its fleet and agree not to go to war without Rome's permission. Although in Spain the Romans faced rebellions – which for seventy years frustrated their attempts to gain control of their new possessions – Rome now dominated the western Mediterranean.

1 The capture of nearby Veii, an Etruscan city, in 396, was the first step in the Roman conquest of Italy.

2 Rome disputed control of Italy with the Samnites, a confederation of the Caraceni, Caudini, Hirpini and Pentri tribes, in a series of wars, from 343 to 290.

3 In the growing rivalry between Rome and Carthage, Sicily was the flashpoint that led in 264 to the outbreak of the First Punic War.

4 In 226 the Ebro was the agreed border between Roman and Carthaginian spheres of influence.

5 A Roman campaign against Illyria was mounted in 229–228 to suppress pirates infesting the Adriatic Sea.

6 Hannibal's crossing of the Alps took 15 days: only a handful of his original 38 elephants survived.

7 Hannibal's base for operations in southern Italy was at Tarentum until the Romans retook the city in 209.

8 Numidia's Berber kingdoms, longtime suppliers of cavalry to Carthage, sided with Rome at Zama in 202.

See also 2.13 (growth of the Roman empire)

Soon after the Second Punic War, Rome was drawn into further wars to protect its position in Italy, Spain and Greece. Cisalpine Gaul was re-conquered by 191. The need to protect the new Spanish provinces from native attack drew Rome into a piecemeal conquest of the whole peninsula. Rome also launched a punitive campaign in 200 against Macedon, which had allied itself with Carthage in the Second Punic War. In 197, after the battle of Cynoscephalae, Macedon was forced to liberate the Greek city-states. At this time Rome took no territory for itself. However, the weight of constant disputes among the Greek cities and the Hellenistic kingdoms had become so onerous by 146 that the Romans imposed direct rule on Greece: opposition was ruthlessly suppressed. Also in 146 a Roman army, which had been besieging Carthage for three years, finally razed the city to the ground, its territory becoming the Roman province of Africa. Expansion into the Middle East began in 133, when the last king of Pergamon bequeathed his kingdom to Rome, and Pergamon became the province of Asia. Southern Gaul was conquered and became the province of Gallia Narbonensis in 121.

As the empire grew, the booty of successful campaigns – treasure and slaves – flooded back to Rome. The largest class of the early republic had been peasant freeholders, but they could not compete with the new slave-run estates of the rich and were forced off the land to swell the ranks of the urban poor. Demands for constitutional reform led to bitter class conflict in Rome, as defenders of aristocratic privilege resorted to acts of violence, such as the murder of the reformist tribune Tiberius Gracchus in 133. Gaius Marius then reformed the Roman army, opening recruitment for the first time to landless citizens. These soldiers looked to their commanders to reward their service with grants of land to settle on when discharged. This had a dramatic effect on Roman politics as successful generals could usually count on their armies to support their political ambitions. Success in war was now the surest route to political power: it was the main motive for Pompey's

campaigns in Anatolia and Syria (67–64 BC), Julius Caesar's conquest of Gaul (58–51 BC) and Crassus's ill-fated attack on Parthia, which ended in his death at Carrhae, in 53 BC. The generals' need to reward their veterans led to the foundation of colonies throughout the empire in the late republic: these became important agents of Romanization.

The competition for power between generals led to civil war in 49 BC and ultimately to the fall of the republic. The victor was Caesar, who defeated his opponent Pompey at Ilerda in Spain (49 BC) and Pharsalus in Greece (48 BC). By 44 BC Caesar had crushed all military opposition, but a month after he declared himself dictator for life he was murdered by republican conspirators. Instability and civil war continued until Caesar's nephew Octavian, later known as Augustus, defeated Mark Antony and Cleopatra at Actium in 31 BC. In 27 BC Augustus introduced a new constitutional settlement, which he claimed "restored the republic" but in reality

	Roman empire, c.201 BC
	gains by 100 BC
	gains by 44 BC
	gains by AD 14
	gains by AD 117
	temporary gain, with dates held
	kingdom of Pontus under Mithradates VI, 112–66 BC
■	pre-Augustan Roman colony
■	Augustan Roman colony
■	post-Augustan Roman colony
—	Roman provincial boundary, early 2nd century AD
🏛	Roman provincial capital
🦅	Roman legion stationed, early 2nd century AD
✸	rebellion against Roman rule, with dates
AC	Alpes Cottiae (Roman province)
AM	Alpes Maritimae (Roman province)
AP	Alpes Poeninae (Roman province)

	200 BC	100 BC	AD 1	AD 100
	Republican period		Julio-Claudian dynasty	Flavian dynasty
Political change	**202** The Second Punic War ends in Carthaginian defeat	**121** Gallia Narbonensis becomes a Roman province	**48 BC** Caesar defeats Pompey in the civil war	**AD 14** Augustus dies and is succeeded by Tiberius
	168 Rome defeats Macedon at the Battle of Pydna	**107–100** Gaius Marius reforms the Roman army	**44 BC** Caesar is murdered by pro-republican conspirators	**43** Claudius initiates the Roman conquest of Britain
	149–146 The Third Punic War. The city of Carthage is razed to the ground	**91–89** The Social War: revolt by Rome's Italian armies (socii) is contained	**31 BC** Octavian (Augustus) is victorious at Actium.	**68–69** The "Year of Four Emperors" brings civil war
	146 Greece becomes a Roman province	**89–66** Three wars against Mithradates VI of Pontus	**27 BC** Augustus "restores the republic" but in reality introduces imperial rule	**106** Dacia is conquered by the emperor Trajan
	133–80 Social conflicts trouble Rome	**58–51 BC** Caesar completes his conquest of Gaul	**AD 9** The Roman army is defeated in Germany	**115–17** Trajan conquers Armenia and Mesopotamia
Cultural change	**c.254–184** Plautus: writer of comedies on Greek models		**c.30–19 BC** The poet Virgil (70–19 BC) writes the *Aeneid*	**c.AD 27** Architect Vitruvius writes *de Architectura*	**113** Trajan's column is erected in Rome
	c.200 Greek influences begin to appear in Roman art		**c.30 BC** Livy (59 BC–AD 17) begins his history of Rome	**AD 64** Christians begin to be persecuted in Rome
	196 The first triumphal arches are built in Rome		**c.8 BC** Ovid (43 BC–AD 17) completes his *Metamorphoses*	**c.100** Tacitus begins writing his *Histories* and the *Annals*
	200 BC	100 BC	AD 1	AD 100

GAULS were respected opponents of the Romans in the west and in Anatolia; this statue of a dying Gaul was made in Pergamon, 2nd century BC.

introduced a monarchical type of government. He took the title *princeps* (first citizen), leaving it to his successors to call themselves *imperator* (emperor).

Expansion continued under the emperors. In Augustus' reign Egypt and Galatia were annexed, the last native resistance was extinguished in Spain, the Alpine tribes were conquered, and the empire's northern frontier was pushed to the Danube. Augustus also tried to conquer Germany but gave up the attempt after a humiliating defeat at the battle of the Teutoburgerwald in AD 9. This defeat convinced Augustus that the empire had reached its natural limits and he advised his successors not to seek any more territories. Despite this advice, the empire continued to expand for another century after the death of Augustus. Much of the expansion was simply a tidying-up operation. The annexation of Lycia (AD 43) and the client kingdom of Mauretania (AD 44)

gave Rome control of the entire Mediterranean coastline. In AD 43, Claudius, a weak emperor who needed a triumph to strengthen his position, began the conquest of Britain but only the southern two-thirds of the island were actually brought under Roman rule. The last emperor to pursue an all-out expansionist policy was Trajan. Between 101 and 106 Trajan conquered the Dacian kingdom, which posed a threat to the security of the Danube frontier. His ambition was to conquer the Parthian empire, and he brought Armenia and Mesopotamia under Roman rule. However, his successor Hadrian (r.117–38), judging these eastern conquests to be undefendable, withdrew from all of them except Edessa. Later in the 2nd century the border was pushed northward in Britain, and northern Mesopotamia was wrested from the Parthians, but from this time on the empire was mainly on the defensive.

[1] Willed to the empire by the king of Pergamon, Asia became Rome's first Anatolian province in 133 BC.

[2] Rebellions – the "Social War" – forced Rome to concede equal political rights to non-Roman Italians.

[3] Mithradates VI of Pontus fought Rome in three wars from 89 until his final defeat in 66 BC.

[4] Augustus' victory at Actium in 31 BC ended the civil war and brought Egypt under Roman rule.

[5] Carthage, refounded as a Roman colony, became the center of Roman administration in Africa in 29 BC.

[6] The Roman conquest of Britain began in AD 43, nearly a century after Caesar's raids in 55 and 54 BC.

See also 2.06 (religion); 2.10 (Hellenistic kingdoms); 2.11 (Persia); 2.14 (later Roman empire)

The Roman empire created a vast free-trade area with a single currency where commerce could flourish without the threat of piracy or war. Good roads, bridges and harbors further aided trade. The empire's prosperity began to falter only in the 3rd century when the high cost of defending the empire caused emperors progressively to debase coinage, setting off runaway inflation.

The vast majority of the population of the Roman empire were peasant farmers or slaves whose needs were adequately met by local producers, but there was also considerable long-distance trade in both luxury goods and basic commodities such as metals, pottery and foodstuffs. The lifestyles of the small wealthy class were geared to conspicuous consumption, and luxury products such as silk, spices, aromatic resins, pigments and ivory were imported from as far afield as China, the East Indies and equatorial Africa to satisfy their tastes. Moralistic Romans worried that these expensive imports were a drain on the wealth of the empire; but finds of Roman metal and glassware, as well as coinage, from India and southeast and central Asia suggest that there was also a healthy demand for Roman exports. Luxury goods apart, the empire was essentially self-sufficient in everyday necessities and what was lacking in one region could easily be supplied by another. Most trade was generated by the needs of the empire's growing urban populations. Rome itself had to import 400,000 tons of grain annually, most of which came from Egypt, Africa and Sicily. The army also generated trade. Over 100,000 tons of grain were needed for rations each year; while the tents for one legion alone required the hides of 54,000 calves. The needs of the army stimulated agriculture and metalworking in the border areas, where most troops were stationed, but also called for much to be brought from elsewhere.

The empire's system of roads was built primarily to provide the army with fast all-weather routes, but they also promoted local trade. However, land transport was expensive because the volumes that could be transported were small. Long-distance cargoes therefore went by water, both by sea and along navigable rivers. Sea-going merchant ships capable of carrying up to 350 tons made it cheaper for

1 The main port for Rome was Puteoli until Claudius improved the harbor at Ostia, though this remained unsafe until Trajan rebuilt it in the early 2nd century.

2 Rome, with about a million inhabitants, was the largest city in the empire. Some 200,000 people relied on state handouts of grain for survival.

3 Egypt was the main granary of the Roman empire: the fertile Nile flood plain was the most productive agricultural area in the empire.

4 Carnuntum was the main center for trading Baltic amber with the German tribes.

5 Northwest Spain was one of the most important mining regions in the Roman empire.

6 Palmyra was a desert city which became an important trading destination for trans-Asian caravans.

7 The Rhineland was an important center of glass manufacturing: much was exported across the Rhine.

the city of Rome to import grain from across the Mediterranean than to cart it into the city from the surrounding countryside. For the same reason the Romans preferred to run frontiers along navigable rivers providing access to border garrisons – and fleets were maintained on the Rhine and the Danube for this purpose.

Although trade was essential to its survival, the empire's commercial classes remained small and enjoyed neither the wealth nor the status of the landowning aristocracy. Goods such as pottery were mass-produced in factories, but most production in the empire was small-scale and under-capitalized, the rich preferring to invest in land. It is in any case doubtful, in view of the poverty of most of the empire's population, whether the markets existed to support a greater degree of industrial production. This is probably one of the factors behind the surprising lack of technological innovation in the empire. Although the Romans were excellent engineers, they did not extensively exploit their under-

standing of the principles of water and wind power. The ready availability of cheap slave labor may also have deterred investment in expensive machinery.

The wealth and population of the empire were not evenly spread: the eastern half was wealthier, more densely urbanized and had a higher population than the western half which, outside Italy, was relatively underdeveloped. In most of the west, as in Gaul and Britain, urbanization was still in its early stages at the time of the Roman conquest, and the promotion of town life became part of the program of Romanization. The Romans founded dozens of new towns, each complete with baths, theaters, amphitheaters and other trappings of Roman civilization. But most of the west was too poor and underpopulated to support this level of urbanization and towns remained primarily administrative or military centers. This contrast between east and west was to have an important bearing on the fate of the empire in the 5th century.

The Roman empire united many different ethnic groups into a single state, but over time, helped by the progressive extension of citizenship, local

TIMELINE

Economic change

AD 1	150	300
40 BC Glass-blowing techniques replace the hand-molding of glassware	**c.100** Trajan devalues the coinage and institutes a range of economic reforms	**c.250** A period of high inflation points to impending economic crisis
27 BC Augustus reduces the army to 28 legions and settles more than 100,000 veterans in frontier colonies	**100** Trajan extends the corn dole in Rome to poor children, as well as to their parents	**286** The empire is divided into eastern and western parts
24–20 BC Augustus organizes regular grain handouts for the Roman poor, using grain from Egypt		**301** Diocletian, in an attempt to end the inflation, issues an edict on prices
	165–67 A plague epidemic sweeps through the empire	
AD 32 There are protests in Rome over grain shortages; riots recur in 51.	**212** Roman citizenship is granted to all inhabitants of the empire, allowing more taxes to be raised	

Transport

AD 1	150	300
c.AD 1–50 The first non-stop trading voyages from Egypt to India are undertaken	**c.200** The empire's arterial road system is effectively completed	
AD 42 Claudius improves the harbor at Ostia		
AD 1	150	300

Vänern
furs

Vättern

Baltic Sea

amber

Lake
Peipus

amber

Roman empire, c.AD 117
main concentration of cities
city with population over 100,000
city with population over 30,000
main road
sea and river route
caravan route
division between Greek
and Latin languages
CELTIC local language surviving
within Roman empire
furs source of goods from
outside Roman empire

goods traded within Roman empire
copper · slaves
gold · brass and bronze
iron · glass
lead · pottery
silver · timber
tin · marble
grain · textiles
olive oil · purple dye
wine

0   600 km
0   400 mi

*animal hides,
slaves*

Colonia Agrippina
Augusta Treverorum

Vistula

Elbe

Odr

Dniepr

*animal hides,
honey, grain*

Dnieper

Castra Regina

Birne

Danube

Carnuntum

C A R P A T H I A N   M T S

Olbia

Panticapaeum

*flax, wine,
iron*

A L P S

Aquileia

Sarmizegethusa

Sava

Danube

Tomi

Black Sea

Sinope

Trapezus

Genua

Ravenna

Singidunum

Salonae

Ancona

Naissus

Byzantium

Nicomedia

Ancyra

Megalopolis

*wild animals
from Asia*

Ostia

Rome

Dyrrhachium

THRACIAN

ILLYRIAN

Amida

Edessa

Puteoli

Brundisium

Thessalonica

A N A T O L I A

Pergamon

Tarsus

Antiochia

*silk
from China*

Sardinia

Corsica

Smyrna

Ephesus

Aphrodisias

Athens

Corinth

Dura Europus

Palmyra

Sicily

Syracusae

Rhodus

Rhodes

Cyprus

Paphus

*ARAMAIC/
SYRIAC*

Ctesiphon

Carthage

Malta

Crete

Gaza to Byzantium - 10–12 days

Tyrus

Damascus

Carthage to Ostia - 3–5 days

Theveste

*Mediterranean
Sea*

Caesarea to Rome - 20 days

Alexandria to Puteoli - 15–20 days

Caesarea

Bostra

Jerusalem

Gaza

NABATAEAN

Petra

Cyrene

Leptis Magna

*slaves and wild
animals
from tropical Africa*

Alexandria

Memphis

Clysma

LIBYAN

*DEMOTIC/
COPTIC*

Myos Hormus

Thebes

Berenice

Syene

*perfume,
spices and
muslin
from India*

*slaves, ivory, ebony
and wild animals
from tropical Africa*

*aromatic
resins
from Arabia*

identities were weakened, and by the 4th century the vast majority of the empire's citizens considered themselves Roman. In the west local languages were gradually replaced by Latin. Distinct local dialects of Latin developed in Italy, Iberia, Dacia and Gaul, eventually developing into the Romance languages – Italian, Spanish, Portuguese, Romanian and French. Celtic languages survived in Britain, Basque in the Pyrenees and Libyan in much of North Africa. Latin made little headway in the east. Here it was Greek which gradually replaced local languages, such as Phrygian, in Anatolia. However, Greek did not take over as completely as Latin did in the west and there remained large communities of Demotic (late ancient Egyptian) and Aramaic speakers.

MERCHANT ships were slow and heavy but were capable of ocean-going voyages: this illustration comes from Trajan's Column in Rome (AD 113).

See also 2.06 (religion and culture);
2.11 (Persia); 2.13 (Diocletian's reforms);

After Hadrian withdrew from Trajan's eastern conquests in 117, the borders of the Roman empire remained stable for almost 150 years. The only significant change was in the east, where successful campaigning by Septimius Severus between 195 and 198 wrested northern Mesopotamia from the Parthians. The 2nd century was a time of unrivaled peace and prosperity for the empire but this was not to last. The wealth of the empire was attractive to the Germanic tribes along the Rhine and Danube frontiers, and these began to unite in powerful confederations and raid Roman territory. In 167 Marcomannic raiders crossed into Italy, and though the emperor, Marcus Aurelius, successfully secured the borders, pressure on the northern frontier was thereafter continuous. Another problem was the imperial succession: there was no accepted way of deposing an incompetent or tyrannical emperor, nor of selecting a new emperor if a dynasty died out or was overthrown. When the incompetent, tyrannical Nero was overthrown in AD 68 the frontier armies promoted their own candidates for the succession, who then fought it out in a civil war. The same happened after the murder of the mad Commodus.

Pressure on the northern frontiers became critical in the 3rd century, and a new threat appeared in 226 when the Parthians were overthrown by the aggressive Persian Sasanian dynasty. In these conditions, the emperor had to be above all a good soldier. While rival candidates for power, promoted by different legions, fought each other for control of the empire, the borders were left undefended and open to invasion. For example, when Valerian (r. 253–60) withdrew troops from the Rhine to fight a usurper, the Franks immediately invaded Gaul. The efforts of emperors to buy the loyalty of their troops led them to debase the coinage to raise money, but this added runaway inflation to the empire's woes. Urban life now declined, especially in the west, where many towns shrank to a fortified administrative core. Civil war and invasion were incessant between 235 and 284: of the twenty-six emperors who ruled in this period all but one died by violence.

Not all the usurpers aimed at control of the whole empire. After Valerian was captured by the Persians at Edessa in 260, defense of the east devolved on Odenathus, ruler of the desert city of Palmyra. He defeated the Persians but then built an independent kingdom for himself. Under his wife and successor Queen Zenobia, it came to include Egypt, Syria and much of Anatolia. In the west the usurper Postumus founded an independent Gallic empire, winning over the people of Gaul, Britain and Spain; he promised to concentrate on defending the frontiers and not to march on Rome.

The Roman empire began to revive in the reign of Aurelian, with the reconquest of Palmyra (272) and the Gallic empire (274), though Dacia was permanently abandoned to the Germans. Political and economic stability were restored by Diocletian (r. 284–305), who reformed the whole structure of the empire. Diocletian greatly expanded the army and reformed the tax system to pay for it. Price regulation was introduced to curb inflation, though it drove goods off the markets. To restore respect to the imperial office, elaborate court ritual was introduced and the idea of the emperor as "first citizen" was abandoned: he was now "lord and god." Civilian and military authority were separated: provinces

▭	Roman empire, c.235
▨	Roman territory lost permanently, 163–378
⬭	kingdom of Palmyra, 260–72
⬭	Gallic empire, 260–74
⠿	strong Christian communities by 300
Goths	major Germanic peoples, 3rd century
Picts	other barbarians, 3rd century
→	attacks on Roman empire, with dates
⬥	city sacked
⊗	Roman victory
⊗	Roman defeat
⊗	battle between Roman forces
⩗	frontier wall or rampart
Italia	Diocletianic diocese
– –	borders of Diocletianic dioceses

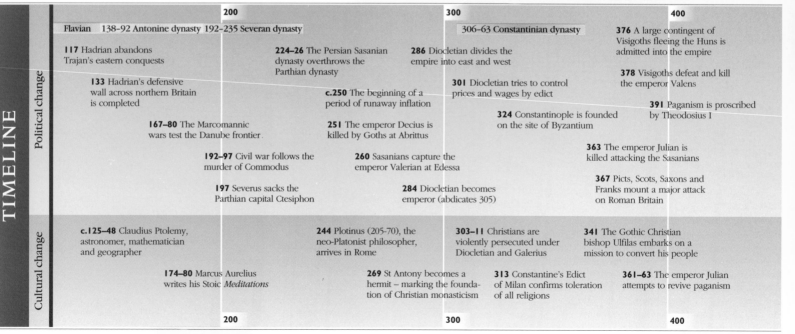

1 In the late 3rd century a chain of forts built on the east and south coasts of Britain was organized into an anti-piracy command, later known as the Saxon Shore.

2 After the Marcomanni attacked Aquileia in 167, the northern frontier was constantly threatened.

3 The importance of Rome declined in the 3rd and 4th centuries as it was abandoned by the emperor in favor of bases closer to the troubled frontiers.

4 Dacia could not be defended, and in 272 Aurelian abandoned it to the Goths and the Gepids.

5 Frankish invaders seized ships at Tarraco in 260 to launch pirate raids on north Africa.

6 Constantine the Great chose the small town of Byzantium as the site of a new capital for the empire.

7 After the emperor Julian was killed at Phrygia in 363 his army bought its freedom by ceding eastern Mesopotamia.

8 A network of ramparts, ditches, military roads and forts was built in the 3rd century to defend Rome's African frontier.

CHRISTIANITY spread widely before toleration was introduced in 313. This 2nd-century carving shows the khi-rho *symbol for Christ.*

were subdivided and organized in dioceses under "vicars" who were directly responsible to the emperor. Diocletian realized that the problems of defending the empire were too great for one ruler and in 286 he appointed Maximian as co-emperor to rule the west while he concentrated on the east.

In the 4th century the empire underwent a cultural transformation as traditional paganism was supplanted by Christianity. The pagan Roman empire was a tolerant state and was prepared to accept any religion that did not involve human sacrifice, so long as its devotees were prepared to pay lip-service to the state gods. Christians were not prepared to do this and had faced frequent persecutions as a result, one of the worst being ordered by Diocletian. Despite this, Christianity had spread steadily through the urban lower and middle classes, and by 300 it

was well established throughout the empire. In 312 the emperor Constantine (r. 306–37) became convinced that the Christian God had helped him win a victory over a rival at the Milvian Bridge, and in 313 he granted Christian toleration. Constantine subsequently presided over church councils, founded churches and was baptized on his deathbed. There is no reason to doubt the sincerity of his conversion, but he may also have seen Christianity as a unifying force for the embattled empire. Constantine's successors continued to promote Christianity and, despite a short-lived pagan revival under Julian (r.361–63), the new religion began to exert a strong influence on all aspects of Roman life, from personal morality to art and literature. Christianity finally became the empire's official religion in 391, when Theodosius I abolished pagan worship.

See also 2.11 (Sasanians): 2.14 (earlier Roman empire); 2.16 (fall of the empire); 2.19 (Germans)

2.16 The fall of the western Roman empire • AD 376 – 480 •

The fragile stability of the 4th-century empire was maintained at great cost to its citizens. Taxation was kept at a high level to pay for the large armies needed to defend the frontiers against increasingly well organized Germanic barbarians; yet the economy, particularly in the west, was in decline. The rich used their political influence to avoid paying taxes, so the tax burden fell heavily upon the poorer classes. Even in Egypt's fertile Nile valley, peasant farmers could not afford to pay their taxes and abandoned their fields. The empire's population contracted and manpower shortages began to affect the armies. The western army relied increasingly on barbarian mercenaries to fill its ranks.

In the 370s pressures on the empire's northern frontier increased dramatically. The Huns, a Turkic nomad people, migrated to the eastern European steppes from central Asia and, around 372, crushed the Ostrogoths. The defeat of this the most powerful Germanic tribe caused panic among the rest. In 376 the Visigoths, seeking sanctuary from the Huns, requested permission to settle in the Roman empire. The eastern emperor, Valens, who saw the Visigoths as a valuable source of recruits for the army, settled them on vacant lands in Thrace. There, however, they were treated badly by the corrupt officials in charge of their settlement; and in 378 they rebelled, defeating and killing Valens in battle at Adrianople. Under a new agreement in 382 the emperor Theodosius gave the Visigoths the status of federates (allies); but they rebelled again in 395 under their ambitious new leader, Alaric. He had previously commanded Gothic troops in the Roman army, but now ravaged Greece and Dalmatia before invading Italy in 401. Stilicho, a Roman general of Germanic origin, drove the Visigoths back into Dalmatia; but the situation deteriorated in 406 when a coalition of Vandals, Suevi and Alans invaded Gaul before crossing the Pyrenees into Spain in 409. They were followed into Gaul by Franks, Burgundians and Alemanni. In 410 Alaric rebelled yet again, and when his demands were refused the Visigoths sacked Rome. Though no longer the administrative capital of the empire, Rome remained a potent symbol of its history and power, and the attack was deeply shocking. Alaric died soon afterward, and his successors were more inclined to cooperate with the Romans. In 418 the Visigoths, as allies of the Romans, attacked the Suevi, Alans and Vandals in Spain, before being settled on rich lands in Aquitaine as federates under nominal Roman suzerainty.

Although the Huns were indirectly responsible for the empire's woes, they initially maintained good

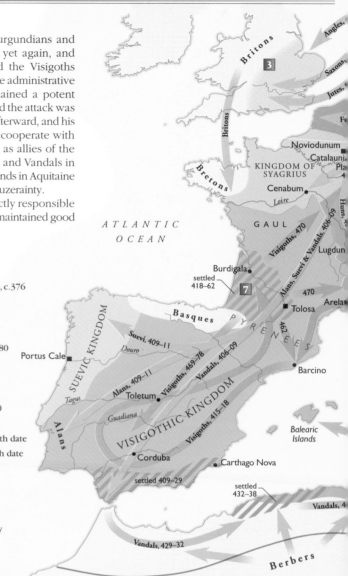

——	border of Roman empire, 378
– –	division between eastern and western Roman empires, 395
——	northern limit of Germanic peoples, c.376
▨	eastern Roman empire, 480
▨	kingdom of Odoacer, 480
▨	kingdom of Syagrius, 480
▨	Burgundian kingdom (Germanic), 480
▨	Franks (Germanic), 480
▨	Ostrogoths (Germanic), 480
▨	Vandal kingdom (Germanic), 480
▨	Visigothic kingdom (Germanic), 480
▨	other Germanic peoples, 480
▨	temporary settlement of Vandals, with date
▨	federate settlement of Visigoths, with date
➤	Hun migration
➤	Alan, Suevi and Vandal migration
➤	Visigoth migration
➤	other migration
Goths	major Germanic people, 4th century
Huns	other barbarian peoples
■	capital city

TIMELINE

Western Empire

402 Ravenna becomes the capital of the western empire

406 Vandals, Suevi and Alans invade Gaul

410 Visigoths under Alaric sack Rome

418 Visigoths are settled as federates in Aquitaine

429 The Vandals cross from Spain to north Africa

c.450 Beginning of Anglo-Saxon settlements in Britain

451 Aetius defeats Attila at the Catalaunian Plain

455 Vandals sack Rome

462–78 Visigothic expansion occurs in Gaul and Spain

476 Odoacer is proclaimed king of Italy

480 Death of Julius Nepos, the last legitimate western emperor

Eastern Empire

c.372 The Huns conquer the Ostrogoths

378 The Visigoths rebel; and the eastern emperor Valens is killed in battle at Adrianople

395 Death of Theodosius I. The division of the empire is made permanent

396–98 The Visigoths ravage Greece

413 The Theodosian walls are built in Constantinople

421–22 War with Sasanians

441 The Huns defeat the Romans at Naissus

453 Constantinople wins ecclesiastical supremacy over Alexandria at the Council of Chalcedon

■ The arrival of the Huns in eastern Europe around 370 completely destabilized the Germanic tribes, causing many to seek refuge in the Roman empire.

■ In 402 the capital of the western empire was moved from Rome to Ravenna, allowing more rapid communication with the northern frontier and Constantinople.

■ Most of Britain's garrison was withdrawn in 407 by the usurper Constantine to fight in a civil war. In 410 Honorius told the Britons to see to their own defenses.

■ Rome was sacked twice in the 5th century: in 410 by the Visigoths; and in 455 by the Vandals.

■ Saxons, Angles and Jutes from north Germany and Denmark began to settle in eastern Britain c.450.

■ The position and strong fortifications of Constantinople saved Anatolia from barbarian invaders in the 5th century.

■ In the 460s Visigoths, settled by the Romans in Aquitaine in 418, expanded into Gaul and Spain.

■ In 476 Italy came under the rule of Odoacer, a barbarian general, who deposed the "last" western emperor: the puppet usurper Romulus Augustulus, who was still a boy.

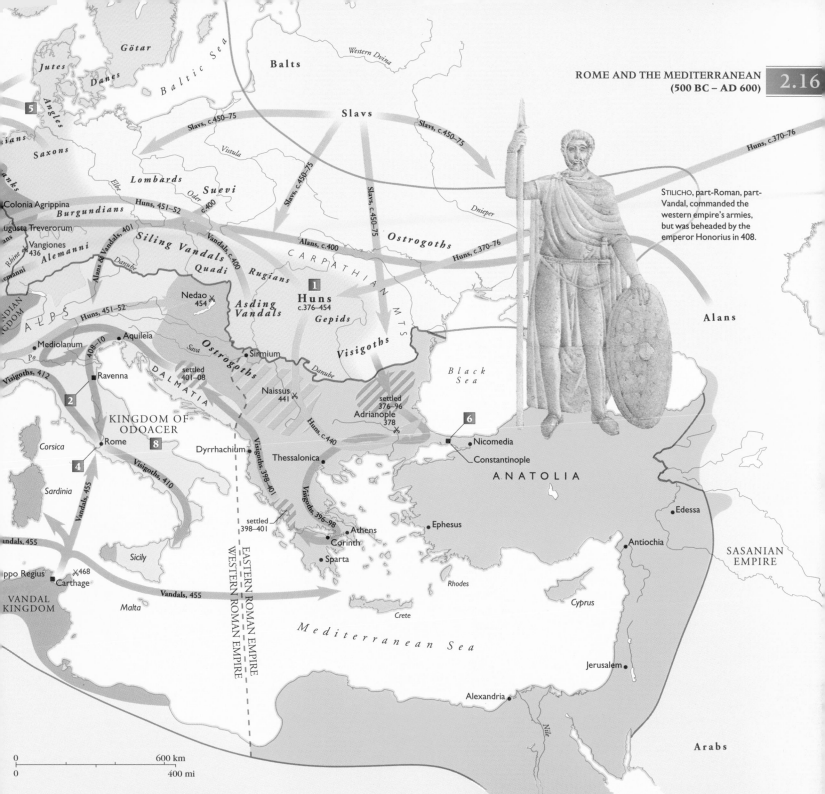

STILICHO, part-Roman, part-Vandal, commanded the western empire's armies, but was beheaded by the emperor Honorius in 408.

Götar

Jutes

Danes

Anglos

Saxons

Baltic Sea

Balts

Western Dvina

Slavs

Slavs, c.450–75

Slavs, c.450–75

Huns, c.370–76

Vistula

Lombards

Suevi

Colonia Agrippina

Burgundians

Augusta Treverorum

Vangiones 436

Alemanni

Huns, 451–52

Oder c.400

Elbe

Alans & Vandals, 401

Siling Vandals

Quadi

Vandals, c.400

Rugians

Slavs, c.450–75

Slavs, c.450–75

Alans, c.400

Dnieper

Ostrogoths

Huns, c.370–76

Alans

Danube

Asding Vandals

1 Huns c.376–454

Gepids

CARPATHIAN MTS

Nedao 454 ×

ALPS

Huns, 451–52

408–10

Aquileia

Mediolanum

Po

Visigoths, 412

Ravenna

2

Ostrogoths

settled 401–08

DALMATIA

Sirmium

Sava

Naissus 441 ×

Visigoths

Huns, c.440

settled 376–96

Adrianople 378 ×

Black Sea

Nicomedia

6

Constantinople

KINGDOM OF ODOACER

Corsica

Rome

8

4

Sardinia

Vandals, 455

Dyrrhachium

Visigoths, 398–401

Thessalonica

Visigoths, 410

Visigoths, 396–98

settled 398–401

Athens

Corinth

Sparta

Rhodes

ANATOLIA

Ephesus

Edessa

Antiochia

SASANIAN EMPIRE

ndals, 455

ppo Regius

× 468

Carthage

VANDAL KINGDOM

Sicily

Malta

Vandals, 455

Crete

Mediterranean Sea

Cyprus

EASTERN ROMAN EMPIRE
WESTERN ROMAN EMPIRE

Jerusalem

Alexandria

Nile

Arabs

0   600 km
0   400 mi

relations with Rome. The Roman general Aetius used Hun mercenaries widely in the 430s to impose federate status on the Burgundians and other barbarian settlers in Gaul, but in 441 Attila turned on the empire, ravaging the Balkans and pushing his western border to the Rhine. In 451 Attila invaded Gaul but was defeated by a coalition of Romans, Visigoths, Burgundians and Franks under Aetius at the Catalaunian Plain. After Attila's death in 453 the Huns' German subjects rebelled, breaking their power at the battle of Nedao in 454. The collapse of the Huns in fact worked against Rome: fear of them had kept Rome's Germanic allies reasonably loyal, now they had less cause to be cooperative.

In 429 the Vandals had crossed from Spain to Africa and in 439 captured Carthage and set up a completely independent kingdom. This was the most serious blow the barbarians had so far struck against the empire, as north Africa was Italy's main source of grain. The Vandals turned to piracy, and in 455 went on to sack Rome itself. The assassination in

this year of Aetius, the west's most able general, and of Valentinian III, last of the Theodosian dynasty, were further blows. The western empire now began to crumble and by the 470s was reduced to little more than Italy. The last legitimate western emperor, Julius Nepos, was driven out of Italy in 475 by a palace coup which placed a boy usurper, Romulus Augustulus, on the throne. The following year Odoacer, a barbarian general, deposed Augustulus and was proclaimed king by his soldiers. Odoacer recognized the suzerainty of the eastern emperor Zeno and offered to rule Italy as imperial viceroy. The deposing of Augustulus in 476 is widely accepted as marking the end of the western Roman empire, but Julius Nepos continued to rule a rump empire in Dalmatia from 475 until his death in 480. Dalmatia then became part of Odoacer's kingdom.

The main cause of the fall of the western Roman empire was its exposure to barbarian attack – far greater than in the east, which had only a short northern frontier. This problem was exacerbated by

the division of the empire in the 4th century, which deprived the poorer, less populated and more vulnerable west of the resources of the richer east. Eastern emperors did assist their western colleagues, but their main priority was ensuring that the east did not go the same way as the west. The west was also politically less stable than the east. From the time of Honorius onward western emperors were dominated by overbearing generals. After the death of Valentinian III in 455, the western emperors became the puppets of barbarian generals: when they outlived their usefulness or tried to act independently, they were murdered. The high cost of defending the empire undermined positive loyalty to it. There was little popular resistance to the barbarians and, as they were inefficient tax collectors, most people probably felt themselves better off without the empire.

See also 2.11 (Sasanians); 2.17 (rise of Byzantium); 2.19 (Germans and Slavs); 2.20 (steppe peoples)

For twelve years after Odoacer's takeover of Italy, Zeno, the eastern emperor, did nothing. Then in 488 he commissioned Theodoric, king of the Ostrogoths, to overthrow Odoacer and rule Italy until he, the emperor, was able to claim sovereignty in person. By 493 Odoacer was dead and Theodoric was master of Italy. Under Theodoric, who wished to preserve Roman civilization, Italy enjoyed peace and prosperity, but there was no assimilation between Roman and Goth. The main barrier was religion. The Goths had converted to Christianity in the 4th century but were followers of the teachings of Arius, who denied the divinity of Christ – which their Roman subjects regarded as heretical. The Burgundians, Visigoths and Vandals were also Arians and assimilation was equally limited in those kingdoms. Arianism also prevented good relations between the barbarian kingdoms and the eastern emperor, who regarded himself as the guardian of orthodox Christianity. The only barbarians to escape the taint of heresy were the Franks, who converted directly from paganism to orthodox Christianity around 500. This earned them the friendship and support of the eastern emperors and the loyalty and cooperation of their Gallo-Roman subjects. Because of this the Frankish kingdom became the strongest power in western Europe by 600.

Although it was frequently at war with Sasanian Persia, the eastern empire prospered after the fall of the west. The emperor Anastasius (r. 491–518) even managed to cut taxes and still leave his successor, Justin (r. 518–27), with a full treasury. Justin was succeeded by his nephew Justinian (r. 527–65), the last great Roman emperor. Justinian had a very clear idea of the responsibilities of a Roman emperor, chief of which was maintaining the territorial integrity of the empire. To Justinian it was a disgrace that the western provinces of the empire were occupied by barbarians and he launched a concerted effort to recover them. In 533 he sent a force under Belisarius which, against expectations, destroyed the Vandal kingdom in north Africa. The Vandal campaign had been made possible by the cooperation of the pro-Roman Ostrogothic queen Amalasuntha,

who allowed the invasion fleet to use Sicily as a base. Amalasuntha's murder in 534 was used as a pretext for the invasion of Italy in 535. By 540 the Ostrogoth capital at Ravenna had fallen, but resistance was revived by Totila (r. 541–52). War with Persia diverted Roman forces to the east and the resulting stalemate in Italy was only broken in 552 when a new Roman army under Narses arrived from Constantinople. By 554 all of Italy south of the Po was in Roman hands, but north of the river Ostrogothic resistance continued until 562. The last of Justinian's conquests was southern Spain, seized opportunistically during a Visigothic civil war in 554.

Justinian's reconquests restored Roman control of the Mediterranean but put the empire under serious economic strain. The concentration of forces in the west left the Balkans exposed to Slavic raiding and settlement, and the Persians made serious

incursions in the east. Italy was devastated by years of war and much of the province was soon lost again following an invasion by the Lombards in 572. However, north Africa and Sicily proved to be valuable additions to the empire's resources.

In about 560 a new wave of nomads, the Avars, arrived in eastern Europe. The Romans paid them to wipe out the remnants of the Huns, but in 580 a dispute over possession of Singidunum (modern

Key

- Eastern Roman empire, 527
- Burgundian kingdom, 527
- Frankish kingdom, 527
- Ostrogothic kingdom, 527
- Vandal kingdom, 527
- Visigothic kingdom, 527
- other Germanic kingdoms and peoples
- Frankish kingdom on death of Clothar I, 561
- Roman empire on death of Justinian, 565
- Lombard settlement, with dates
- Sasanian occupation, 607–628
- → Roman campaign under Belisarius, 533–34
- → Roman campaign under Belisarius, 535–40
- → other Roman campaign, 552–54
- → Persian-Avar campaigns, with date
- → migration, with date
- ⋈ place fortified by Justinian
- ⊕ patriarchal see

0 _____ 600 km
0 _____ 400 mi

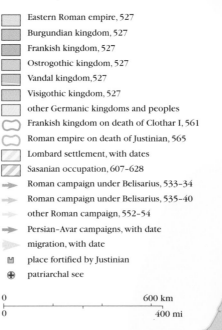

TIMELINE

Political change

500	550	600
486 Clovis, founder of the Frankish kingdom, defeats Syagrius, the last Roman ruler in Gaul, at Soissons	**554** Justinian reconquers southern Spain	**592–602** The emperor Maurice campaigns against the Avars
526 Theodoric dies		
532 Justinian quells an anti-reform uprising in Constantinople	**561** The Frankish kingdom is divided between the sons of Clothar I	**607–27** War against Sasanian Persia ends with defeat of the Persians
489–93 Theodoric, king of the Ostrogoths, defeats Odoacer and wins Italy	**533–34** Justinian's general Belisarius conquers the Vandal kingdom in Africa	**568–82** The Lombards invade northern Italy	**610–22** Heraclius restructures the eastern Roman empire, creating what we now call the Byzantine empire
c.503 Clovis becomes a convert to Christianity	**536–62** Belisarius and Narses conquer the Ostrogothic kingdom in Italy	**571** The Visigoths recapture Cordoba	
507 Clovis defeats the Visigoths at Vouillé, driving the Visigoths into the Iberian peninsula	**540** The Sasanian Persians sack Antiochia		**638** Arabs capture Jerusalem

Cultural change

500	550	600
529 Justinian closes the Academy at Athens	**565** Procopius (c.499-566) publishes the last of his histories of Justinian's reign	**591** Gregory of Tours (c.538-94), completes his *History [of the Franks]*
529–34 Justinian codifies Roman law		**596–97** Pope Gregory the Great dispatches a mission to convert the Anglo-Saxons
c.535–40 St Benedict (c.480-c.550) writes his monastic rule		

Danes

Baltic Sea

Balts

Thuringians

Saxons

Slavs

Vistula

Elbe

Oder

Avars, 533–62 **4**

Don

Dnieper

Huns

C A R P A T H I A N   M T S

Bulgars

540s–80s

Alans

Lombards **6**

568–72

OSTROGOTHIC
KINGDOM

Danube

626

Gepids

Singidunum

Cherson

Black Sea

Mediolanum

Po

572–82

Ravenna **3**

Busta
Gallorum
552

Salonae

Naissus

Sava

Narses

7

Danube

Trapezus

Adrianople

8

Nicomedia

1

Rome ⊕

Narses

Corsica

Thessalonica

Constantinople ⊕

Nicaea

A N A T O L I A

626

Mons
Lactacius
552

Neapolis

Sardinia

EASTERN
ROMAN EMPIRE

Nineveh
627

Sicily

Athens

Ephesus

Antiochia

Tigris

Tricameron
533

2 Catana

Syracusae

Rhodes

540

Persians

Carthage
ad Decimum
533

Cyprus

Palmyra

Ctesiphon

Malta

Liberius

Crete

Damascus

SASANIAN
EMPIRE

*M e d i t e r r a n e a n
S e a*

Jerusalem ⊕

Leptis Magna

Cyrene

Alexandria ⊕

Nile

Arabs

JUSTINIAN was portrayed in this
mosaic at Ravenna, supported by
religious and military forces.

Belgrade) led to war. For ten years the Avars raided
the Balkans until the emperor, Maurice, launched a
series of effective counterattacks in 592. Maurice was
close to breaking Avar power, when his army
mutinied in 602: he was deposed and murdered by
his successor, Phocas, an incompetent despot. The
administrative structure of the empire now began to
fall apart. Slavs and Avars overran the Balkans and
the Persians took the fortresses of Roman Mesopotamia one by one. The chaotic state of the empire

prompted the governor of Africa to equip his son
Heraclius with an army in 610 and send him to
Constantinople to overthrow Phocas.

The reign of Heraclius was a turning point. The
structure of the empire of Diocletian, Constantine
and Justinian could not be revived. Heraclius spent
the first years of his reign rebuilding the administrative and military structure of the empire. Greek,
which had always been the majority language in the
eastern empire, replaced Latin in official documents.
Heraclius worked closely with the patriarch of
Constantinople, who willingly used the wealth and
authority of the church to support the state. While
Heraclius was reforming the empire, the war with
Persia continued to go badly and by 616 Syria,
Palestine and Egypt had been lost. In 622 Heraclius
launched a bold campaign directly into the heart of
the Sasanian empire and five years later destroyed
the Persian army at Nineveh, bringing the war to an
end. Heraclius had saved the empire, but his reforms
are considered to mark the end of the eastern
Roman empire and the beginning of the medieval
Greek Byzantine empire (named for the old Greek
name for Constantinople).

1 Rome regained importance in the 6th century as
the chief center of Christianity in western Europe.

2 The Ostrogothic queen Amalasuntha allowed
Justinian's general Belisarius to use Sicily as a base for
his attack on the Vandals in 533.

3 Ravenna, the Ostrogothic capital, was taken by
Belisarius in 540; resistance continued for many years.

4 The Avars, a Mongol people, migrated to Europe
after being defeated by the Turks in central Asia (552).

5 Civil war in the Visigothic kingdom gave Justinian
the opportunity to reconquer southern Spain in 554.

6 Originally Roman allies against the Ostrogoths, the
Lombards invaded and settled Italy 568–82.

7 Justinian's concentration on the west left the
Balkans exposed to frequent Slav raids and settlement.

8 A joint Persian–Avar attack on Constantinople in
626 failed when the Byzantine fleet prevented the two
attacking armies from uniting.

See also 2.16 (fall of the western empire);
2.20 (barbarian invaders)

The name Celts was used by Greek writers from the 5th century BC onward to describe a group of peoples of central and western Europe. Roman writers called the same peoples Gauls. The origins of the Celts are uncertain but are probably to be found in the northern Alps in the Bronze Age Urnfield (from mid-2nd millennium BC) and the late Bronze–early Iron Age Hallstatt cultures (1200–450 BC). There were at least two waves of Celtic migration out of central Europe. The first, from around 1000, took the Urnfield culture across western Europe into northern Spain by the 7th century; and a second, beginning in the 8th century, had by 500 BC spread the Hallstatt culture across France, Spain, Portugal, Germany, the Low Countries, and southern Britain.

A new phase of Celtic history began around 450 BC with the development in Germany and France of the La Tène culture. This was distinguished by a vigorous art style based on geometrical patterns and stylized animal images. It developed from Hallstatt art but also showed the influence of Etruscan and Scythian styles. The La Tène culture spread quickly across central and western Europe and reached the British Isles by about 400 BC, passed on partly by trade contacts and partly by smallscale migrations of continental Celts, such as the Parisii, who settled in Yorkshire. The La Tène culture did not spread to Spain, where the earlier Celtic settlers and the native population had become assimilated, forming a distinctive Celtiberian culture.

Around 400 BC there were major migrations of Celtic peoples into Italy and the lower Danube region. In Italy the Celts raided widely, sacked Rome, permanently weakened the Etruscans, and settled densely in the Po valley. The Celts on the lower Danube began to migrate into the Balkans in the 3rd century BC. A major raid on Delphi was repulsed, but the Hellenistic kingdom of Thrace was destroyed by their attacks. Three tribes crossed the Dardanelles and settled in central Anatolia, from where they raided the surrounding kingdoms.

The early 3rd century marked the high tide of Celtic expansion. The Romans began the conquest

of the Celts of the Po valley at the battle of Telamon in 225 and captured the last center of resistance in Italy at Bononia (modern Bologna) in 192. The Thracians restored their kingdom around 220; and the Anatolian Celts were pacified by Pergamon in 230. In the 230s the Carthaginians began the conquest of the Celtiberians, and this was continued by the Romans after they had expelled the Carthaginians from Spain in 206. The Roman victory at Numantia in 133 brought them control of most of Spain, but Celtiberian resistance continued in the northwest until 19 BC. By the first century AD the continental Celts were caught firmly in a vise between the northward expansion of the Roman empire and the southward and westward expansion of the Germanic tribes and the Dacians. Between 58

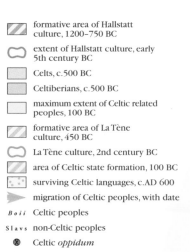

formative area of Hallstatt culture, 1200–750 BC

extent of Hallstatt culture, early 5th century BC

Celts, c.500 BC

Celtiberians, c.500 BC

maximum extent of Celtic related peoples, 100 BC

formative area of La Tène culture, 450 BC

La Tène culture, 2nd century BC

area of Celtic state formation, 100 BC

surviving Celtic languages, c.AD 600

migration of Celtic peoples, with date

Boii Celtic peoples

Slavs non-Celtic peoples

⊗ Celtic *oppidum*

⊗ other important Celtic site

⊗ La Tène vehicle burial

northern limit of Roman empire, 60 BC

northern limit of Roman empire, AD 79

expansion of non-Celtic peoples, with date

```
0                    600 km
0              400 mi
```

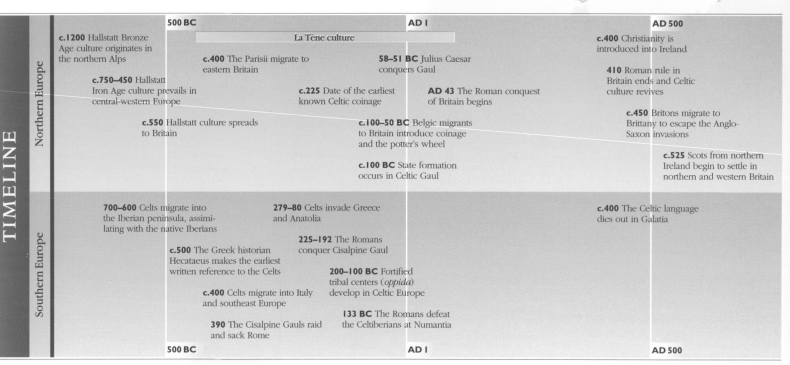

Northern Europe

500 BC

AD 1

AD 500

La Tène culture

c.1200 Hallstatt Bronze Age culture originates in the northern Alps

c.750–450 Hallstatt Iron Age culture prevails in central-western Europe

c.400 The Parisii migrate to eastern Britain

c.550 Hallstatt culture spreads to Britain

c.225 Date of the earliest known Celtic coinage

58–51 BC Julius Caesar conquers Gaul

AD 43 The Roman conquest of Britain begins

c.100–50 BC Belgic migrants to Britain introduce coinage and the potter's wheel

c.100 BC State formation occurs in Celtic Gaul

c.400 Christianity is introduced into Ireland

410 Roman rule in Britain ends and Celtic culture revives

c.450 Britons migrate to Brittany to escape the Anglo-Saxon invasions

c.525 Scots from northern Ireland begin to settle in northern and western Britain

Southern Europe

700–600 Celts migrate into the Iberian peninsula, assimilating with the native Iberians

c.500 The Greek historian Hecataeus makes the earliest written reference to the Celts

c.400 Celts migrate into Italy and southeast Europe

390 The Cisalpine Gauls raid and sack Rome

279–80 Celts invade Greece and Anatolia

225–192 The Romans conquer Cisalpine Gaul

200–100 BC Fortified tribal centers (*oppida*) develop in Celtic Europe

133 BC The Romans defeat the Celtiberians at Numantia

c.400 The Celtic language dies out in Galatia

500 BC

AD 1

AD 500

HORSES, chariots and armor were important elements in the Celtic love of display. This bronze head comes from Yorkshire, Britain.

1 The Celts (Gauls) sacked Rome in 390 BC, after defeating a Roman army at the river Allia.

2 An invasive Celtic migration as far south as Delphi was turned back by Greek resistance in 279 BC .

3 Celtic raids in Anatolia ceased after the victory of Attalus I of Pergamon around 230 BC.

4 Survivors of the Celtic attack on Delphi in 279 founded a kingdom in Thrace that lasted until 213 BC.

5 The main Celtiberian resistance to Roman rule was broken when, after a 20-year siege, Numantia fell in 133 BC.

6 Trade contacts with the Roman empire led to the formation of tribal states in southern Gaul in the 1st century BC.

7 Julius Caesar's victory over Vercingetorix at Alesia in 52 BC, the climax of an eight-year campaign (58–51 BC), secured Roman control of Gaul.

8 The Iceni, led by their queen, Boudicca, rebelled unsuccessfully against Roman rule in AD 60.

9 Celtic culture and art revived in Britain after the end of Roman rule in AD 410.

---

and 51 BC Julius Caesar conquered the Celts of Gaul. Under Augustus the tribes of the Alps and Pannonia were brought under Roman rule. By AD 1 the only independent Celts on mainland Europe were enclaves in German territory north of the Danube.

Celtic society was hierarchical and competitive and by the 2nd century BC was in the early stages of state formation. Fortified centers, or *oppida*, spread across Europe: some, such as Manching on the Danube, were large towns by the 1st century BC. Coinage and, in some areas, writing came into use. In southern Gaul small tribal states in direct contact with the Roman empire had developed by 60 BC. The Roman conquest prevented the Celts from developing a full urban civilization of their own.

The Celtic resistance to Rome failed for two main reasons. The Celts were politically disunited and the Romans easily exploited rivalries between states or

tribes to their own advantage. Also, Celtic warriors saw war as an opportunity to seek personal glory and this put them at a disadvantage to the drilled and disciplined legions. After the Roman conquest the La Tène culture died out on the continent and Celtic language was gradually replaced by Latin; but Celtic religion continued to be practiced. *Oppida* were superseded by planned Romanized towns.

Apart from two punitive raids by Caesar in 55–54 BC, it was AD 43 before the Romans began to subjugate the Celts in Britain. By this time contacts with the Romans across the Channel had already led to considerable Romanization of the southern British tribes and to the development of *oppida* and small tribal states. The Romans could never conquer all of Britain: the closest they came was in AD 83 when they defeated the Caledonians at "Mons Graupius". Harsh weather, mountainous terrain and long lines

of communication meant that the highland tribes of Scotland stayed independent, as did the Celts in Ireland, where pagan Celtic culture survived into the early Middle Ages. La Tène art died out in southern Britain in the 2nd century AD, but Celtic art traditions continued in the far north and Ireland, while Celtic languages survived throughout the British Isles. After the end of Roman rule in Britain in 410, Celtic art revived but was strongly influenced by late Roman and Anglo-Saxon art. The introduction of Christianity to Ireland in the 5th century inspired the development of a Celtic monastic civilization which, through missionary activity, had begun to exert a strong influence in Britain and the continent by 600.

See also 2.13 (growth of the Roman empire); 2.19 (Germans)

The Germans originated in southern Scandinavia and the north German plain in the first half of the 1st millennium BC, probably descended from peoples long settled there. The first contact between the Germans and the Mediterranean civilizations occurred around 350 BC, when the Greek navigator Pytheas of Massilia explored the North Sea coasts. However, his account of his voyage was not widely believed and Mediterranean writers first became aware of the Germans as a group distinct from the Celts only at the end of the 2nd century BC. At this time the Germans' society and way of life resembled that of the Celts, but showed no evidence of power centralization or urban development.

In the second half of the 1st millennium BC the Germans expanded out of north Germany, mainly at the expense of the Celtic peoples to their south and west. These movements were for the most part gradual, but around 120 the Cimbri and the Teutones, two peoples from Jutland, began a twenty-year migration that took them across west-central Europe. When the tribes attacked the Taurisci in 113, their Roman allies sent an army to protect them. The Cimbri and Teutones crushed this army at Noreia but then headed northwest into Gaul. In 109 the tribes invaded southern Gaul and inflicted a succession of defeats on Roman armies, culminating in their victory at Arausio (Orange) in 105. At this point the tribes split up, the Cimbri invading Spain and the Teutones going to northern Gaul. The Roman dictator Marius used the respite to reorganize the legions, and when the Teutones returned to southern Gaul in 102, he defeated them at Aquae Sextiae (Aix-en-Provence). In 101 Marius defeated the Cimbri – who had finally invaded Italy – at Vercellae. Fear of future Germanic invasions was a major motive for Roman expansion northward in the 1st century BC.

Julius Caesar conquered the tribes on the west bank of the Rhine in 56 BC, but these were to be the only Germans permanently under Roman rule. By AD 6 the Germanic tribes as far east as the Elbe were pacified, but a rebellion under Arminius destroyed the Roman army of occupation in AD 9. After AD 12

Key:
- Germanic peoples, c.750 BC
- spread of Germanic peoples, c.50 BC
- spread of Germanic peoples, c.AD 360
- probable formative area of the Slavs (Chernoles complex, c.750 BC)
- Slavs, c.AD 550
- northern frontier of Roman empire, AD 14
- under temporary Roman control, 12 BC–AD 9
- migration of Cimbri and Teutones, 120–101 BC
- Germanic raids and migrations, AD 1–200
- Germanic raids and migrations, AD 200–400
- Slavic migration, AD 540–70
- other migrations
- *Rugii* major Germanic peoples, AD 1–200
- *Rugii* major Germanic peoples, AD 200–400
- Aesti other peoples

TIMELINE

Germans

500 BC	AD 1	AD 500
c.500 Iron working is introduced into Scandinavia		167 The Marcomanni sack Aquileia
c.350 Pytheas of Massilia explores the German and Scandinavian coast		c.200 Germanic tribes form a powerful confederation
	120–101 Migrations of the Cimbri and Teutones	251 The Goths defeat and kill the Roman emperor Decius at Abrittus
	c.70 BC German invasion of Gaul under Ariovistus	c.372 The Huns defeat king Ermanaric of the Ostrogoths
	56 BC Caesar defeats the Germans to west of the Rhine	376 Fleeing Visigoths find refuge in the Roman empire
	AD 9 Germans rebel against Roman rule	406 Vandals, Suevi and Alans invade Gaul
	AD 41 Chauci mount pirate raids along the coast of Gaul	c.450 Anglo-Saxon migrations to Britain begin

Slavs

c.750–c.500 The Iron Age Chernoles complex culture, associated with Slav origins		c.450 Slavs raid and settle in the Balkans
		c.560 Avars migrating westward conquer the Slavs

| 500 BC | AD 1 | AD 500 |

1 The Balts were farming peoples whose cultural identity emerged as early as 1800 BC.

2 Two Roman armies were destroyed by the Cimbri and Teutones at Arausio in 105 BC.

3 In AD 9 Rome lost three legions at the battle of the Teutoburgerwald against Germans under Arminius.

4 A Germanic farming village of fifty houses occupied from the 1st century BC to the 5th century AD was found at Feddersen Wierde.

5 Votive offerings were a feature of Germanic religion: one of the richest finds, at Hjortspring, included a ship and many weapons sunk in a bog.

6 A 3rd-century kingdom centered in Stevns controlled the flow of Roman trade in the southern Baltic.

7 The Goths, Burgundians and other Germans believed they had migrated from Scandinavia – called "the womb of peoples" – in the 6th century AD.

8 Some historians think that the "Scythian farmers" were Slavs living under Scythian domination.

9 In the 540s–60s, while the armies of the eastern Roman emperor Justinian (r.527–65) campaigned in Italy, the Slavs raided and settled in the Balkans.

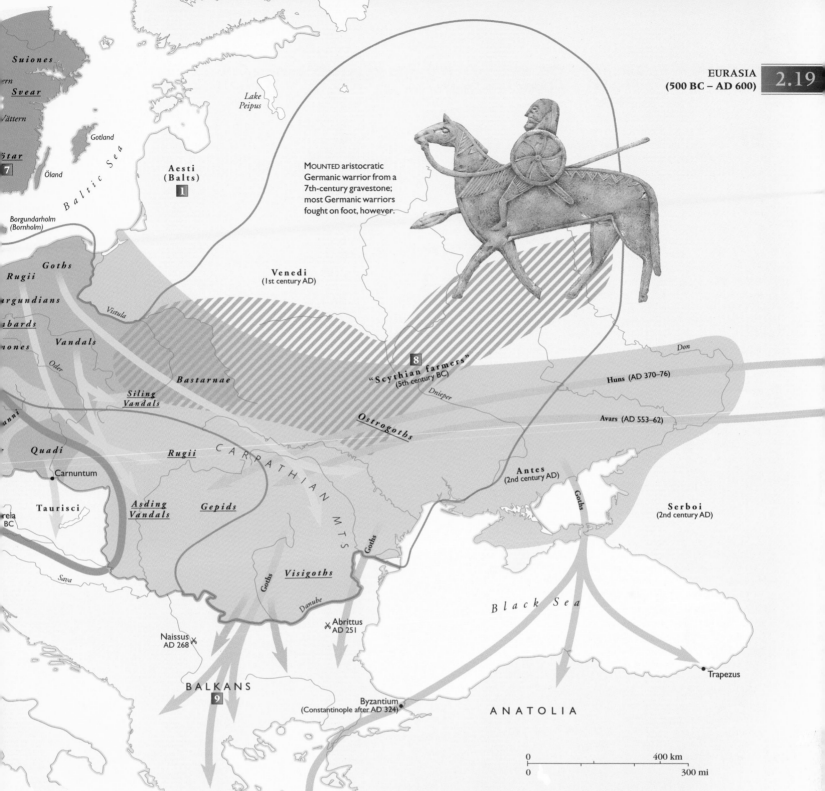

Suiones

Svear

Vättern

Götar

7

Gotland

Öland

Baltic Sea

Lake Peipus

Aesti
(Balts)
1

*Borgundarholm
(Bornholm)*

Goths

Rugii

Burgundians

Lombards

..nones

Vandals

Oder

Vistula

*Siling
Vandals*

Bastarnae

Venedi
(1st century AD)

Mounted aristocratic
Germanic warrior from a
7th-century gravestone;
most Germanic warriors
fought on foot, however.

Don

8

"Scythian farmers"
(5th century BC)

Dnieper

Ostrogoths

Huns (AD 370–76)

Avars (AD 553–62)

Quadi

• Carnuntum

Rugii

C A R P A T H I A N   M T S

Antes
(2nd century AD)

Goths

Serboi
(2nd century AD)

Taurisci

**..reia
BC**

*Asding
Vandals*

Gepids

Sava

Goths

Goths

Visigoths

Danube

✕ Abrittus
AD 251

B l a c k   S e a

Naissus ✕
AD 268

BALKANS
9

Byzantium •
(Constantinople after AD 324)

A N A T O L I A

• Trapezus

• Athens

| 0 | | | | 400 km |
| 0 | | | 300 mi | |

Rome made no serious attempts to conquer the Germans again, despite many punitive expeditions against troublesome tribes.

There was considerable trade across the border between the Germans and Romans, who gave diplomatic and material support to friendly tribes against their enemies. Many Germans were recruited into the Roman army. These contacts with Rome led to dramatic changes in the social structure of the Germanic tribes in the late 2nd–early 3rd centuries. Small tribes merged to form powerful confederations: thus, on the Rhine, the Chasuarii, Chamavi, Bructeri, Tencteri and other tribes emerged as the Frankish confederacy in the early 3rd century. These confederations were dangerous enemies and the empire suffered from Germanic invasions in the 3rd century. Many tribes, like the Burgundians, moved closer to the borders of the Roman empire, hoping to share in

the spoils of raiding and trade. These movements were disruptive and some tribes split up. A migration of the Gepids around 300 split the Goths into two halves – Visigoths and Ostrogoths. The Ostrogoths embarked on a rapid expansion across the steppes to the Don. Here they ran into the Huns, who defeated them. The Ostrogoth kingdom collapsed; the Gepids were crushed next; and the Visigoths fled into the Roman empire.

The earliest records of the Slavs date from the mid-6th century AD when they began to raid and settle in the Balkans. They were tribal farming peoples, ruled by warrior chiefs. By this time Slavs occupied much of eastern Europe, so peoples speaking Slavonic languages must have existed long before this. However, their origins are obscure. The Venedi, Antes, Serboi and the Scythian farmers – all eastern European peoples mentioned by classical

writers – have at some time been claimed by historians as Slavs, but these identifications are contentious. Archeological evidence is inconclusive, because of the disruptions in eastern Europe caused by migrations of steppe nomads and Germanic peoples. The early Iron Age Chernoles complex (750–500 BC), centered between the Vistula and the Don, has been described as proto-Slavic, but there is no certain link with the historical Slavs. Probably the Slavs emerged over a wide area of eastern Europe from a number of cultures. For much of their early history they lived under the domination of the Scythians, Sarmatians, Ostrogoths and Huns, and they were conquered in the late 6th century by the Avars. When Avar power declined in the 7th century, the Slavs emerged to play an important role in the formation of early medieval Europe.

See also 2.15 (Roman empire);
2.18 (Celts); 2.20 (steppe peoples)

The steppes are a vast area of grassland stretching from eastern Europe across central Asia to Manchuria, which were colonized in the 5th millennium BC by farmers from western Eurasia. The harsh climate was not well suited to arable farming, so the steppe farmers relied primarily on their herds of cattle, horses, sheep and goats. Around 3500 BC wheeled vehicles came into use. This new mobility allowed the farmers to develop a transhumant lifestyle (moving their flocks and herds between summer and winter pastures), significantly increasing the grazing resources available to them. In the second half of the 2nd millennium BC bits and bridles were introduced, which made horseback riding possible. This allowed the steppe peoples to manage large herds over vast ranges, and led to the adoption of a fully nomadic way of life around 900.

The earliest nomads were Iranian-speakers who occupied the steppes as far east as the Ordos desert in China by the 8th century. The Cimmerians on the Russian steppes in the early 1st millennium were the first known nomad power. About 700 they were eclipsed by the Scythians, another Iranian people from central Asia or Siberia. Pursued across the Caucasus by the Scythians, a group of Cimmerians migrated to Anatolia, destroying the Phrygian kingdom on the way. This was the first instance of conflicts on the steppes setting off migrations that had destructive effects on remote urban civilizations – a frequent cycle over the next two millennia.

The Scythians were ruled by powerful chiefs, who were buried in underground chambers with offerings of weapons, jewelry, horses, wagons and human sacrifices, and covered with a *kurgan*, or barrow. An important group of burials at Pazyryk in the Altay mountains, revealed that the Scythians

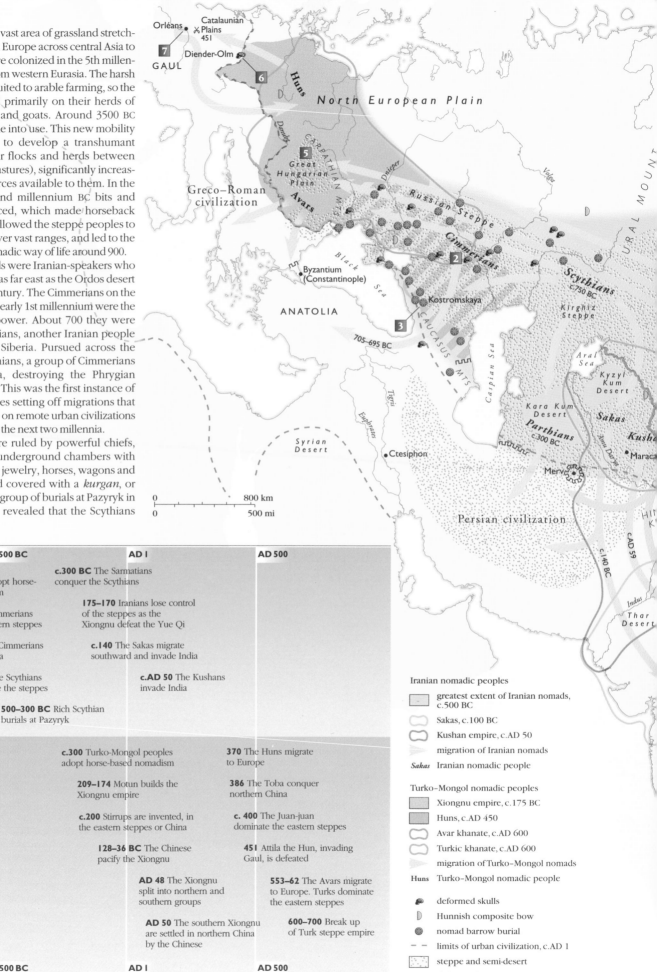

TIMELINE

Iranian nomads

c.900 The Iranian steppe peoples adopt horse-mounted nomadism

c.900–700 The Cimmerians dominate the western steppes

705–695 The Cimmerians invade Anatolia

c.700–300 The Scythians now dominate the steppes

500–300 BC Rich Scythian burials at Pazyryk

c.300 BC The Sarmatians conquer the Scythians

175–170 Iranians lose control of the steppes as the Xiongnu defeat the Yue Qi

c.140 The Sakas migrate southward and invade India

c.AD 50 The Kushans invade India

Turko-Mongol nomads

c.300 Turko-Mongol peoples adopt horse-based nomadism

209–174 Motun builds the Xiongnu empire

c.200 Stirrups are invented, in the eastern steppes or China

128–36 BC The Chinese pacify the Xiongnu

AD 48 The Xiongnu split into northern and southern groups

AD 50 The southern Xiongnu are settled in northern China by the Chinese

370 The Huns migrate to Europe

386 The Toba conquer northern China

c. 400 The Juan-juan dominate the eastern steppes

451 Attila the Hun, invading Gaul, is defeated

553–62 The Avars migrate to Europe. Turks dominate the eastern steppes

600–700 Break up of Turk steppe empire

Iranian nomadic peoples

greatest extent of Iranian nomads, c.500 BC

Sakas, c.100 BC

Kushan empire, c.AD 50

migration of Iranian nomads

Sakas Iranian nomadic people

Turko-Mongol nomadic peoples

Xiongnu empire, c.175 BC

Huns, c.AD 450

Avar khanate, c.AD 600

Turkic khanate, c.AD 600

migration of Turko-Mongol nomads

Huns Turko-Mongol nomadic people

deformed skulls

Hunnish composite bow

nomad barrow burial

- - limits of urban civilization, c.AD 1

steppe and semi-desert

defensive barrier

WAGONS, such as this 5th-century BC example from Pazyryk, made the nomadic lifestyle possible.

1 Burials in the Tarim basin indicate that European-type peoples were settled in the eastern steppes around 2000 BC.

2 The Cimmerians, the first steppe peoples to adopt a fully nomadic way of life, dominated the steppes c.900–700 BC.

3 Site of the barrow burial of a Scythian chieftain of the 7th or 6th century BC which included offerings of weapons and sacrificed servants and horses.

4 Chinese rulers began to build great defensive walls to deter nomad raiders, in the 4th century BC.

5 The Hungarian plain, the most westerly area of steppe capable of supporting large herds of horses, became the center of the Hun and Avar empires.

6 Hunnish burials are notable for their distinctively deformed skulls caused by binding children's heads.

7 Orleans, besieged by the Huns in AD 451, was the farthest west that steppe nomads ventured.

Motun (r.209–174 BC) they raided the Han empire of China, exacting huge amounts in tribute. In 170 the Xiongnu defeated the Iranian Yue Qi nomads and drove them to the west, in turn forcing the Sakas to move south around 140 through the Parthian empire into India, where they founded a kingdom which lasted until about AD 400. The dominant Yue Qi clan, the Kushans, built an empire which by AD 50 extended from the Aral Sea to the Indian Ocean and controlled the Asian trade routes.

Between 128 and 36 BC the Chinese fought a series of campaigns that succeeded in reducing the Xiongnu to tributary status. In AD 48 the Xiongnu split into two groups; and they finally disappeared from history around AD 400. In the late 4th century the Huns, a Turkic people, migrated west from central Asia to the steppes of east Europe, destabilizing the Germanic tribes and causing them to invade the Roman empire in search of safer lands to settle. The Huns reached the height of their power under Attila (r.434–53), but their empire collapsed after his death. Another Hunnish people, the Ephthalite ("White") Huns, invaded Persia and India in the late 5th century, preventing the Sasanians from exploiting the problems of the Roman empire and destroying the declining Gupta empire.

For several centuries after the collapse of Xiongnu power, no one people achieved dominance on the eastern steppes. At times of internal weakness China was raided, and in 386 the north was conquered by the Toba nomads, who held power there for over 150 years. Around 400 the Juan-juan, a Mongol-dominated confederation, built an empire which covered much the same area as the earlier Xiongnu empire. The Juan-juan were themselves overthrown in 553 by their Turkish subjects, who went on to create an empire that stretched from Manchuria to the Aral Sea by 600. Part of the Juan-juan confederation, the Avars, fled west and in 562 arrived in eastern Europe where, in alliance with the Sasanians, they almost destroyed the eastern Roman empire. To save the empire reforms had to be introduced – changes so far-reaching that historians consider them the beginning of the Byzantine empire.

decorated their bodies with elaborate tattoos. The Scythians produced a vigorous art style based on stylized animals, and imported Greek metalwork and other goods. Scythian power waned in the 3rd century and their place on the western steppes was taken by the Sarmatians. The defeated Scythians were probably not exterminated, but absorbed by the Sarmatians.

The practice of assimilating defeated rivals explains both the rapid rise of steppe peoples and their rapid extinctions. The numbers of a successful tribe were swelled by assimilated enemies and by other tribes who joined voluntarily to share in the prestige and plunder of the victors. By the same means an apparently numerous and powerful people could suddenly vanish. Although very destructive, nomad armies rarely made lasting conquests outside the

steppe zone. Only on the steppes was there sufficient grazing for the huge numbers of horses that nomad armies needed. Where nomads did make lasting conquests outside the steppe zone, as in India and China, they abandoned their lifestyle and became assimilated into the culture of the more numerous settled population.

The Turko-Mongol peoples of the eastern steppes made the transition from transhumant pastoralism to full horse-mounted nomadism around 300 BC. In the short composite bow (made of glued strips of horn and wood) the Turko-Mongol nomads had a weapon ideally suited to fast moving cavalry warfare, and they soon proved a formidable threat to Iranian nomads and urban civilizations alike. The first nomad power of the eastern steppes was the Xiongnu, a Turkic dominated confederation. Under

See also 2.19 (Germans);
2.23 (Kushans and Guptas); 2.24 (China)

The earliest African state formed in Egypt's Nile valley, where a centralized kingdom had emerged by 3000 BC. By this time desertification had turned the Sahara into a major barrier to travel and the only easy land route between Egypt and tropical Africa lay along the narrow valley of the middle Nile through Nubia. By 2500 several chiefdoms had emerged in Nubia. These were consolidated by 1700 into a large state, known to the Egyptians as Kush, whose capital was at Kerma. Nubia was rich in natural resources, especially gold, and was subjected to Egyptian plundering expeditions. It may, therefore, have been the impetus to organize an effective defense against the Egyptians that provided the impetus for state formation in this area. Kush was conquered by the Egyptians about 1500 at the start of Egypt's imperialistic New Kingdom period. When Egyptian power declined at the end of the New Kingdom (1070 BC), Kush regained its independence. In 770 the kings of Kush conquered southern Egypt and in 712 Shabaka (r.712–698) brought the whole kingdom under Nubian rule. Assyrian attacks on Egypt drove the Nubians from northern Egypt, and by 657 they had lost control of the whole country. The Egyptians expelled the Assyrians in 653 and launched campaigns into Nubia, forcing the Nubians to move their capital south to Meroë around 590. The kingdom of Meroë, as Kush is subsequently known, remained a major power that was taken seriously by the Persians, Greco-Macedonians and Romans who in turn ruled Egypt after 525 BC. In the 4th century Meroë suffered attacks from desert nomads; it collapsed about 350, after the capital was taken by the Axumites. Three small states, Nobatia, Makkura and Alwa, arose as successors to Meroë but Makkura conquered Nobatia in the 8th century.

Nubia was strongly influenced by Egyptian religion, kingship and culture. Until about 200 BC, when an indigenous Meroitic script was developed, Egyptian scripts and language were used for inscriptions, and the use of pyramids for royal burials continued into the Christian era, long after the practice had ceased in Egypt. Christianity was introduced to

Nubia in the 6th century and remained strong until the region was put under pressure by the Arabs in the 13th century.

The second state to develop in tropical Africa, Axum emerged in northern Ethiopia in the 1st century AD. Urban development had begun at sites such as Yeha in the 5th century BC and the cultural development of the area was strongly influenced by the Sabeans of Arabia, whose alphabet, architecture and religion were adopted. In the 1st century AD the port of Adulis was exporting ivory, rhinoceros horn, tortoise-shell, obsidian and aromatic resins to the Roman empire via Red Sea trade routes. The city of Axum itself included complexes of monumental buildings and palaces. Among the most remarkable monuments at Axum are monoliths carved to resemble multistory buildings: the tallest still standing is 69 feet (21 meters) high. The kingdom of Axum reached a peak in the reign of King Ezana around 350. About this time also, Ezana converted to Christianity, the first African ruler to do so. In 522 the Axumites invaded and conquered the Yemen and held it until driven out by the Sasanians in 574. In the 8th century, attacks by the Arabs accelerated the decline of Axum, and by the 10th century power had shifted to the Ethiopian highlands.

Another area of Africa in which state formation occurred was the Maghrib, where the Berber kingdoms of Numantia and Mauretania emerged around 200 BC in the power vacuum left by the defeat of Carthage in the Second Punic War (226–201 BC). However, these states were soon swallowed up by the expanding empire of Rome. The most significant development in north Africa was the introduction of the camel to the Sahara around 100 BC. Camels were ideal for desert warfare, and settled communities on the fringes of the desert soon suffered badly from nomad raids. Camels also had the endurance for long desert crossings – horses, mules and bullocks had previously been the main beasts of burden in the Sahara. Now cross-desert trade began to expand, and by AD 500 camel caravans forged strong trade links between the Mediterranean and west Africa

(maritime links were never established, because of adverse winds south of Cape Bojador).

The earliest Iron Age culture of west Africa, the Nok culture of Nigeria (c. 500 BC– AD 400), is noted for its sophisticated terracotta sculptures, which are often seen as being ancestral to the art styles of the medieval Ibo and Yoruba peoples. By AD 600 many areas of west Africa had dense farming populations, and one city, Jenne-jeno, had developed as a regional trading center. Many large burial mounds in this region point to the emergence of powerful elites and the beginnings of state formation.

The major development in Africa south of the Equator was the expansion of the Bantu-speaking peoples, mixed farming and, later, iron working. The Bantu languages belong to the Niger-Kordofanian group, confined to tropical west Africa in the second millennium BC. The original homeland of the Bantu was in southern Nigeria and Cameroon, but around 2000 BC Bantu-speakers began to spread into central and east Africa, and by AD 500 they had reached southern Africa. Bantu languages were spread partly by migrations of iron-using farmers, but also by the assimilation to Bantu culture of the Khoisan-speaking Stone Age herders and hunter-gatherers of eastern and southern Africa.

Map legend

Nok early Iron Age culture, 6th century BC–5th century AD

maximum extent of Nubian power, 712–671 BC

kingdom of Meroë, 590 BC–AD 350

kingdom of Axum under Ezana, c.AD 350

Axumite occupation, AD 522–74

kingdom of Numidia, 2nd century BC

kingdom of Mauretania, 2nd century BC

origin of Bantu-speaking peoples, 2000 BC

northwestern Bantu by AD 500

eastern Bantu by AD 500

western Bantu by AD 500

spread of Bantu, with date

Niger–Kordofanian languages, 2nd millennium BC

border of Roman empire, AD 1

sub-Sahara African early Iron Age site

with evidence of iron production

other site

trading post, 1st–3rd century AD

early Christian church, 4th–6th century AD

probable trans-Saharan route

sea route

desert

tropical rainforest

Cape Bojador

1

Akj

Senegal

Gambia

0 — 1000 km

0 — 800 mi

TIMELINE

Northern Africa

600 BC	AD 1	AD 600
712–671 Egypt is under Nubian rule	c.200 Berber kingdoms emerge in north Africa	c.350 Fall of the kingdom of Meroë
590 Meroë becomes the capital of Nubia	146 The Romans destroy the city of Carthage	c.350 King Ezana of Axum converts to Christianity
525–523 Egypt is conquered by Persia	c.100 BC The camel is introduced into the Sahara	522–74 The kingdom of Axum rules in the Yemen
c.500 Sabeans settle in Ethiopia, later contributing to rise of the kingdom of Axum	AD 1–100 The kingdom of Axum emerges	c.540 The Nubians are converted to Christianity

Southern Africa

600 BC	AD 1	AD 600
700–600 Iron working is first known in the central Sahara region	c.200 Date of the earliest occupation at Jenne-jeno	c.400 City walls are built at Jenne-jeno
c.480 Taruga, Nigeria, flourishes as an iron working center	c.AD 1 Khoisans in southern Africa are herding sheep	400–500 Iron working reaches southern Africa
400–300 Iron working is established in the east African highlands	AD 1–100 Madagascar is settled by Austronesians from southeast Asia	500–600 Cattle and iron working are widespread in southern Africa
	100–300 Greco-Roman merchants sail to east Africa for ivory	

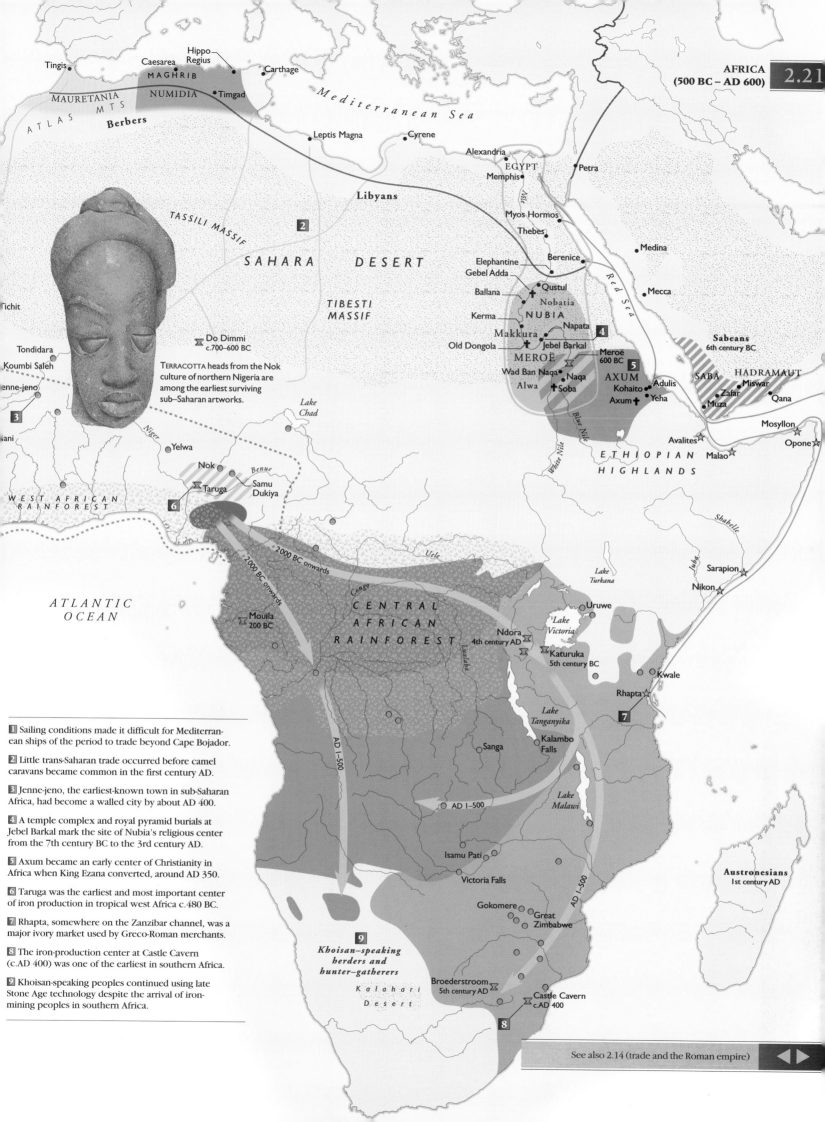

Tingis
Caesarea
Hippo Regius
MAGHRIB
Carthage
MAURETANIA
NUMIDIA
Timgad
ATLAS MTS
Berbers
Mediterranean Sea
Leptis Magna
Cyrene
Alexandria
EGYPT
Memphis
Petra

SAHARA DESERT

TASSILI MASSIF

Libyans

Myos Hormos
Thebes
Berenice
Medina
Elephantine
Gebel Adda
Qustul
Mecca
Ballana
Nobatia
Kerma
NUBIA
Napata
Red Sea
Sabeans
6th century BC
Makkura
Jebel Barkal
Meroë
600 BC
SABA
HADRAMAUT
Old Dongola
MEROË
AXUM
Miswar
Wad Ban Naqa
Naqa
Adulis
Zafar
Kohaito
Yeha
Muza
Qana
Alwa
Soba
Axum

Do Dimmi
c.700–600 BC

TERRACOTTA heads from the Nok culture of northern Nigeria are among the earliest surviving sub–Saharan artworks.

Tichit
Tondidara
Koumbi Saleh
enne-jeno
ani
Lake Chad
Niger
Yelwa
Nok
Benue
Taruga
Samu
Dukiya
WEST AFRICAN RAINFOREST

ETHIOPIAN HIGHLANDS
White Nile
Blue Nile

Mosyllon
Avalites
Malao
Opone

ATLANTIC OCEAN

2,000 BC onwards
2,000 BC onwards
Uele
CENTRAL AFRICAN RAINFOREST
Congo
Mouila
200 BC

Lake Turkana
Sarapion
Nikon

Lualaba
Uruwe
Ndora
4th century AD
Lake Victoria
Katuruka
5th century BC
Kwale
Rhapta

AD 1–500

Sanga

Lake Tanganyika
Kalambo Falls

Lake Malawi

AD 1–500

AD 1–500

Isamu Pati

Victoria Falls

Austronesians
1st century AD

Gokomere
Great Zimbabwe

9
Khoisan–speaking herders and hunter-gatherers

Kalahari Desert

Broederstroom
5th century AD
Castle Cavern
c.AD 400
8

Shabelle
Juba

1. Sailing conditions made it difficult for Mediterranean ships of the period to trade beyond Cape Bojador.

2. Little trans-Saharan trade occurred before camel caravans became common in the first century AD.

3. Jenne-jeno, the earliest-known town in sub-Saharan Africa, had become a walled city by about AD 400.

4. A temple complex and royal pyramid burials at Jebel Barkal mark the site of Nubia's religious center from the 7th century BC to the 3rd century AD.

5. Axum became an early center of Christianity in Africa when King Ezana converted, around AD 350.

6. Taruga was the earliest and most important center of iron production in tropical west Africa c.480 BC.

7. Rhapta, somewhere on the Zanzibar channel, was a major ivory market used by Greco-Roman merchants.

8. The iron-production center at Castle Cavern (c.AD 400) was one of the earliest in southern Africa.

9. Khoisan-speaking peoples continued using late Stone Age technology despite the arrival of iron-mining peoples in southern Africa.

See also 2.14 (trade and the Roman empire)

In 500 BC northern India was divided into several Hindu kingdoms, the most powerful being Magadha, ruled by king Bimbisara. Southern India was still dominated by tribal peoples under Hindu influence. In 364 Magadha came under the control of the expansionist Nanda dynasty, which by about 340 dominated northern India. The Nandas' reputation for oppressive taxation, however, led to their overthrow in a coup by Chandragupta Maurya (r. 321–c.293). Chandragupta's origins are obscure but he appears to have been a military commander in the northwest border provinces at the time of Alexander the Great's invasion of the Indus valley: he fought against Greek outposts in the area and may have met Alexander.

By 311 Chandragupta had extended his kingdom to the Indus, bringing him into conflict with Seleucos, who had seized power after Alexander's death. In 305 Chandragupta defeated Seleucos and was ceded control of the whole Indus valley in return for a gift of 500 war elephants. Chandragupta maintained a large standing army and imposed a harsh penal code on his people. He also created an effective central bureaucracy, which controlled economic activity and carried out road building, irrigation and other public works. In about 293 he abdicated in favor of his son Bindusara (r.c. 293–268) and became a Jain monk, dying around 286. Bindusara continued the expansionist program of his father and extended the Mauryan empire far into southern India. In 268 he was succeeded by his son Ashoka, one of India's most remarkable rulers. Reportedly overcome with remorse after a bloody conquest of the east-coast district of Kalinga in 261, Ashoka converted to Buddhism in about 260.

Buddhism had its origins in the teachings of Siddhartha Gautama, the Buddha, (c.563–483), in the heartland of late 6th-century Magadha. It was just one among many sects influenced by, but reacting against, India's traditions of Brahmanic Hinduism,

A CARVING of about AD 100 from Sanchi , exemplifying a common Hindu theme of a dancing woman with a flowering tree.

until the missionary work started by Ashoka in 258 began its transformation from minor sect to major world religion. Ashoka adopted the Buddhist principles of right conduct and non-violence, assured neighboring states of his goodwill, ameliorated his grandfather's penal code and sought to rule as far as possible by moral authority alone. To spread Buddhist values he had edicts on morality and the way of compassion carved on rock-faces and pillars throughout his empire. Over thirty of these survive, forming the most important source of information about Ashoka's reign. Ashoka intervened in doctrinal matters and it was his initiative that led to the defining of the Buddhist canon at the Third Buddhist council at Pataliputra around 240. Ashoka also promoted Buddhism abroad, sending missions to Indonesia, southern India, Ceylon, the Greek states of western Asia and the nomads of central Asia.

Although Ashoka's empire was the largest state to exist in India before the coming of the Mughal empire in the 17th century AD, it did not long survive

Arabian Sea

UTTARAPATHA

Herat

Kandahar

Marakanda

TIMELINE

Political change

500 BC

c.540–490 Magadha, under king Bimbisara, becomes the leading Hindu kingdom

c.483 King Vijaya founds the first state in Ceylon

364–321 Under the Nanda dynasty Magadha dominates the Ganges plain

327–325 Alexander the Great conquers the Indus valley

321 Chandragupta Maurya seizes power in Magadha and founds the Mauryan empire

c.293 Chandragupta abdicates in favor of Bindusara

c.293–268 Bindusara Maurya conquers southern India

250 BC

268–233 The reign of the Mauryan king Ashoka

c.185 The last Mauryan king is deposed

141 The Sakas invade northwest India

c.94 BC A Saka kingdom is founded in northwest India

AD I

c.AD 50 King Kharavela of Kalinga dominates eastern and central India

AD 50–75 The Kushans invade and conquer northwest India

Cultural change

528 Siddhartha Gautama the Buddha (c.563–483) attains "Enlightenment"

c.500 Sinhalese migrate to northern Ceylon

c.260 Ashoka converts to Buddhism

c.250 Ashoka introduces Buddhism into Ceylon

500 BC   **250 BC**   **AD I**

Legend

empire of Alexander the Great, c.325 BC

kingdom of Magadha under Nanda dynasty, c.324 BC

Mauryan empire

territory gained by Chandragupta Maurya, 320–305 BC

territory gained by Bindusara, c.293–268 BC

territory gained by Ashoka, 268–260 BC

maximum extent of empire under Ashoka, c.260 BC

weak or nominal Mauryan control

provincial capital

VANGA province under Ashoka

Ashokan rock edict

Ashokan pillar edict

heartland of Satavahanihara kingdom late 1st century BC

maximum extent of Saka rule, 1st century BC

Western Sakas, 2nd century AD

formative area of Buddhism

Buddhist monument, before 187 BC

Buddhist monument, 187 BC–AD 50

migration of peoples

ancient river course

modern coastline where altered

his death in 233. Much of the empire was only loosely held and the south was lost almost at once, while by 200 the Bactrian Greeks had conquered the Indus valley and restored Alexander's frontier in India. In the 180s the Bactrians briefly extended their control as far south as Barygaza and as far east as Mathura. The last Mauryan king was overthrown in 185 by Pushyamitra Shunga, one of his generals. Under the Shunga dynasty Magadha continued to be a major power, but after the dynasty fell in 73 BC the kingdom's power collapsed completely and it became just one minor state among many on the Gangetic plain. By this time power had shifted to the northwest where the Sakas, nomadic invaders from central Asia, had established a powerful kingdom around 94 BC. By AD 1 the Saka kingdom was in decline, but around AD 50 a second wave of nomads, the Kushans, invaded and founded another major kingdom in the northwest.

The advent of the Mauryan empire accelerated state formation in southern India – trade contacts, colonies of northerners and Buddhist missions ending the area's relative isolation. The first considerable state in the region, Kalinga, dominated eastern India and extended its power into the Gangetic plain in the middle of the 1st century BC under King Kharavela. Soon after Kharavela's death, however, it sank back into obscurity. More stable was the state of Satavahanihara, centered around Pratisthana, which also rose to prominence in the 1st century BC and remained the dominant power in the south until the 3rd century AD. Ceylon was colonized by Sinhalese from southern India around 500 BC and the native Veddas were pushed into the interior. Traditionally the first state in Ceylon was founded around 483, by King Vijaya in the north of the island. Ashoka's missionaries took Buddhism to Ceylon, where the religion set down particularly deep roots.

1 The trading city of Taxila, occupied successively by Persians, Greeks, Mauryans, Sakas and Kushans, became a melting pot of different cultures.

2 Bodh Gaya, where Buddha gained "Enlightenment" c.528 BC, was and remains a sacred site of Buddhism.

3 Anuradhapura was founded in 437 BC as the capital of a Sinhalese kingdom of northern Ceylon.

4 Pataliputra was capital of Magadha and the Mauryan empire and one of the largest cities in the ancient world, defended by a timber wall with 500 towers.

5 A dam, reservoir and irrigation project of the Mauryan period at Junagadh was one of the first such large projects to be built under government direction.

6 Southern India was (most probably) conquered by Chandragupta's son Bindusara (r. c.293–268 BC).

7 Amaravati was the main Buddhist center in southern India from the 3rd century BC to the 14th AD.

8 A complex of rock-cut Buddhist temples and monasteries with fine wall paintings was built at Ajanta from the 2nd century BC to the 5th AD.

9 Trade in pearls, diamonds and gold led to state formation in southern India by the 1st century BC.

See also 2.09 (Alexander's empires);
2.20 steppe peoples; 2.23 (Guptas)

Around AD 50 the Kushans made northwest India part of an empire stretching from the Ganges to the Aral Sea. They were a clan of the Yue Qi nomads who had overrun the Greek kingdom of Bactria around 135 BC. The Kushan state was set up in Bactria around AD 25 by Kujala Kadphises, who invaded India and conquered Gandhara and the Northern Sakas around AD 50. Kujala's successor, Vima Kadphises (r.c.75–100), conquered the Indus valley and much of the Gangetic plain. The empire reached its peak under Kanishka (r.c.100–130). He was a devout Buddhist and a patron of the arts, supporting both the Indo-Hellenistic school of Gandhara and the Hindu school of Mathura. Under Kanishka's successors, the Kushan empire maintained its borders until the 3rd century, when most of the empire's western provinces were conquered by the Sasanian King Shapur I. Although the Kushans briefly regained their independence in the 4th century, the united Kushan empire was not restored.

The Kushan empire was never highly centralized and the king ruled through a host of dependent sub-kings or *yaghbus*. Kushan rulers used an eclectic range of titles, including *maharaja* (great king), *rajatiraja* (king of kings), the Greek title *basileus* (king) and *kaisara* (from the Latin *caesar*). They also instituted a cult of ruler worship and used the title *devaputra* (son of God). Kushan culture was equally eclectic, mixing Hellenistic, Indian and central Asian styles. Kushan rulers were tolerant in matters of religion. Most of the early rulers were Buddhists and the later ones Hindus, but all showed respect for a wide range of Persian, Greek and even Roman deities. The empire was always wealthy, prospering by its control of all the major trans-Asian overland trade routes. High-quality gold coinage was made by melting down gold Roman coins flooding into the empire to pay for luxury goods such as Chinese silk.

The Kushans did not have a monopoly on east–west trade. By the 1st century AD, Mediterranean seafarers had discovered how to exploit the monsoon winds to sail across the Indian Ocean, bringing increased trade between the Roman empire and southern India. The region's most valuable exports were spices, which the Romans paid for in gold. South Indian rulers did not issue their own coinage and Roman coins circulated freely. The most powerful south Indian state at this period was Satavahanihara; but the influx of wealth led to the formation of several small tribal kingdoms and cities in the region.

The decline of Kushan power made possible the rise of the Gupta kingdom in the 4th century. Minor princes in the Varanasi area in the later 3rd century, the Guptas may have been feudatories of Magadha. The dynasty began with the reign of Chandragupta I (r.320–35), who made an advantageous marriage alliance with the Licchavis. This brought him control of Magadha, the fertile and densely populated heartland of the former Mauryan empire. Chandragupta was succeeded by his son Samudragupta (r.335–80), whose long reign saw the kingdom expand across northern India, reducing the Kushans to tributary status. Samudragupta also fought a major campaign in the southeast, reducing many rulers to tributaries. He formed strong alliances with the Sakas and the Vakatakas (in power in Satavahanihara), but his son and successor, Chandragupta II (r.380–414), turned on the Western Sakas, conquered their kingdom and imposed direct rule. The empire ruled by Chandragupta II was almost as large as the Mauryan empire, but was very loose-knit. Gupta inscriptions approximately cover the area in which the dynasty exercised direct rule – the rest of the empire was ruled by tributary kings and barely-subdued tribes.

The Guptas were patrons of the arts and sciences and the period was one of great creativity. They were devout Hindus and some of the main features of Hinduism, such as image-worship, appeared under their rule. The Hindu epics of the *Ramayana* and the *Mahabharata* reached their final form at this time. Sanskrit poetry and drama flourished, causing the Gupta period to be regarded as the classical age of Indian literature. Advances were made in astronomy and mathematics, including the invention of the decimal system of numerals, later adopted by the Arabs and, through them, by the Europeans.

After the death of Chandragupta II, the empire ceased expanding but remained powerful, and under Skandagupta (r.c.455–67) defeated a major Hunnish invasion. However, a war of succession followed Skandagupta's death and the empire went into decline as tributary kings and nominally conquered tribes reasserted their independence. The final blow came from an invasion of the Hunas (Ephthalite Huns) in 505–11, who founded a kingdom in northwest India, destroying the last remnants of the Kushans. In 528 a coalition of Indian princes defeated the Hunas, but the Guptas played only a minor role in this campaign. Gupta rulers continued in Magadha until around 720, but only as mere princes. Except for a brief period under Harsha (r.606–47) of Kanauj, who united the states on the Gangetic plain, no supraregional state reappeared in India until the 13th century.

core area of Kushan state, c.AD 25
Kushan empire, mid 2nd century AD
Satavahanihara, mid 2nd century
Gupta kingdom of Chandragupta I, c.AD 320
Gupta empire of Samudragupta, c.AD 370
additions to Gupta empire by Chandragupta II, c.AD 410
VANGA minor kingdom
Comari important seaport for Roman trade
hoard of Roman coins
Gupta inscription
trade route
southern campaign of Samudragupta, c.AD 360
migration of Kushans/Yue Qi
migration of Ephthalites (Hunas)
ancient river course
modern coastline where altered

to Persia and the Mediterranean

to Persia

0   400 km
0   300 mi

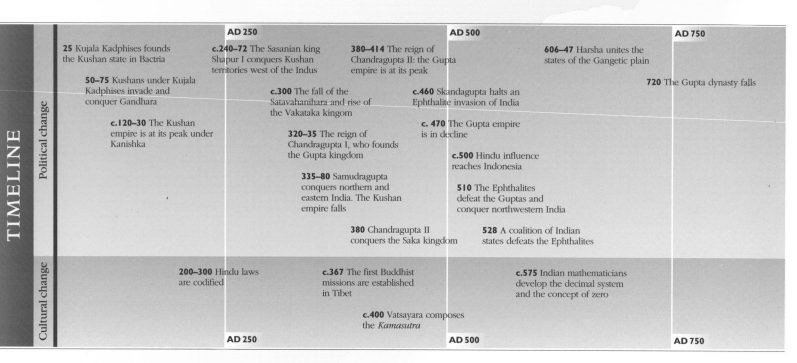

TIMELINE

Political change

25 Kujala Kadphises founds the Kushan state in Bactria

50–75 Kushans under Kujala Kadphises invade and conquer Gandhara

c.120–30 The Kushan empire is at its peak under Kanishka

AD 250

c.240–72 The Sasanian king Shapur I conquers Kushan territories west of the Indus

c.300 The fall of the Satavahanihara and rise of the Vakataka kingom

320–35 The reign of Chandragupta I, who founds the Gupta kingdom

335–80 Samudragupta conquers northern and eastern India. The Kushan empire falls

380 Chandragupta II conquers the Saka kingdom

AD 500

380–414 The reign of Chandragupta II: the Gupta empire is at its peak

c.460 Skandagupta halts an Ephthalite invasion of India

c.470 The Gupta empire is in decline

c.500 Hindu influence reaches Indonesia

510 The Ephthalites defeat the Guptas and conquer northwestern India

528 A coalition of Indian states defeats the Ephthalites

AD 750

606–47 Harsha unites the states of the Gangetic plain

720 The Gupta dynasty falls

Cultural change

200–300 Hindu laws are codified

c.367 The first Buddhist missions are established in Tibet

c.400 Vatsayara composes the *Kamasutra*

c.575 Indian mathematicians develop the decimal system and the concept of zero

AD 250   AD 500   AD 750

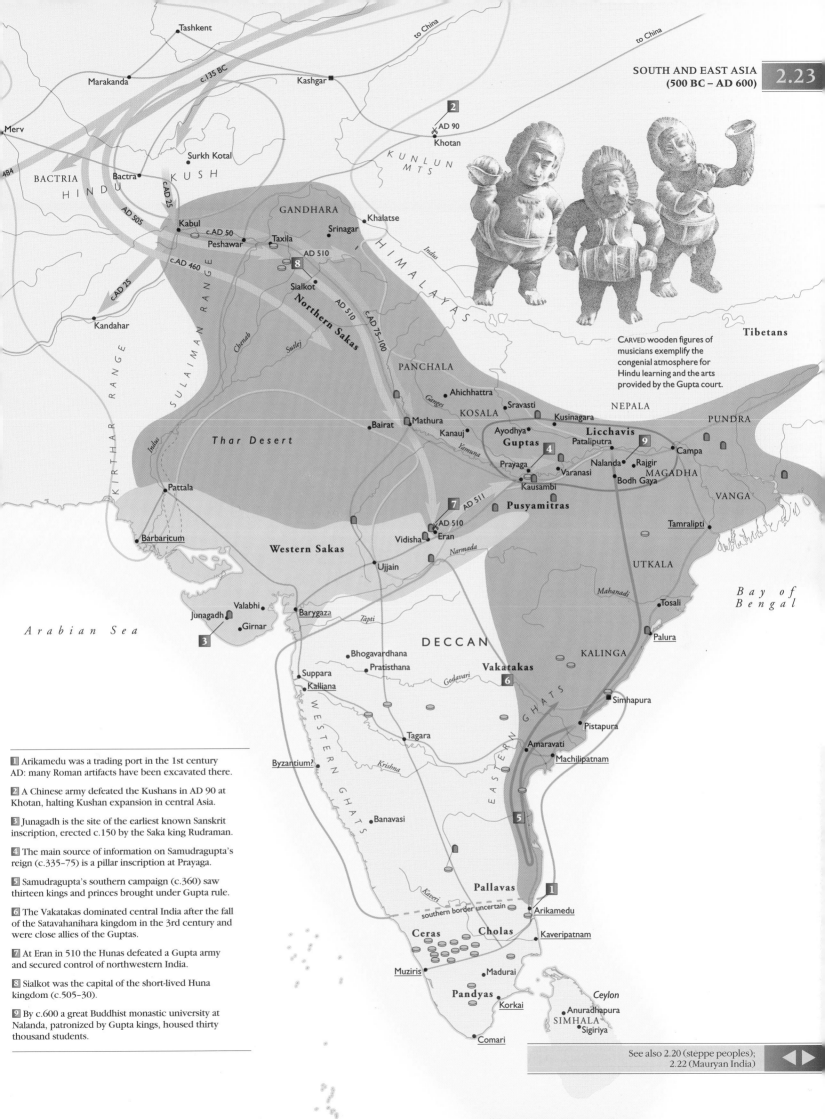

to China

to China

Tashkent

Marakanda

c.135 BC

Kashgar

Merv

484

2

AD 90

Khotan

BACTRIA

Surkh Kotal

HINDU

Bactra

KUSH

KUNLUN

MTS

Kabul

c.AD 50

GANDHARA

Khalatse

AD 25

Peshawar

Taxila

Srinagar

Indus

AD 505

c.AD 460

AD 510

HIMALAYAS

Kandahar

8

Sialkot

Northern Sakas

AD 510

c.AD 75–100

Chenab

Sutlej

PANCHALA

NEPALA

CARVED wooden figures of
musicians exemplify the
congenial atmosphere for
Hindu learning and the arts
provided by the Gupta court.

Tibetans

Ahichhattra

SULAIMAN RANGE

Ganges

KOSALA

Sravasti

Kusinagara

PUNDRA

KIRTHAR RANGE

Indus

Bairat

Mathura

Kanauj

Ayodhya

Licchavis

Thar Desert

Prayaga

Guptas

4

Pataliputra

9

Campa

Yamuna

Varanasi

Nalanda

Rajgir

MAGADHA

Kausambi

Bodh Gaya

VANGA

Pattala

7

AD 511

Pusyamitras

Tamralipti

Barbaricum

AD 510

Eran

Vidisha

UTKALA

Western Sakas

Ujjain

Narmada

Mahanadi

Tosali

Bay of
Bengal

Valabhi

Junagadh

Girnar

Barygaza

Tapti

KALINGA

Palura

Arabian Sea

3

DECCAN

Vakatakas

Simhapura

Bhogavardhana

6

Pratisthana

Godavari

Suppara

Kalliana

Pistapura

EASTERN GHATS

WESTERN GHATS

Tagara

Amaravati

Byzantium?

Krishna

Machilipatnam

Banavasi

5

Pallavas

1

Kaveri

Arikamedu

southern border uncertain

Ceras

Cholas

Kaveripatnam

Muziris

Madurai

Ceylon

Pandyas

Korkai

Anuradhapura

SIMHALA

Sigiriya

Comari

1 Arikamedu was a trading port in the 1st century
AD: many Roman artifacts have been excavated there.

2 A Chinese army defeated the Kushans in AD 90 at
Khotan, halting Kushan expansion in central Asia.

3 Junagadh is the site of the earliest known Sanskrit
inscription, erected c.150 by the Saka king Rudraman.

4 The main source of information on Samudragupta's
reign (c.335–75) is a pillar inscription at Prayaga.

5 Samudragupta's southern campaign (c.360) saw
thirteen kings and princes brought under Gupta rule.

6 The Vakatakas dominated central India after the fall
of the Satavahanihara kingdom in the 3rd century and
were close allies of the Guptas.

7 At Eran in 510 the Hunas defeated a Gupta army
and secured control of northwestern India.

8 Sialkot was the capital of the short-lived Huna
kingdom (c.505–30).

9 By c.600 a great Buddhist monastic university at
Nalanda, patronized by Gupta kings, housed thirty
thousand students.

See also 2.20 (steppe peoples);
2.22 (Mauryan India)

Zhou China (1122–256 BC) was a decentralized feudal state: the king exercised direct authority only over his own domain, while the provinces were held as fiefs by dukes who ruled in his name. Gradually the dukes became, in effect, the rulers of independent states; the Zhou king reigned from his capital at Luoyang but did not rule. The Warring States period (480–221 BC) saw the stronger states eliminate the weaker and absorb their territory: by 300 eleven states were left, and by 256, when the last Zhou king was deposed, there were seven. By 221 one state – Qin – was supreme.

Qin's rise to dominance began under Xiao (r.361–338). Shang Yang, Xiao's prime minister, ended the power of the feudal aristocracy and enacted a series of reforms that turned Qin into a centralized state based on a settled and productive peasantry and a strong army. Qin's frontier position gave it opportunities for expansion at the expense of the tribal peoples to the west, while its mountainous borders protected it from the aggression of other states. By 315 it was the strongest of the surviving states. The Qin dukes had already abandoned the pretence of subservience to the Zhou by adopting the title of king. In the 3rd century Qin waged almost constant warfare against the other Chinese states, which failed to combine against it and were picked off one at a time. The unification of China was completed in a series of lightning campaigns by Zheng (r.246–210) between 230 and 221, after which he adopted the title Shi Huangdi, the "First Emperor".

Shi Huangdi is regarded as the founder of the Chinese empire and the pattern of centralized totalitarian government he established has endured to the present day. Qin laws and institutions were extended to the whole of China. The aristocracies of the defeated states were deported, the remnants of feudalism were abolished and a non-hereditary central and local bureaucracy was created. The empire was divided into 36 districts or commanderies, governed by civilian and military officials responsible directly to the autocratic emperor. Coinage, weights and measures, scripts and even the axle sizes of wagons were standardized. In an attempt to ensure that Chinese history began with him, Shi Huangdi

ordered the destruction of all works of history, along with all "subversive" works of literature: scholars who protested were executed. Military campaigns extended the empire in the south while armies of conscripted laborers linked the frontier walls, which had been built by the Warring States against nomad invasions, into a continuous defensive system.

The cost of Shi Huangdi's reforms ruined the economy and his despotic rule caused such discontent that, after his death in 210, a civil war broke out. In 206 rebels massacred the entire Qin royal family. However, there was no restoration of the old states and the empire passed intact under the rule of Liu Bang, a commoner who had become a Qin official, and who became the first ruler of the Han dynasty. Gaozu (to use his more common posthumous title) ameliorated the severe Qin laws, reduced taxes and introduced reforms to restore prosperity. He rewarded some generals and bureaucrats with small fiefs but these were strictly controlled and the centralized state of Shi Huangdi was preserved.

The Former Han period (206 BC–AD 9) saw major territorial gains in central Asia and the south but northern China suffered severely from raids by the Xiongnu nomads until they were pacified in a long series of Han campaigns between 128 and 36 BC.

A TERRACOTTA army, six thousand men and horses strong, was buried with Shi Huangdi at Xianyang.

Turfan

Dunhuang

Cherchen

Gansu Corridor

QILIAN MTS

Changye

Wu-su

Lake Qinghai

Tibetans

105 BC

108 BC

6

8

- Jin, c.500 BC
- Warring States border, c.300 BC
- Qin state, c.350 BC
- Qin gains by 300 BC
- Qin gains, 300–250 BC
- Qin gains, 230–221 BC
- Qin gains by 206 BC
- empire of the former Han dynasty, c.AD 6
- Han protectorates, c.59 BC–AD 23, AD 73–127
- territorial gains of Later Han dynasty
- independent kingdom of Nan-yue, 206–113 BC
- Warring States capital
- capital of Zhou empire
- capital of Qin dynasty
- capital of former Han dynasty and Later Han dynasty
- Qin fort
- frontier wall
- Chinese campaign
- Xiongnu campaign
- modern coastline and drainage where altered

TIMELINE

	400 BC	200 BC	AD I	AD 200
	Warring States period	Former Han	Later Han	Three kingdoms period

Political change

c.500 Jin becomes the leading Chinese state

c.400 Breakup of the Jin state

361–338 Shang Yang turns Qin into a militaristic state

c. 350–315 Qin becomes the leading state in China

256 Qin deposes the last Zhou king

230–221 King Zheng of Qin unifies China

221–210 Zheng unites China under the Qin dynasty and takes the title Shi Huangdi

209–202 Civil war: the Qin dynasty is overthrown and Han dynasty established

128–36 BC The Han launch a series of campaigns to pacify the Xiongnu

117–115 BC Han conquer Gansu corridor

57 BC Traditional date for foundation of the first Korean state, Silla

AD 9 Courtier Wang Mang overthrows Han dynasty

AD 23 Restoration of Han dynasty

126 Peasant revolts against landowners

189 Provincial warlords seize the Han capital, Luoyang

190 General Tung Cho installs a puppet emperor on Han throne

220 Deposition of last Han emperor: China splits into three kingdoms

Cultural change

c. 500 Sun Tzu writes *The Art of War*

371–289 Mencius (Mengzi), Confucian philosopher

c.350 Crossbow invented

175–150 Iron weapons and tools come into widespread use in China

c. 100 Sima Qian writes the history of China from the beginning to his own times

c.100 Introduction of Buddhism to China

| 400 BC | 200 BC | AD I | AD 200 |

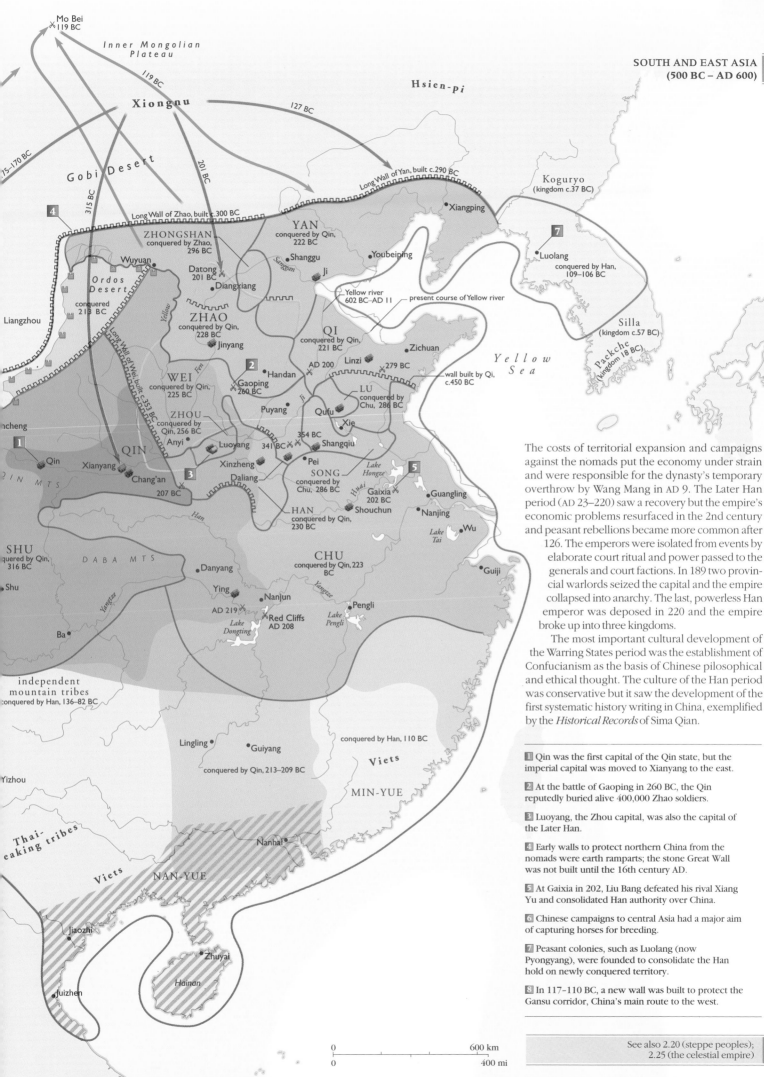

Mo Bei
119 BC

Inner Mongolian Plateau

119 BC

Hsien-pi

127 BC

Xiongnu

201 BC

315 BC

Gobi Desert

175–170 BC

Long Wall of Yan, built c.290 BC

Koguryo
(kingdom c.37 BC)

• Xiangping

4

Long Wall of Zhao, built c.300 BC

ZHONGSHAN
conquered by Zhao,
296 BC

• Wuyuan

*Ordos
Desert*

conquered
213 BC

Datong
201 BC

• Diangxiang

Shanggu

• Youbeiping

• Ji

7

• Luolang
conquered by Han,
109–106 BC

Liangzhou

Yellow river
602 BC–AD 11

present course of Yellow river

Silla
(kingdom c.57 BC)

ZHAO
conquered by Qin,
228 BC

• Jinyang

QI
conquered by Qin,
221 BC

• Zichuan

AD 200

Linzi

279 BC

*Yellow
Sea*

Paekche
(kingdom 18 BC)

2

Handan

wall built by Qi,
c.450 BC

WEI
conquered by Qin,
225 BC

Gaoping
260 BC

Puyang

LU
conquered by
Chu, 286 BC

Qufu

ncheng

ZHOU
conquered by
Qin, 256 BC

Anyi

• Luoyang

354 BC

• Xie

341 BC

Shangqiu

1

• Qin

Xianyang

QIN

3

Xinzheng

• Pei

SONG
conquered by
Chu, 286 BC

*Lake
Hongze*

5

QIN MTS

Chang'an

207 BC

Daliang

Gaixia
202 BC

Shouchun

• Guangling

HAN
conquered by Qin,
230 BC

• Nanjing

*Lake
Tai*

• Wu

SHU
quered by Qin,
316 BC

DABA MTS

Han

CHU
conquered by Qin, 223
BC

• Guiji

• Shu

• Danyang

Yangtze

Ying

AD 219

• Nanjun

Red Cliffs
AD 208

*Lake
Pengli*

• Pengli

• Ba

*Lake
Dongting*

Yangtze

independent
mountain tribes
conquered by Han, 136–82 BC

Yizhou

Lingling •

• Guiyang

conquered by Han, 110 BC

Viets

MIN-YUE

*Thai-
eaking tribes*

conquered by Qin, 213–209 BC

• Nanhai

Viets

NAN-YUE

• Jiaozhi

• Zhuyai

Hainan

uizhen

The costs of territorial expansion and campaigns against the nomads put the economy under strain and were responsible for the dynasty's temporary overthrow by Wang Mang in AD 9. The Later Han period (AD 23–220) saw a recovery but the empire's economic problems resurfaced in the 2nd century and peasant rebellions became more common after 126. The emperors were isolated from events by elaborate court ritual and power passed to the generals and court factions. In 189 two provincial warlords seized the capital and the empire collapsed into anarchy. The last, powerless Han emperor was deposed in 220 and the empire broke up into three kingdoms.

The most important cultural development of the Warring States period was the establishment of Confucianism as the basis of Chinese pilosophical and ethical thought. The culture of the Han period was conservative but it saw the development of the first systematic history writing in China, exemplified by the *Historical Records* of Sima Qian.

1 Qin was the first capital of the Qin state, but the imperial capital was moved to Xianyang to the east.

2 At the battle of Gaoping in 260 BC, the Qin reputedly buried alive 400,000 Zhao soldiers.

3 Luoyang, the Zhou capital, was also the capital of the Later Han.

4 Early walls to protect northern China from the nomads were earth ramparts; the stone Great Wall was not built until the 16th century AD.

5 At Gaixia in 202, Liu Bang defeated his rival Xiang Yu and consolidated Han authority over China.

6 Chinese campaigns to central Asia had a major aim of capturing horses for breeding.

7 Peasant colonies, such as Luolang (now Pyongyang), were founded to consolidate the Han hold on newly conquered territory.

8 In 117–110 BC, a new wall was built to protect the Gansu corridor, China's main route to the west.

See also 2.20 (steppe peoples);
2.25 (the celestial empire)

0   600 km
0   400 mi

China's "period of disunion" between the fall of the Han dynasty in 220 and the reunification of the empire under the Sui in 589 saw constant warfare and nomad invasion. It was also critically important in Chinese cultural and economic history.

None of the warlords whose rivalries had brought down the Han could command universal allegiance, and the empire split into three kingdoms. The strongest – and the most populous – was the northern state of Wei, which included the wealthy Yellow river valley. The weakest and least populated kingdom was Shu, which relied on its mountainous frontiers for protection. Wu was the largest by area but its population was only slightly more than that of Shu. Each kingdom considered itself the legitimate successor to the Han, and wars between them were frequent and devastating: many towns were ruined and the total population of China fell sharply.

The first kingdom to fall was Shu. In 263 the Wei general, Sima Yen, sent an army through hundreds of kilometers of trackless mountain country to descend unexpectedly on Chengdu, the Shu capital. Shu capitulated but many of its nobles and troops fled west, eventually finding a refuge in Persia. Two years later Sima Yen seized power in Wei and, as Wudi (r.265–89), became the first emperor of the Jin dynasty. Wudi's main interest was his harem but he found time to conquer Wu in 280, briefly reuniting China. Shortly after Wudi's death, civil wars broke out between his sons, reaching their peak in the "rebellion of the eight princes" (291–306). To support their struggles the princes recruited troops from among the steppe peoples, but this made the weakness of the empire only too obvious to the nomads, who turned on their employers: northern China fragmented into a mosaic of Chinese and nomad states. Southern China stayed under the stable but oppressive rule of the Jin dynasty until 420, after which several short-lived dynasties ruled until 589.

The destruction afflicting northern China caused large numbers of landowners and peasants to flee

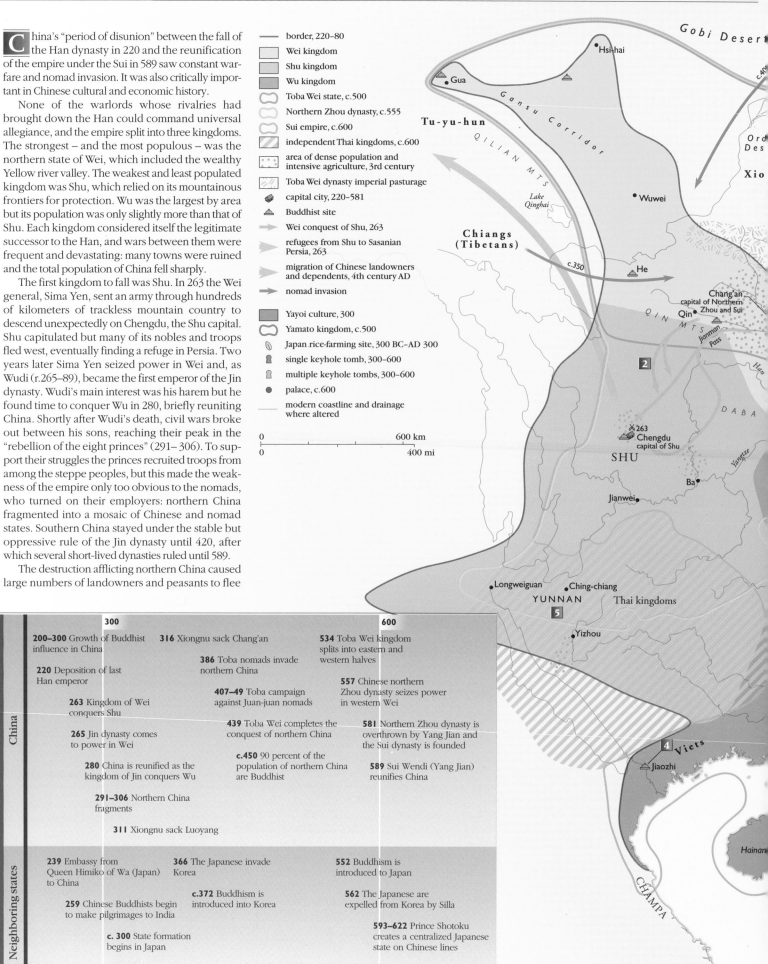

border, 220–80
Wei kingdom
Shu kingdom
Wu kingdom
Toba Wei state, c.500
Northern Zhou dynasty, c.555
Sui empire, c.600
independent Thai kingdoms, c.600
area of dense population and intensive agriculture, 3rd century
Toba Wei dynasty imperial pasturage
capital city, 220–581
Buddhist site
Wei conquest of Shu, 263
refugees from Shu to Sasanian Persia, 263
migration of Chinese landowners and dependents, 4th century AD
nomad invasion

Yayoi culture, 300
Yamato kingdom, c.500
Japan rice-farming site, 300 BC–AD 300
single keyhole tomb, 300–600
multiple keyhole tombs, 300–600
palace, c.600
modern coastline and drainage where altered

0 .... 600 km
0 .... 400 mi

TIMELINE

China

200–300 Growth of Buddhist influence in China

220 Deposition of last Han emperor

263 Kingdom of Wei conquers Shu

265 Jin dynasty comes to power in Wei

280 China is reunified as the kingdom of Jin conquers Wu

291–306 Northern China fragments

311 Xiongnu sack Luoyang

316 Xiongnu sack Chang'an

386 Toba nomads invade northern China

407–49 Toba campaign against Juan-juan nomads

439 Toba Wei completes the conquest of northern China

c.450 90 percent of the population of northern China are Buddhist

534 Toba Wei kingdom splits into eastern and western halves

557 Chinese northern Zhou dynasty seizes power in western Wei

581 Northern Zhou dynasty is overthrown by Yang Jian and the Sui dynasty is founded

589 Sui Wendi (Yang Jian) reunifies China

Neighboring states

239 Embassy from Queen Himiko of Wa (Japan) to China

259 Chinese Buddhists begin to make pilgrimages to India

c. 300 State formation begins in Japan

366 The Japanese invade Korea

c.372 Buddhism is introduced into Korea

552 Buddhism is introduced to Japan

562 The Japanese are expelled from Korea by Silla

593–622 Prince Shotoku creates a centralized Japanese state on Chinese lines

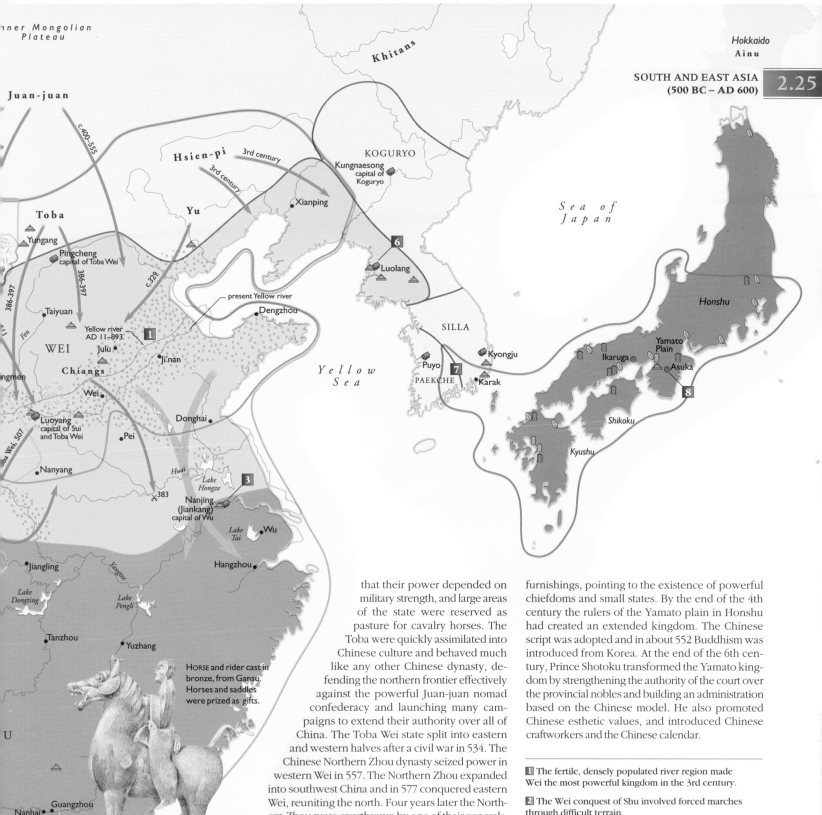

HORSE and rider cast in bronze, from Gansu. Horses and saddles were prized as gifts.

south and settle on the fertile but sparsely populated Yangtze plain. This sparked a period of economic and population growth in southern China which, within a few centuries, saw it overtake the north as the most populous and prosperous part of China.

The position in the north began to stabilize after the Toba, a Turkic nomad confederation, invaded the north in 386–97 and re-established the Wei state. The Toba were a small minority among the Chinese population and they had little administrative expertise. However, they gained the cooperation of the northern landowners who saw the restoration of strong government as a way to protect their interests against a discontented peasantry. The Toba knew

that their power depended on military strength, and large areas of the state were reserved as pasture for cavalry horses. The Toba were quickly assimilated into Chinese culture and behaved much like any other Chinese dynasty, defending the northern frontier effectively against the powerful Juan-juan nomad confederacy and launching many campaigns to extend their authority over all of China. The Toba Wei state split into eastern and western halves after a civil war in 534. The Chinese Northern Zhou dynasty seized power in western Wei in 557. The Northern Zhou expanded into southwest China and in 577 conquered eastern Wei, reuniting the north. Four years later the Northern Zhou were overthrown by one of their generals, Yang Jian, who founded the Sui dynasty. In 589 he launched a campaign against the southern Chen dynasty and reunified China under his rule.

The major cultural development of this period of disunion was the rise of Buddhism. Buddhism was introduced into China in the 1st century AD but it only became popular after the fall of the Han: its emphasis on personal salvation and otherworldliness being attractive to a deeply troubled society. Buddhism introduced Indian art, architecture, philosophy and science and was the strongest outside influence on China before the 19th century AD.

While China was undergoing disunion, the first states appeared in Japan. Complex societies began to develop in Japan in the Yayoi culture (300 BC–AD300) which saw rice farming become established in Kyushu, Honshu and Shikoku. Early in the Yamato period (AD 300–710) large tombs appeared (called "keyhole tombs" for their shape) with rich

furnishings, pointing to the existence of powerful chiefdoms and small states. By the end of the 4th century the rulers of the Yamato plain in Honshu had created an extended kingdom. The Chinese script was adopted and in about 552 Buddhism was introduced from Korea. At the end of the 6th century, Prince Shotoku transformed the Yamato kingdom by strengthening the authority of the court over the provincial nobles and building an administration based on the Chinese model. He also promoted Chinese esthetic values, and introduced Chinese craftworkers and the Chinese calendar.

1 The fertile, densely populated river region made Wei the most powerful kingdom in the 3rd century.

2 The Wei conquest of Shu involved forced marches through difficult terrain.

3 Nanjing (Jiankang) was capital of southern Chinese dynasties 220–280 and 317–589 and was a major cultural center.

4 The Viets, an Austroasiatic people, carried out an unsuccessful rebellion against Chinese rule in 541–47.

5 Thai-speaking peoples of Yunnan founded several independent kingdoms by 600, benefitting from Chinese weakness.

6 Luolang became the capital of Koguryo after its capture in 313.

7 The southern Korean peninsula was conquered by the Japanese 366–562.

8 Asuka, capital of the late Yamato kingdom, was a complex of palaces, tombs and temples, c.550–650.

See also 2.06 (spread of Buddhism);
2.24 (the first emperor)

In AD 600 the Austronesian language group spanned the Indian and Pacific oceans. Austronesian-speaking peoples had originated in Taiwan around 3000 BC. The introduction of rice farming from China a millennium earlier led to population growth, followed by expansion into the Philippines, Indonesia and Malaysia, where Austronesians had become the dominant peoples by about 2000 BC. In the early first millennium BC Austronesians settled the coast of modern Vietnam and in the 1st century AD Austronesians from the Indonesian archipelago sailed west to colonize the uninhabited island of Madagascar.

Australia, New Guinea and the Solomon Islands had been settled many millennia earlier by Australoid peoples. Around 2000 BC Austronesians began moving into the coastal regions of New Guinea (they did not penetrate the highlands) and the islands. The Lapita culture (named for a site in New Caledonia), characterized by tools of shell and by distinctive pottery, developed here around 1600. By 1000 the Lapita culture had spread eastward to New Caledonia, Fiji, Samoa and Tonga. This migration probably followed the inventions of the sail-powered canoe with outrigger and the twin-hulled voyaging canoe.

The Australian Aborigines remained (except in the far north) isolated from the rest of the world, and the hunter–gatherer way of life established at least 40,000 years ago survived, adapting to environmental changes, until European contact in the 18th century AD. Differing styles of art have been found widely dispersed across the continent.

In the middle of the first millennium BC the Lapita culture-area began to divide. In the west the culture was absorbed into the diverse cultural traditions of the long-established Australoid peoples, ancestors of the modern Melanesians. In the Fiji–Samoa–Tonga triangle the Lapita developed into the ancestral Polynesian culture. The early Polynesians lived

TIMELINE

Southeast Asia

500 BC	AD 1	AD 500
c.500 The earliest chiefdoms develop in southeast Asia		**c.400** Hinduism is introduced into southeast Asia
	113 The Chinese expand into Vietnam	**c.450** State formation occurs in island southeast Asia
	AD 50–100 The kingdom of Funan is founded	**c.550** The kingdom of Chen-la overthrows Funan
	c.192 The kingdom of Champa is founded	**c.600** Thai kingdoms in Yunnan are founded
	c.300 Buddhism is introduced into southeast Asia	
	300s The kingdom of Funan builds a regional empire	

The Pacific

500 BC	AD 1	AD 500
c.1600 The Lapita culture develops in the Bismarck archipelago	**c.200** Polynesians settle in the islands of Tahiti	**c.400** Polynesians settle in the Hawaiian islands
c.1500 Austronesian-speaking peoples from the Philippines settle in the Mariana islands	**1–100 AD** Pottery-making skills die out in Polynesia	**900–1000** Polynesians settle in Aotearoa (New Zealand)
c.500–300 Polynesian culture develops in Fiji, Tonga and Samoa	**c.300** Polynesians settle in Easter Island	**c.1200** Chiefdoms develop in Polynesia

| 500 BC | AD 1 | AD 500 |

1 Austronesian languages originated in Taiwan before 3000 BC and began to spread through the southeast Asian islands before 2000 BC.

2 The Lapita culture originated in the Bismarck archipelago (New Britain and New Ireland) c.1600 BC and by 1000 had spread to New Caledonia, Fiji and Tonga.

3 Polynesian culture developed in the Fiji–Samoa–Tonga triangle c.500–300 BC, but was later displaced in Fiji by waves of Melanesian settlers.

4 Important trade routes crossed the Kra isthmus in the early centuries AD, stimulating the growth of several small short-lived kingdoms.

5 Oc Eo was a major trading port in the 2nd and 3rd centuries AD, declining in the 4th century when trade routes shifted to the Malacca straits.

6 By AD 400 the kingdom of Funan dominated most of the territory of modern Cambodia and Thailand.

7 Powerful chiefdoms, megalithic monuments and a system of pictographic writing developed on Easter island in the 17th century AD.

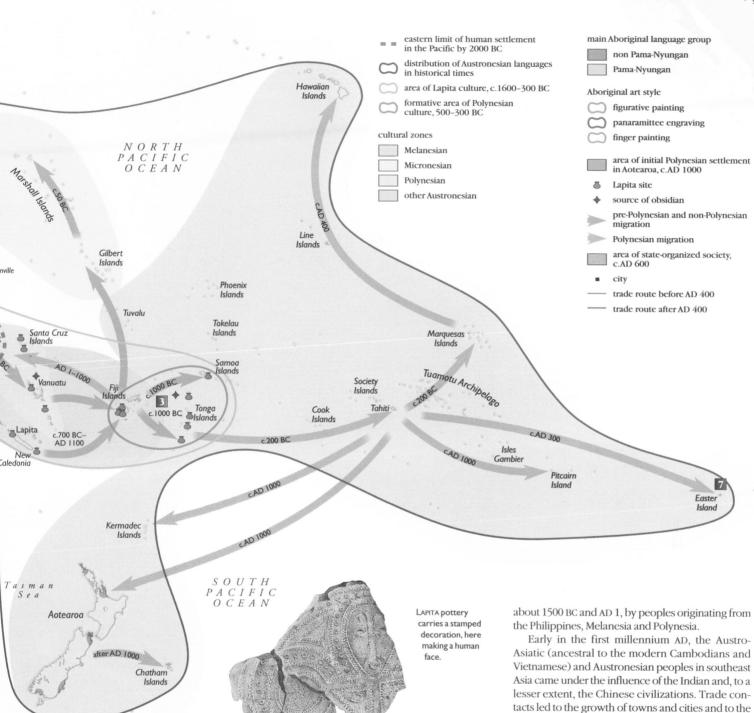

eastern limit of human settlement
in the Pacific by 2000 BC

distribution of Austronesian languages
in historical times

area of Lapita culture, c.1600–300 BC

formative area of Polynesian
culture, 500–300 BC

cultural zones

Melanesian

Micronesian

Polynesian

other Austronesian

main Aboriginal language group

non Pama-Nyungan

Pama-Nyungan

Aboriginal art style

figurative painting

panaramittee engraving

finger painting

area of initial Polynesian settlement
in Aotearoa, c.AD 1000

Lapita site

source of obsidian

pre-Polynesian and non-Polynesian
migration

Polynesian migration

area of state-organized society,
c.AD 600

city

trade route before AD 400

trade route after AD 400

LAPITA pottery
carries a stamped
decoration, here
making a human
face.

by a mixture of farming, fishing and gathering tree-products such as coconuts; their crops and domestic animals – taro, yams, breadfruit, pigs, dogs and chickens – had been brought by their ancestors from southeast Asia.

The Polynesians migrated farther east to Tahiti, the Tuamotu archipelago and the Marquesas Islands by about 200 BC. Polynesian settlement of the Pacific was the result of planned voyages of discovery. Polynesian seafarers accumulated extensive practical knowledge of the stars, weather, ocean wildlife, sea conditions and currents, and this enabled them to navigate accurately across vast distances of open ocean. Easter Island was settled around AD 300 and the Hawaiian islands a hundred years later. The final pulse of Polynesian expansion took place around AD 1000 with the settlement of Aotearoa (New

Zealand). Few of the Polynesians' traditional crops would grow in Aotearoa's temperate climate, so the Maoris cultivated native plants and hunted sea mammals and flightless birds. There was also migration westward in the first millennium AD to the Solomon Islands, but the Polynesians here were cut off from the main Polynesian regions by a Melanesian migration from Vanuatu to Fiji around 1100. Some Polynesians probably made contact with the Americas, as the Maoris and eastern Polynesians cultivated the sweet potato, a native of South America. The Polynesians formed simple tribal societies in the colonization period, but by 1200 chiefdoms appeared throughout the region.

The third Pacific culture-area, Micronesia, has a much more confused history but scattered islands of this region seem to have been settled between

about 1500 BC and AD 1, by peoples originating from the Philippines, Melanesia and Polynesia.

Early in the first millennium AD, the Austro-Asiatic (ancestral to the modern Cambodians and Vietnamese) and Austronesian peoples in southeast Asia came under the influence of the Indian and, to a lesser extent, the Chinese civilizations. Trade contacts led to the growth of towns and cities and to the formation of the first states in the region. One of the earliest states to emerge was Funan, centered on the lower Mekong, which by AD 100 became an intermediary in trade between China and India. In the 4th century Funan became an imperial power and for a time dominated mainland southeast Asia. Another important kingdom was Champa in southern Vietnam. In the 4th and 5th centuries Champa took advantage of Chinese divisions to launch cross-border raids, but its kings were forced to pay tribute to China after 586. State formation began later in island southeast Asia, but by 600 many small Buddhist- and Hindu-influenced states had arisen in Sumatra, Java and Borneo. An important factor here was a shifting of trade routes away from Funan, south to the Malacca straits in the 4th century.

See also 2.05 (the world in 600)

The foundations of Mesoamerican civilization were laid in the Middle Preclassic period (900–300 BC) by the Olmec peoples of the Gulf coast and the Zapotecs of the Oaxaca valley. The influence of the Olmec civilization had declined by the start of the Late Preclassic (300–1 BC), but the Zapotec remained influential, particularly with regard to its hieroglyphic script. However, by the end of the period the Zapotec civilization was overshadowed by Teotihuacán and the Maya.

Teotihuacán first appeared around 200 BC as one of many large, prosperous farming communities in the fertile and well watered Valley of Mexico. The growth of Teotihuacán began at the beginning of the Classic period (AD 1–650), when a monumental ceremonial center, palaces and a large urban settlement were built on a carefully planned grid pattern. At its peak around AD 500, Teotihuacán covered twenty square kilometers (eight square miles) – a greater area than ancient Rome, although with a rather smaller population (between one and two hundred thousand). Considerable areas of the city were devoted to craft workshops, including those of obsidian workers, potters, stonemasons, plasterers and bricklayers. The city also contained quarters for foreign residents, such as Zapotec merchants. Trade was important to Teotihuacán, and it is likely that the caste of armed merchants, known in Aztec times as *pochteca*, had their origins there.

In its heyday Teotihuacán was the most important cultural, religious and economic center in Mesoamerica. The art, architecture, religions and costume of the Olmec, Maya and Zapotecs all show the influence of Classic Teotihuacán. Although the Teotihuacán civilization was probably literate, no inscriptions or other written records have survived. For unknown reasons – possibly soil erosion caused by overcultivation and deforestation – Teotihuacán began to decline around AD 600. Soon after 700 the city was sacked and burned, probably by forces from the nearby city of Cholula. The site continued to be occupied on a small scale, but by the time of the Aztecs – the cultural heirs of Teotihuacán – its origins had been forgotten.

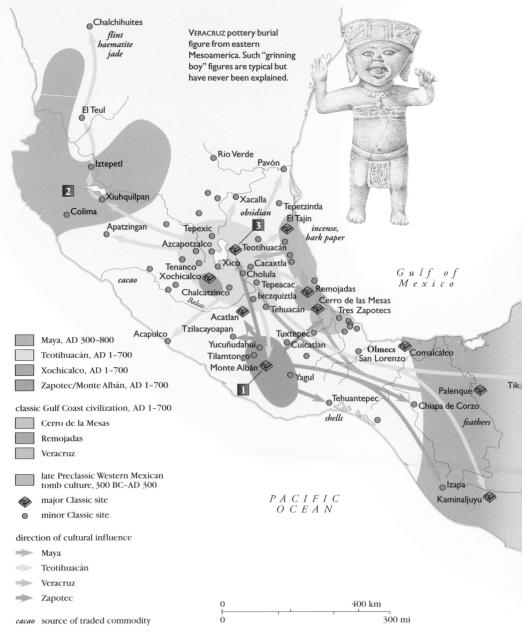

VERACRUZ pottery burial figure from eastern Mesoamerica. Such "grinning boy" figures are typical but have never been explained.

Maya, AD 300–800
Teotihuacán, AD 1–700
Xochicalco, AD 1–700
Zapotec/Monte Albán, AD 1–700

classic Gulf Coast civilization, AD 1–700
Cerro de la Mesas
Remojadas
Veracruz

late Preclassic Western Mexican tomb culture, 300 BC–AD 300
major Classic site
minor Classic site

direction of cultural influence
Maya
Teotihuacán
Veracruz
Zapotec

cacao source of traded commodity

0   400 km
0   300 mi

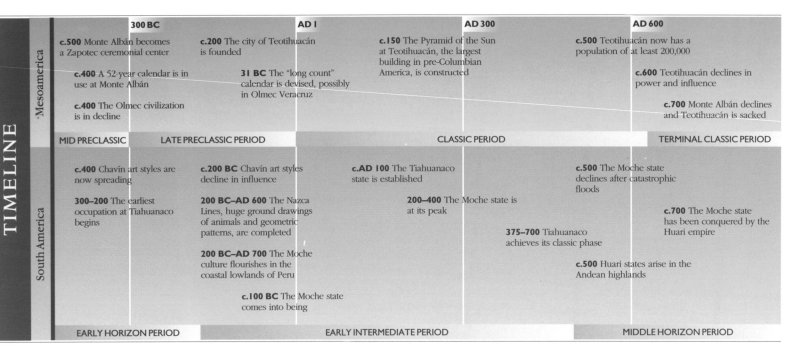

	300 BC	AD 1	AD 300	AD 600
Mesoamerica	**c.500** Monte Albán becomes a Zapotec ceremonial center	**c.200** The city of Teotihuacán is founded	**c.150** The Pyramid of the Sun at Teotihuacán, the largest building in pre-Columbian America, is constructed	**c.500** Teotihuacán now has a population of at least 200,000
	c.400 A 52-year calendar is in use at Monte Albán	**31 BC** The "long count" calendar is devised, possibly in Olmec Veracruz		**c.600** Teotihuacán declines in power and influence
	c.400 The Olmec civilization is in decline			**c.700** Monte Albán declines and Teotihuacán is sacked
	MID PRECLASSIC	LATE PRECLASSIC PERIOD	CLASSIC PERIOD	TERMINAL CLASSIC PERIOD
South America	**c.400** Chavín art styles are now spreading	**c.200 BC** Chavín art styles decline in influence	**c.AD 100** The Tiahuanaco state is established	**c.500** The Moche state declines after catastrophic floods
	300–200 The earliest occupation at Tiahuanaco begins	**200 BC–AD 600** The Nazca Lines, huge ground drawings of animals and geometric patterns, are completed	**200–400** The Moche state is at its peak	**c.700** The Moche state has been conquered by the Huari empire
		200 BC–AD 700 The Moche culture flourishes in the coastal lowlands of Peru	**375–700** Tiahuanaco achieves its classic phase	**c.500** Huari states arise in the Andean highlands
		c.100 BC The Moche state comes into being		
	EARLY HORIZON PERIOD	EARLY INTERMEDIATE PERIOD		MIDDLE HORIZON PERIOD

Intensive irrigation-based agriculture and powerful chiefdoms, sophisticated artistic and architectural traditions all developed in many areas of the central Andes during the Initial period (1800–800 BC) and Early Horizon period (800–200 BC). The dominant cultural influence over a wide area of highland and coastal Peru by about 400 BC was the Chavín art style; its declined about 200 BC and it was succeeded by a variety of local styles.

The decline of Chavín influence marks the start of the Early Intermediate period (200 BC–AD 500), which saw the first states and empires in South America. Warfare was more prevalent and large fortifications were built through the region. The earliest state formed around the coastal site of Moche in about 100 BC. Moche was a vast ceremonial center, including two huge adobe (mud brick) platforms: the pyramids of the Sun and the Moon. Between the two is a cemetery which has yielded richly furnished royal burials. Moche craftsmen were among the most skilled in the New World, producing fine polychrome ceramics, textiles and metalwork in gold, silver and copper. Some pottery was mass-produced using molds. Moche craftsmen were full-time specialists, some of whom worked in teams under the direction of supervisors, while laborers were drafted for work on major public projects as necessary. The Moche economy was based on fishing and agriculture, growing maize, potatoes, cotton, peppers and peanuts in irrigated fields. By AD 200 the Moche culture was spread by conquest to all the neighboring coastal valleys, where provincial capitals and fortresses were built. Moche itself was abandoned around AD 500, after massive flooding, and the capital was moved north to Pampa Grande, where it remained until the Moche state was absorbed by the Huari empire between 600 and 700. At the same time that Moche became an imperial state, other small states were emerging among the coastal Nazca people and among the highland Huarpa and Recuay peoples and, farther south, at Tiahuanaco in the lake Titicaca basin.

The site of Tiahuanaco was first occupied about 300 BC, but its growth as a major power began in the period AD 100–375, when major building and agricultural improvement projects began. At the heart of Tiahuanaco was a precinct of temples, platforms, tombs and palaces around which was a large residential area, housing between twenty and forty thousand people. The outstanding feature of Tiahuanaco architecture is its meticulously finished drystone walls and monolithic sculptures. In its Classic period (AD 375–700) Tiahuanaco built an empire which dominated the southern Andes and extended to the Pacific coast and the edge of the Amazonian rainforest. Expansion to the north was blocked by the rise of the aggressive Huari empire in the 6th century. The motive for the expansion of Tiahuanaco, and all the successive highland empires up to the Inca in the 15th century, was the desire to achieve control over supplies of lowland and coastal products. Both Tiahuanaco and Huari were abandoned around 1000, possibly because of prolonged drought conditions.

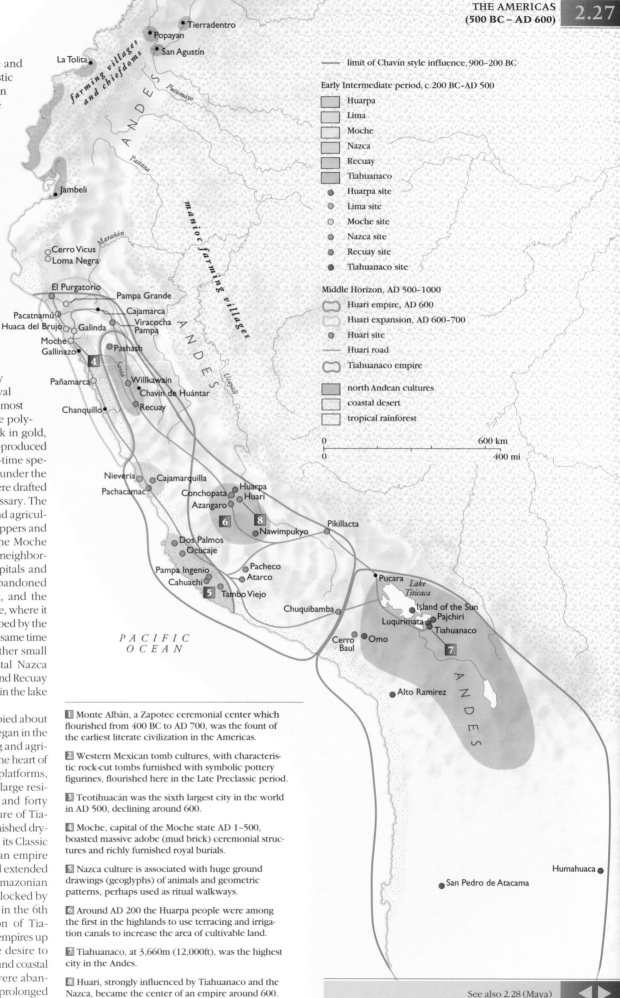

— limit of Chavín style influence, 900–200 BC

Early Intermediate period, c.200 BC–AD 500
- Huarpa
- Lima
- Moche
- Nazca
- Recuay
- Tiahuanaco
- Huarpa site
- Lima site
- Moche site
- Nazca site
- Recuay site
- Tiahuanaco site

Middle Horizon, AD 500–1000
- Huari empire, AD 600
- Huari expansion, AD 600–700
- Huari site
- Huari road
- Tiahuanaco empire
- north Andean cultures
- coastal desert
- tropical rainforest

| 0 | | 600 km |
| 0 | | 400 mi |

1 Monte Albán, a Zapotec ceremonial center which flourished from 400 BC to AD 700, was the fount of the earliest literate civilization in the Americas.

2 Western Mexican tomb cultures, with characteristic rock-cut tombs furnished with symbolic pottery figurines, flourished here in the Late Preclassic period.

3 Teotihuacán was the sixth largest city in the world in AD 500, declining around 600.

4 Moche, capital of the Moche state AD 1–500, boasted massive adobe (mud brick) ceremonial structures and richly furnished royal burials.

5 Nazca culture is associated with huge ground drawings (geoglyphs) of animals and geometric patterns, perhaps used as ritual walkways.

6 Around AD 200 the Huarpa people were among the first in the highlands to use terracing and irrigation canals to increase the area of cultivable land.

7 Tiahuanaco, at 3,660m (12,000ft), was the highest city in the Andes.

8 Huari, strongly influenced by Tiahuanaco and the Nazca, became the center of an empire around 600.

See also 2.28 (Maya)

The most sophisticated of the pre-Columbian civilizations of the Americas was the Maya of Guatemala, Petén and Yucatán. By draining and canalizing the swamplands, agricultural production rose in the Middle Preclassic period (700–300 BC), making it possible to support large populations. Chiefdoms and small states appeared and the first towns and monumental structures were built. During the Late Preclassic (300 BC–AD 300) powerful city-states emerged, writing came into use, advanced mathematical and astronomical studies were pursued, and a calendrical system was adopted. The new states were competitive and warlike and many cities were fortified. Underlying these developments may have been such factors as population pressure, agricultural intensification, long-distance trade and increased warfare. The main influences on the development of Mayan civilization were the Olmecs and the Zapotecs, from whom the Maya received, among other things, the 52-year "long count" calendar, writing and the sacred ball game.

The most important Maya center of the Late Preclassic period was the city of El Mirador, occupied 150 BC–AD 150. It had large temple pyramids, a fortified palace area, marketplaces and a population approaching 80,000. Causeways known as *sacbes* linked El Mirador with its subordinate villages. Although there is some evidence of writing at El Mirador, the best evidence for its use by the Preclassic Maya comes from the southern highland area, where many *stelae* (stone monuments) were erected at sites like Kaminaljuyú, in the 1st and 2nd centuries AD, to commemorate royal ancestors. The earliest known inscription, found at El Baul, carries a "long-count" date equivalent to AD 36. The Maya did not invent writing themselves, but their hieroglyphic script was the only pre-Columbian script that could fully express the spoken language. The Mayan script included both ideographic and phonetic elements. About 800 glyphs are known. The southern Maya declined in the 3rd century AD and the tradition of erecting commemorative *stelae* died out. The cause was probably a volcanic eruption that blew apart

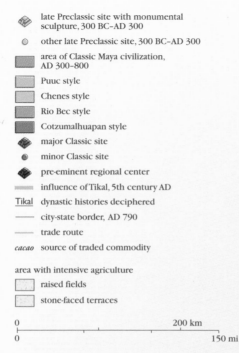

◈	late Preclassic site with monumental sculpture, 300 BC–AD 300
◎	other late Preclassic site, 300 BC–AD 300
�	area of Classic Maya civilization, AD 300–800
▢	Puuc style
▢	Chenes style
▢	Rio Bec style
▢	Cotzumalhuapan style
◈	major Classic site
◉	minor Classic site
◈	pre-eminent regional center
▬	influence of Tikal, 5th century AD
Tikal	dynastic histories deciphered
────	city-state border, AD 790
────	trade route
cacao	source of traded commodity

area with intensive agriculture
| ▢ | raised fields |
| ▢ | stone-faced terraces |

0 ————————— 200 km
0 ————————— 150 mi

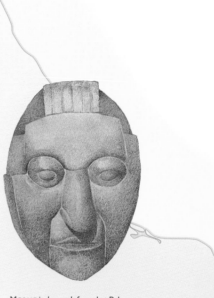

MOSAIC jade mask found at Palenque, possibly a representation of Pacal, ruler of Palenque in the 7th century.

Mount Ilopango, covering thousands of square kilometers with ash and ruining agriculture for years.

Commemorative *stelae* with hieroglyphic inscriptions began to be erected by the Maya in the central lowland rainforest area around AD 300, a development that marks the beginning of the Classic period (AD 300–800). The earliest show clear stylistic links with the highland Maya. Until about AD 400 *stelae* were only erected at Tikal, Uaxactún and a few nearby centers, but thereafter the practice spread throughout the central area. Palenque, Yaxchilán, Copán and Calakmul all developed into major regional powers, but the dominant city-state for much of the Classic period was Tikal, with a population of 75,000–100,000. At its peak under King Stormy Sky (r.411–57), Tikal dominated most of the central area and maintained cultural and trade links

with Teotihuacán, the greatest power in Mesoamerica. Tikal went into decline after its defeat by Caracol in 562; and although it recovered under Ah Cacau (r.682–723) it did not regain its preeminence.

Warfare was common among the Classic Maya city-states, although the aim was more often to exact tribute and take prisoners than to annex territory permanently. The normal fate of prisoners was ritual torture and mutilation, after which they were sacrificed to the gods. Human sacrifices were needed to dedicate new temples, to accompany the dead and to mark important events such as the completion of calendrical cycles. Mayan rulers were expected to take part in painful bloodletting rites as a means of communicating with ancestral spirits. Marriage alliances were the usual means of forging friendly relations between states.

TIMELINE

	400 BC	AD I	AD 400	AD 800
Political change	**500–100 BC** Mayan forms of kingship develop		**c.200–250** The eruption of Mount Ilopango devastates the southern Maya	**695** King Jaguar Paw of Calakmul is captured and sacrificed by Ah Cacau of Tikal
	c.350–300 BC The earliest Maya city-states appear			
		c.150 BC–AD 150 El Mirador is the largest center of Mayan civilization	**300–600** Teotihuacán is an influence on the Maya	**800s** The central Maya states are in decline
			411–57 Tikal is the dominant Maya center during the reign of King Stormy Sky	**c.900** Chichén Itzá becomes the dominant Maya center
			562 Tikal is defeated by the state of Caracol	
	LATE PRECLASSIC PERIOD		CLASSIC PERIOD	POSTCLASSIC PERIOD
Cultural change	**200–100 BC** The earliest known Mayan writing dates from this time		**c.300** Corbeled arches and vaults first appear in Mayan architecture	**799** The last monuments are erected at Palenque
				800 The "long count" calendar falls into disuse
		AD 36 The earliest Mayan calendrical inscriptions, at El Baul, date from this year		**889** The last monuments are erected at Tikal
			292 Earliest known lowland inscription – found at Tikal	
	400 BC	**AD I**	**AD 400**	**AD 800**

1 El Mirador was the largest Maya center in the Late Preclassic period, before being abandoned c.AD 150.

2 Lake Ilopango now fills the crater left by the catastrophic eruption of Mount Ilopango c.AD 200-250, which caused the decline of the southern Maya .

3 Tikal was the largest Maya city. It reached its peak under King Stormy Sky (r.AD 411-57) and dominated the central Maya until conquered by Caracol in 562.

4 Classic Maya ceremonial centers were often aligned on astronomical events. The earliest such center, at Uaxactún, was aligned on the midwinter, equinoctial and midsummer sunrises.

5 Copán, a major Maya center during the Classic period, was supplanted by Quirigua in 738.

6 The raised causeway, or *sacbe*, linking Cobá with Yaxuná runs for some 100 kilometers (62 miles).

7 Murals at Bonampak celebrating a victory of King Chan Muan c.790 provide vivid evidence of the warlike character of Maya civilization.

8 Power and population moved to the north in the Early Postclassic period (AD 900-1200), when Chichén Itzá became the dominant Maya center.

Gulf of Mexico

Komchen
Dzibilchaltún
Izamal
Acanceh
feathers slaves
Chichén Itzá
Cobá
feathers slaves
Oxkintok
Uxmal
Mul-Chic
Chacchob
Yaxuná
Tancah
Jaina
Kabah
Loltun
Xcalumkin
Sayil
Chacmultún
Keuic
Labná
Xcocha
Xcichmook
Yucatán Peninsula
Xtampak
Dzibilnocac
Huntichmul
Edzná
NORTHERN AREA
Hochob

Pechal
cacao

Becan
Xpuhil
Hormiguero
Pasión del Cristo
Uaacbal
Rio Bec
Cohunlich
Cerros
Oxpemul
La Muñeca
Nohmul
Cuello
Calakmul
El Pálmar
Colhá
Naachlún
Altamira
Ucal
Balakbal
Altun Ha
El Mirador
Rio Azul
Lamanaí
CENTRAL AREA
La Honradez
cacao
Nakum
San José
PETÉN
Uaxactún
Baking Pot
El Perú
Xullún
Naranjo
Tikal
Palenque
El Porvenir
Uolaritún
Yaxhá
Xunantunich
Piedras Negras
Motul de San José
Mountain Cow
Lago Peten Itzán
Caracol
La Mar
El Cayo
Pomona
Toniniá
Yaxchilán
Lacanhá
cacao
Sacul
Bonampak
Itzán
El Caribe
Ixtutz
Nimli Punit
Agua Escondida
La Armelia
Seibal
Lubaantin
Santa Elena Poco Uinic
Altar de Sacrificios
Dos Pilas
Machaquitá
Pusihá
Chinkultic
Aguateca
Cancuén
marine products and shells
Quen Santo
Salinas de los Nueve Cerros
feathers obsidian salt
Chamá
cacao
Lagartero
cacao
Lago de Izabal
Nebaj
Quirigua
Santa Rica
La Lagunita
San Agustin Acasaguastlán
Los Higos
SOUTHERN AREA
El Paraiso
cacao
cacao feathers
Guatemalan Highlands
Motagua
cacao jade
Izapa
jade
Copán
Takalik
Lago de Atitlán
obsidian
Kaminaljuyú
jade
Yarumela
El Jobo
Chucumuk
Asuncion Mita
Salinac la Bianca
Tiquisate
El Baul
Amatitián
Chalchuapa
Lempa
Pantaleon
obsidian
Monti Alto
Obero
Tazumal
Finca Arizona
Lake Ilopango
Usulutan

PACIFIC OCEAN

The civilization of the Classic Maya was not uniform: several regional decorative styles are known, and there was considerable variation in architectural styles. The Maya were highly skilled craftsmen, producing monumental stone sculpture, jade carving, pottery, paintings and obsidian tools of the highest quality. A few gold and copper objects have been found at Mayan sites, but metals were little used before Postclassic times.

The Classic period came to an end around the beginning of the 9th century, when the city-states of the central lowlands began to collapse. The population declined dramatically, new building ceased, and the tradition of erecting commemorative *stelae* was abandoned. The last monuments were erected at Palenque in 799, at Yaxchilan in 808, at Quirigua 810, at Copán in 822 and Tikal in 889. By 950 all the major central Mayan cities lay in ruins. The "long count" calendar fell out of use.

The collapse is thought to be an indirect consequence of the fall of Teotihuacán around 750. Mayan rulers competed, through warfare and by commissioning more and more ambitious building projects, to fill the power vacuum created by the fall of Teotihuacán. Pressures on the peasantry to supply food and labor increased to such a point that the agricultural economy collapsed; malnutrition, population decline and political collapse followed. Classic Mayan civilization did not die out, but continued to flourish in the semiarid north of the Yucatán peninsula until around 1000, when the area was invaded by the Toltecs, from central Mexico.

See also 2.27 (Teotihuacán)

Cross-referencing

References to other dictionary entries are identified in small capitals (e.g. CHRISTIANITY *); references to map spreads are denoted by the use of an arrow (e.g.* ▷ 2.21 *).*

Dating

For the purposes of this dictionary, the end of the Paleolithic period of early human prehistory, about 10,000 BC/12,000 years ago (i.e. the end of the Pleistocene Ice Age), is taken as the boundary between geological and historical time. Earlier dates are therefore given in years ago (ya), while dates after the end of the Paleolithic are given using the conventional BC/AD system.

Chinese spellings

Since 1979 the standard international system for the transliteration of Chinese names into Roman characters has been Pinyin and this is the system used throughout this dictionary.

ACADEMY

Originally a gymnasium (training ground for athletes) on the outskirts of ATHENS, named after the hero Academeus. The philosopher PLATO (429–347 BC) turned it into a school for the training of philosophers. It remained in use until it was closed down by the Christians in the 6th century AD. ▷ 2.08, 2.17

ACTIUM, BATTLE OF

Battle of 31 BC in which Octavian (AUGUSTUS) blockaded the fleet of MARK ANTONY and CLEOPATRA at Actium on the Ambracian Gulf in northwest GREECE. Although Mark Antony and Cleopatra managed to evade the blockade and escape south, this defeat meant the loss of their campaign. ▷ 2.02, 2.13

ADRIANOPLE

City of northern Thrace, funded by HADRIAN in about AD 125. It was the site of a battle in AD 378, at which the Roman emperor VALENS was defeated and killed by the VISIGOTHS, supported by the OSTROGOTHS. As a result of the defeat, the new emperor THEODOSIUS supplied food to the GOTHS in return for help in defending the border against other intruders. The city was taken by the Turks in 1361 and renamed Edirne. ▷ 2.16

ADULIS

An ancient port on the Red Sea coast of AXUM (now in Eritrea) and important staging post in the trade between the Mediterranean and southern Arabia, east Africa and the Indian Ocean. It was probably founded by the Egyptians and rose to prominence in the mid-3rd century BC, boosted by PTOLEMAIC trade. ▷ 2.21

AEGOSPOTAMI, BATTLE OF

Aegospotami, at the entrance to the Black Sea, was the site of a devastating defeat of the Athenian navy by the Spartan commander Lysander, in 405 BC. The battle marked the end of the PELOPONNESIAN WAR. ▷ 2.08

AESCHYLOS

Athenian playwright (c.525–456 BC) seen as the founder of Greek tragedy, though very few of his plays survive. For the first time, individual characters rather than a chorus were used to tell a story. His famous trilogy, the *Oresteia*, dealt with the problems of justice and revenge in the city-state. ▷ 2.07

AETIUS

(c.AD 390–454) One of the last effective generals of the ROMAN EMPIRE, who was responsible for the defeat of ATTILA and the HUNS at the Battle of the Catalaunian Plains in AD 451. Despite his success, the empire continued to crumble under BARBARIAN pressure, and Aetius was assassinated by the emperor VALENTINIAN III in 454. ▷ 2.16

AETOLIA

Mountainous region of west-central GREECE that remained outside the mainstream of Greek history until the 4th century BC, when the settlements of the area united in the Aetolian league. The league absorbed neighboring cities and shrines, including DELPHI, in the 3rd century BC, but its forces were defeated by ROME in 168 BC. ▷ 2.08

AGRI DECUMATES

Roman name for a region of southwestern Germany, north of the Danube and east of the Rhine. It was annexed to the ROMAN EMPIRE from about AD 75 but abandoned in 263 to the ALEMANNI. ▷ 2.13, 2.15

AH CACAU

Ancient MAYAN king of TIKAL (r.AD 682–723). Under his reign Tikal began its second major period of expansion and key monuments were built. His magnificently furnished tomb was discovered in 1961. ▷ 2.28

AHURA MAZDA

The chief god of ZOROASTRIANISM – the religion of Achemenid and Sasanian PERSIA first preached by Zoroaster in the 7th century BC. Ahura Mazda – also known as Ormazd or "supreme knowledge" – was said to have created the world and created the twin spirits of good and evil, though he was associated with the spirit of good in its struggle against evil. ▷ 2.06

AJANTA

Sacred Buddhist site in Maharashtra state, western India, some 106 kilometers (66 miles) northwest of Aurangabad. It comprises temples and monasteries carved by hand from the rock face between the 1st century BC and the 7th century AD, and adorned with fine carvings and frescoes of Buddhist legends. The caves were rediscovered in 1819. ▷ 2.22

ALANS

Sarmatian pastoral nomad tribe from the Black Sea steppes, first recorded in the 1st century AD raiding the Persian empire. In the late 4th century they were driven westward by the HUNS. They entered the ROMAN EMPIRE in 406; some settled in GAUL, others became closely associated with the VANDALS and migrated to southwest Spain and north Africa. ▷ 2.16, 2.17, 2.19

ALARIC

Powerful leader of the GOTHS who created a fighting force from refugee VISIGOTHS in the ROMAN EMPIRE. His main aim was to find land in which they could settle, but when the Romans refused to negotiate with him he sacked Rome in AD 410. He died shortly afterwards. ▷ 2.16

ALBION

Ancient name for Britain – first used by GREEK writers in the 4th century BC – that is presumed to refer to the white chalk cliffs of Dover. It was also used by medieval CELTIC writers and later became applied specifically to England.

ALEMANNI

Literally meaning "all men", a grouping of Germanic peoples who began raiding across the borders of the ROMAN EMPIRE in the mid-3rd century AD, sometimes reaching as far south as Italy. They were never truly defeated. The French word for Germany, "Allemagne", is a reminder of their impact. ▷ 2.15, 2.16, 2.19

ALESIA

Celtic stronghold in Central GAUL (modern France) and the site of the last stand of VERCINGETORIX – the most formidable of the Celtic leaders – against JULIUS CAESAR in 52 BC. The defeat of Vercingetorix after a long and difficult siege allowed Gaul to become incorporated into the ROMAN EMPIRE. ▷ 2.13, 2.18

ALEXANDER THE GREAT

One of the great conquerors in world history, Alexander inherited the throne of MACEDONIA in 336 BC from his father, PHILIP II. A charismatic leader who always fought at the front of his troops, Alexander subdued mainland GREECE before invading the Persian Achemenid empire in search of the treasure and prestige he needed to maintain his position. After spectacular victories at the rivers Granicus (334) and Issus (333), and at Gaugamela in Assyria (331), Persian resistance collapsed. In 330 Alexander captured Persepolis, the Persian capital: DARIUS III, the last Achemenid king, was murdered shortly afterwards. Alexander spent another four years subduing the Persian empire's eastern provinces and invading India (326) before his army mutinied, forcing him to end his campaigns.

Alexander's conquest of the Persian empire made Greco-Macedonian civilization the dominant cultural influence as far east as India. The strain of constant fighting, effects of wounds and heavy drinking took their toll, and Alexander died in 323 BC aged only 32, probably in the belief that his victories had earned him the status of a god. Alexander had not given his empire any centralized institutions, and it fell apart during the WARS OF THE DIADOCHI. ▷ 2.08, 2.09, 2.11, 2.22

ALEXANDRIA
City on the Egyptian coast founded by ALEXANDER THE GREAT in 332 BC and seat of the PTOLEMAIC DYNASTY. The Ptolemies successfully preserved its independence from Egypt proper, but used Egyptian wealth to make it one of the most flourishing cities of the ancient Mediterranean. Its MUSEUM and library made it a center for mathematicians, scientists and poets. Alexandria was incorporated into the ROMAN EMPIRE, along with the rest of Egypt, in 30 BC, after the death of the last Ptolemaic queen, CLEOPATRA. ▷ 2.09, 2.10, 2.16, 2.21

ALKIBIADES
(451–404 BC) Ambitious, aristocratic Athenian general who persuaded the Athenians to launch an ill-fated campaign in Sicily in 415 BC. He then defected to Sparta and, though he later commanded an Athenian fleet, never regained the trust of the city. ▷ 2.08

ALTAIC LANGUAGES
A subfamily of the Ural-Altaic languages found in eastern Europe and across Russia, that comprises the TURKIC, MONGOLIAN and TUNGUSIC languages.

AMALASUNTHA, QUEEN
Daughter of THEODORIC, the Ostrogothic king of Italy. On his death in AD 526 she became regent for her son. She respected Roman culture and built links with JUSTINIAN, the emperor in the east, that led to her murder by OSTROGOTH nobles in AD 534. ▷ 2.17

AMARAVATI
Buddhist site in Andhra Pradesh state, eastern India, the most important Indian Buddhist site from the 3rd century BC to the period of Islamic rule, and the capital of the Buddhist kingdom of Andhra. Its STUPA (from 200 BC) was of exceptional size and contained sculptures of fine detail and narrative power. The Amaravati style spread throughout southern India, as far as southeast Asia. ▷ 2.22

AMBROSE
Formidable Christian bishop of Milan from AD 374 to 397. Appointed because of his administrative skills, he turned out to be a powerful upholder of Christian orthodoxy (against the ARIANS) and a scourge of PAGANISM. He even excommunicated the emperor THEODOSIUS I for the massacre of some opponents.

ANASTASIUS
Ruler of the eastern ROMAN EMPIRE (r.AD 491–518). Although elderly when he came to the throne, Anastasius was an excellent administrator and left a full state treasury. He was disliked in his capital, Constantinople, for favoring the eastern provinces of his empire above the city. ▷ 2.17

ANGLES
Germanic tribe of northern Germany and southern Denmark from the early centuries AD, and one of the three main groups to invade Britain in the mid-5th century. They settled mainly in Northumbria, Mercia and East Anglia, and gave their name to England. ▷ 2.16, 2.19

ANGLO-SAXONS
The Germanic invaders and settlers of southern and eastern Britain in the 5th century AD, made up of the ANGLES, Saxons and JUTES. About 200 years later the three groups had merged into a single Anglo-Saxon identity. The term was used by GALLIC writers to distinguish the invaders from the Romano-British population. Anglo-Saxon England flourished until the Norman invasion of 1066. ▷ 2.16, 2.17, 2.19

ANTIGONOS
(c.382–301 BC) Macedonian commander whose ambitions were to win control of the empire of ALEXANDER THE GREAT after the latter's death. The task was too great for any one man, and Antigonos was continually outmaneuvered by rivals until he was killed at the BATTLE OF IPSUS. His grandson (also Antigonos) managed to regain control of MACEDONIA and establish a stable kingdom there. ▷ 2.09

ANTIOCH, ANTIOCHIA
The royal capital of the SELEUCID KINGDOM founded in 300 BC on the banks of the Orontes in Syria. It flourished as both an administrative and trading center, and later became the capital of the Roman province of Syria. It was home to an important and influential early Christian community. ▷ 2.11, 2.17

ANTIOCHUS III
The most successful of the SELEUCID kings, (r.223–187 BC). Known as "the Great", he re-established his dynasty's control over much of the old Persian empire, including Babylon. An attempt to regain influence in GREECE led to a successful counteroffensive by Rome. Antiochus was humbled and his kingdom lost the west coast of Asia. ▷ 2.10

ANTIOCHUS IV
The ambitious son of ANTIOCHUS III and a SELEUCID king from 174 to 163 BC. His attempt to take over Egypt was thwarted by the Romans, and his plans to Hellenize JUDAEA led only to a successful Jewish revolt. He died while campaigning in PERSIA. ▷ 2.10

ANTONINE DYNASTY
Roman dynasty composed of the emperors ANTONINUS PIUS (AD 138–61), MARCUS AURELIUS (AD 161–80) – who initially shared the reign with his adoptive brother Lucius Verus (AD 161–69) – and COMMODUS (AD 177–92), the son of Marcus Aurelius. ▷ 2.15

ANTONINE WALL
Built for ANTONINUS PIUS in AD 139–42 by Q. Lollius Urbicus, this was a massive undertaking – a frontier wall running 59 kilometers (37 miles) across modern Scotland, from the Forth to the river Clyde. Made of turf on a cobbled foundation with a ditch in front, it had 17 forts as well as signaling platforms and fortlets. Excavation has revealed two main phases of occupation, between about 139 and 164. The circumstances of its abandonment are not known. ▷ 2.15

ANTONINUS PIUS
Roman emperor (r.AD 138–161) who served as proconsul in Asia during the 120s. He was adopted by the emperor HADRIAN and on succeeding him in 138 ruled the empire efficiently and frugally. He was succeeded by MARCUS AURELIUS.

ANTONY, MARK
(c.83–30 BC) Roman statesman and general. After the assassination of JULIUS CAESAR in 44 BC, Antony formed the Second Triumvirate with Lepidus and Octavian (AUGUSTUS) against the republican conspirators. Following Antony's defeat of Cassius and Brutus at Philippi in 42 BC, the triumvirs divided the empire between them, Antony taking the rich eastern Mediterranean. In Egypt Antony met CLEOPATRA (41 BC) and they became lovers. They also allied politically to challenge Octavian's dominance in the west. However, Antony's relationship with Cleopatra allowed Octavian to cast him in the role of a traitor. In 31 BC Antony and Cleopatra were defeated by Octavian at ACTIUM; Antony committed suicide in 30 BC as Octavian entered Alexandria. ▷ 2.13

ANTONY, ST
(c.AD 251–356) Ascetic Christian who lived much of his long life in the Egyptian desert. Often seen as the founding figure of Egyptian monasticism, he was idealized in a famous Life (357), the first of many to glorify early saints. ▷ 2.15

ANURADHAPURA
Ceylonese city, the capital of a kingdom of the same name from the 5th century BC. The city was abandoned following raids from southern India in the 10th century AD, and the capital moved to Polonnaruva. During its period of supremacy Anuradhapura became a cultural center for the arts. Later forgotten, the city was not rediscovered until the late 19th century. Its remains include vast STUPAS and imposing statues. ▷ 2.22

APOLLONIUS OF PERGE
Greek mathematician (fl.c.200 BC) whose work on cones remained the standard text on the subject for centuries.

AQUILEIA
In 181 BC the Romans founded a Latin colony here at the head of the Adriatic – a strategic position controlling routes across the Julian Alps, the trade in Baltic amber and local gold deposits. Aquileia became a great military, commercial and industrial center, and one of the largest cities in the world, with about 100,000 inhabitants. It was sacked by ATTILA in AD 452 but revived in the medieval period. ▷ 2.15, 2.19

AQUITANIA, AQUITAINE
The area enclosed by the Garonne, Pyrenees and Bay of Biscay. It was inhabited by the Gaulish tribes of the Aquitani, who were conquered by the Romans between 56 and 27 BC. Under AUGUSTUS, Aquitania became an imperial province extending as far north as the Loire, and prospered from agriculture and trade. It was settled by the VISIGOTHS in the early 5th century. ▷ 2.13, 2.16, 2.18

ARACHOSIA
Ancient province of the Persian and Alexandrian empires, now in southern Afghanistan. Its capital was probably at the modern city of Kandahar. ▷ 2.09

ARAUSIO, BATTLE OF
Defeat in southern France (near modern Orange) of the Romans (105 BC) at the hands of the CIMBRI and TEUTONES. Following this defeat, GAIUS MARIUS became Roman consul and reorganized the army. ▷ 2.19

ARCHIMEDES
Outstanding Greek mathematician (c.287–212 BC) of the ancient world. His fertile mind transcended conventional mathematical thinking in fields as varied as astronomy, the measurement of volumes, hydrostatics and notation. He is also remembered for his inventions, such as a screw used to raise water, and ingenious devices to protect his native city SYRACUSE from a Roman siege in which he was killed. ▷ 2.10

ARDASHIR
Two kings of Sasanian PERSIA. Ardashir I (r.c.AD 220–40) was the grandson of SASAN, after whom the dynasty was named. He was king of Persia and founded the SASANIAN DYNASTY by overthrowing the Parthian dynasty in 224–26. Ardashir II (r.379–383) succeeded SHAPUR II. A weak king, he was soon deposed. ▷ 2.11

ARIANISM
The early Christian belief, developed by Arius (a priest in ALEXANDRIA) and others, that JESUS was a distinct creation of God the Father. ARIANISM was condemned as a heresy at the COUNCIL OF NICAEA in 325 (which proclaimed the orthodox view that Jesus had always been part of God), but remained strong in the eastern empire.

ARIKAMEDU
Trading port near Pondicherry on the coast of southeast India in the early centuries AD. Roman artifacts, including coins and pottery, have been excavated there since 1945. It may have been known as Poduce in ancient times. It has been suggested that contact with the Mediterranean began well before the Roman period. ▷ 2.23

ARIOVISTUS
Germanic leader who invaded eastern GAUL in about 70 BC and fought with the Sequani CELTS before dominating the region in the 60s BC. Despite an earlier alliance with Rome, JULIUS CAESAR defeated him in eastern Gaul in 58 BC. ▷ 2.19

ARISTAGORAS OF MILETUS
(c.505–496 BC) Powerful figure in the Ionian city of MILETUS who played a leading part in organizing a revolt of the Ionian cities against their Persian overlords. He failed to coordinate the cities and their resources effectively, and died while fighting in Thrace. ▷ 2.07

ARISTARCHOS OF SAMOS
Greek astronomer of the early 3rd century BC, and the first to propose that the sun revolved around the stars. He also assumed that the Earth moved on an axis and attempted, unsuccessfully, to measure the size of the solar system. ▷ 2.10

ARISTOTLE
Greek philosopher born in the northern Aegean (384–322 BC). Aristotle studied with PLATO in ATHENS before embarking on an extraordinary intellectual career which penetrated almost every area of philosophy, the sciences, ethics and politics. He is chiefly remembered for his system of logic, as a founder of the discipline of zoology and for his thoughts on the nature of man. His work dominated medieval scientific thinking and some aspects of it were of value as late as the 19th century. ▷ 2.08, 2.09

ARMAGH
Ancient city in Ireland (now in Northern Ireland) and the ecclesiastical capital established by ST PATRICK in about AD 445.

ARMINIUS
GERMAN war leader born in about 19 BC who inflicted a humiliating defeat on the Romans in the TEUTOBURGERWALD (near modern Osnabruck) in AD 9, effectively ending the Roman attempt to conquer Germany. ▷ 2.19

ARSACIDS
Dynasty ruling the Parthian empire in PERSIA, founded by Arsaces I (r.c.247–c.211 BC). He was a king of the IRANIAN-speaking PARNI peoples, who asserted the independence of the kingdom of Parthia from the SELEUCIDS in 238 BC. His successors extended their rule over Persia and Mesopotamia, notably under Mithradates I in the 2nd century BC. Under their rule the Parthians emphasized continuity with the Achemenids, but adopted a great deal of HELLENISTIC culture. The dynasty was overthrown by the SASANIANS in the 3rd century AD. ▷ 2.10, 2.11

ARVERNI
Celtic tribe of southern GAUL (in modern Auvergne), whose leader, VERCINGETORIX, led a revolt against the Romans. It was eventually crushed by JULIUS CAESAR at ALESIA (52 BC). ▷ 2.18

ASHOKA
MAURYAN king of India (r.268–233 BC) who brought the Mauryan empire to its zenith by conquering KALINGA in 261. Horrified by the violence of the conquest, Ashoka converted to BUDDHISM, which he made the state religion, promulgating its teachings throughout his empire in laws carved on rock faces and pillars. He convened a Buddhist council at PATALIPUTRA that confirmed the Buddhist canon. His empire broke up through internal factionalism and external pressures in the 50 years after his death. ▷ 2.22

ASIA (ROMAN PROVINCE)
Originally the kingdom of PERGAMON. Made the Provincia Asia in 133 BC, and enlarged under the empire, it occupied much of modern west-central Turkey. A fertile region with abundant natural resources, it was known for its manufactured goods, such as woollen fabrics. It flourished in the early empire but suffered Gothic invasions in the AD 250s and 260s. Many fine archeological remains have survived. ▷ 2.13

ASUKA
Capital of YAMATO Japan from the mid-6th century AD to 710, when Nara became the first permanent capital. The city was a center of Buddhist culture. ▷ 2.25

ATHENS
The dominant Greek city-state of the 5th century BC. Its large territory, ATTICA, and fine trading connections led to Athens' increasing wealth in the 6th century BC. In the 5th century it pioneered a democratic system of government, led the Greeks successfully against two Persian invasions and established a large Aegean empire. Athens brimmed with self-confidence. Culturally it fostered the birth of drama and was an important center for vase painting and sculpture. The PARTHENON, the temple to Athena on the Acropolis, was an architectural and sculptural masterpiece. In the late 5th and 4th centuries BC Athens was home to the philosophers SOCRATES, PLATO and ARISTOTLE. After its defeat by Sparta in

404 BC Athens sank into decline, but the city remained a major cultural center for centuries. ▷ 2.07, 2.08, 2.09, 2.10

ATREBATES

A Gaulish people (probably of continental origin) encountered by the Romans in the area between west Sussex and the rivers Thames and Test. They made treaties with Rome and three *civitates* ("communities") were created: of the Atrebates (capital at Silchester), of the BELGAE (capital at Winchester) and of the Regni (capital at Chichester). ▷ 2.18

ATROPATENE

One of the successor kingdoms of ALEXANDER THE GREAT's empire in northern PERSIA and the Caucasus (now Azerbaijan) set up by the Persian general, Atropates, in 328 BC. Its capital was at Gazaca. It came under Roman control (in the 1st century BC), Parthian and later Sasanian control. ▷ 2.09, 2.10, 2.11

ATTALIDS

Dynasty of kings who ruled over PERGAMON, a kingdom in western Asia Minor carved from the SELEUCID empire, from 241 to 133 BC. Their capital, Pergamon, was an important center of HELLENISTIC culture. ▷ 2.10

ATTALUS I

Founding king (r.238–197 BC) of the ATTALID dynasty, following a major defeat of the (Celtic) Galatians of Asia Minor. He later fought successfully as an ally of Rome against the resurgent power of MACEDONIA. ▷ 2.18

ATTILA

King of the HUNS (r.AD 435–53), Attila undertook a series of military campaigns against Rome from AD 442 until his death in 453. He attacked the Balkan Roman province (442–43, 447), invaded GAUL, where he was defeated by Roman and allied forces at the Catalaunian Plain (451), and finally sacked various Italian cities (452). ▷ 2.16, 2.20

AUGUSTINE, ST

(AD 354–430) Major theologian and preacher who was appointed bishop of Hippo in his native north Africa. Augustine is remembered above all for his autobiographical *Confessions* and *City of God* (which proclaimed that the heavenly kingdom was more important than any earthly city). Augustine was dedicated to upholding the authority of the Latin church as it moved away from its roots in the Greek world and redefined itself.

AUGUSTULUS, ROMULUS

Last emperor (r.AD 475–76) of the western ROMAN EMPIRE who came to power – and was overthrown – while still a child. ▷ 2.16

AUGUSTUS

Born in 63 BC under the name of Octavian, and adopted by JULIUS CAESAR as his heir, he was a skilled and ruthless politician and military leader. He had a long struggle to gain the leadership of Rome, finally defeating MARK ANTONY (his leading opponent) and CLEOPATRA at ACTIUM in 31 BC. In 27 BC Augustus introduced a new constitutional settlement, which he claimed "restored the republic" but in reality introduced a monarchical type of government. He took the title of *princeps* (first citizen), leaving it to his successors to call themselves *imperator* (emperor) – a term derived from *imperium*, the supreme power to execute the law and command in war, which had belonged to the kings of Rome and then to consuls and other officials.

He received from the senate the title "Augustus" and ruled until his death in AD 14. He enlarged the empire and did much to improve and modernize the living conditions and city control of Rome through such measures as the introduction of safeguards against flood, fire and famine. He also enhanced both Rome's and his own prestige with a major building program that included a new forum, temples, and the creation of the splendid suburb of the Campus Martius. ▷ 2.03, 2.04, 2.13, 2.14, 2.18

AURELIAN

(r.AD 270–75) Born in about AD 215 in the Danube region, he rose to fame by the common route of military success and became emperor in 270 on the death of Claudius II. In his short reign he protected Rome from BARBARIAN invasions (this included the construction of the great Aurelianic wall around Rome), defeated the VANDALS in PANNONIA and the Carpi on the Danube, crushed revolts in PALMYRA and conquered the GALLIC EMPIRE with his defeat of Tetricus in 274 at Chalons. He was murdered in 275 on a campaign against PERSIA. ▷ 2.15

AURELIUS, MARCUS

(AD 121–80) Born in Baetica (Spain), he was related to HADRIAN, of whom he became a favorite. He succeded ANTONINUS PIUS as emperor in 161 and ruled jointly with his adoptive brother, Lucius Verus, until the latter's death in 169. He successfully defended the empire's frontiers in Britain, Spain, Upper Germany, along the Danube and in the east, but by allowing his patently unworthy son COMMODUS to succeed him, he condemned the empire to a long period of political instability. Marcus Aurelius was widely admired as a STOIC philosopher and his *Meditations*, as well as some of his correspondence have survived. ▷ 2.15

AUSTRALIAN ABORIGINALS

The original inhabitants of Australia who first reached the continent 40,000–60,000 ya, at a time when the land bridge with New Guinea still existed. The first settlements in southern Australia and Tasmania date from about 30,000 ya. They lived as hunter-gatherers, most being nomadic. Engraved and painted figurative art developed about 29,000 ya, and different cultural areas have been identified, based on techniques. Exchange of stones, shells and pigments along a complex of long-distance trade and cultural routes ensured an overall cultural unity, despite the diversity imposed by linguistic and environmental differences (some 260 language groups have been identified). This was expressed above all in the concept of "dreamtime", an awareness of the spirit in the environment.

At the time of the first European contact, there were perhaps 3 million Australian Aboriginals, of whom the largest concentration was in the Murray-Darling region of southeastern Australia. ▷ 2.26

AUSTRO-ASIATIC PEOPLES

Ancestral peoples of mainland southeast Asia – especially Cambodia and Vietnam. Rice farmers, they settled the region before 2000 BC. The relationship between the Austro-Asiatic and AUSTRONESIAN languages is a subject of continuing dispute. ▷ 2.26

AUSTRONESIAN

Cultural group of southeast Asia based on the Austronesian language group that originated in Taiwan before 2000 BC. They spread through the Indonesian and Malayan archipelagoes and into the Pacific islands, where the POLYNESIAN culture developed. Austronesians from Sumatra settled Madagascar in the 1st century AD. The term is also applied to the modern languages of Malaya and Indonesia. ▷ 2.26

AVANTI

Ancient kingdom (*mahajanapadas*) of west-central India. In about 600 BC its capital was at Mahismati (later moved to UJJAIN). It was a major regional power until it was conquered by MAGADHA in the late 4th century BC. The kingdom revived after the fall of the SAKAS but the region gradually became known as Malwa. ▷ 2.22

AVARS

Nomadic people originating from the eastern Asiatic steppes who were driven westward from the region in the mid-6th century AD. By 600 they had established a khanate based on the Great Hungarian Plain and encompassing much of modern Ukraine and eastern Europe. They unsuccessfully besieged Constantinople in 626 in alliance with the Sasanians. They were defeated by CHARLEMAGNE in 791, finally submitting in 795. ▷ 2.17, 2.20

AXUM, AXUMITES

Important trading kingdom in northern Ethiopia that successfully exploited its position on the Red Sea to survive for nearly 1,000 years (1st to 10th centuries AD). CHRISTIANITY arrived at the time of its most powerful king, EZANA, in the mid-4th century, opening up links with Byzantine Egypt. In the 6th century the Axumites temporarily occupied southern Yemen. ▷ 2.21

BACTRIA

Ancient region of central Asia, with its capital at Bactra (modern Balkh), and a province of the Achemenid empire from the 6th century BC. It broke away from the SELEUCID KINGDOM to become an independent HELLENISTIC kingdom in 239 BC, extending its sway into the Indus valley in the early 2nd century BC and campaigning deep into central India. Bactrian influence helped to introduce Hellenistic culture to India. The kingdom was overrun by KUSHAN nomads in about 135 BC. ▷ 2.09, 2.10, 2.11, 2.22, 2.23

BALLCOURT, MESOAMERICAN

Distinctive feature of Mesoamerican cultures from Preclassic times, a large I-shaped court with retaining walls and (in examples from the Classic period) sloping playing areas. The ball game was played between two teams who had to pass a solid rubber ball through a stone ring attached to the side wall. Players wore body protection. The game had cosmological significance and was sometimes associated with human sacrifice.

BARBARIAN

Originally used by the Greeks as a term of abuse for anyone who did not speak GREEK; in the CLASSICAL PERIOD it became a general term for the peoples of north and east Europe and the Asian steppes who did not enjoy a settled or civilized existence. ▷ 2.15, 2.16, 2.17

BASKETMAKER CULTURE

Aceramic cultural group of hunter-gatherers and early farmers in the southwestern region of North America, and precursors of the Pueblo and Anasazi. The tradition began in the early 1st millennium BC (Basketmaker I); Basketmaker II (185 BC–AD 500) saw initial maize cultivation; Basketmaker III (from 500) saw more complex agriculture and developed into the Anasazi tradition. ▷ 2.03, 2.04, 2.05

BASQUES

Indigenous people of northern Spain, culturally distinct since Paleolithic times. Known as Vascones, they successively resisted Roman, VISIGOTH and Moorish rule. In the 3rd century AD they were converted to CHRISTIANITY. In the 9th century AD they nominally recognized the overlordship of Charlemagne, but they maintained their own language and identity, and fought for autonomy from France and Spain into the late 20th century. ▷ 2.14, 2.16, 2.17

BELGAE

JULIUS CAESAR subdued a group of this name to the north of the rivers Seine and Marne (modern northern France). They were said to have settled in southeast Britain, but archeological evidence suggests that there were close contacts across the Channel, rather than major movements of people. ▷ 2.18

BELGICA

The Roman province of Gallia Belgica was formed some time after the Gallic BELGAE were subdued by JULIUS CAESAR in 57 BC. Both archeological remains and ancient sources indicate that this was not an area of uniform culture. ▷ 2.13

BELISARIUS

(c.AD 500–65) General of the eastern ROMAN EMPIRE who reconquered northern Africa and parts of Italy, including Rome, for the emperor JUSTINIAN in the 530s. When Belisarius took RAVENNA in 540 the OSTROGOTHS offered to make him king of Italy. Although he declined the offer, Justinian never trusted him again. ▷ 2.17

BENEDICT, ST

(c.AD 480–c.550) Italian founder of the Benedictine monastic order and author of the famous rule of St Benedict, which served as a model for monastic life throughout the Middle Ages. It stressed obedience, silence and humility. Benedict's first foundation was at Monte Cassino in central Italy. ▷ 2.17

BENEVENTUM (BENEVENTO)

A center, named Malventum, of the Hirpini Samnites that was taken by the Romans some time after 300 BC. It became a flourishing Latin colony, with the more auspicious name of Beneventum, in 268 BC. Under the empire it became a colony for veteran soldiers, and the famous arch of TRAJAN was erected in AD 114. ▷ 2.12

BERBERS

Indigenous people of the northern Sahara and Mediterranean region of north Africa, mainly sedentary farmers in the CLASSICAL PERIOD. Berbers are shown in Egyptian Old Kingdom tomb paintings (c.2400 BC). The Berber kingdoms of NUMANTIA and MAURETANIA arose in about 200 BC but were colonized by the Romans and conquered by the Arabs in the 7th century AD. In the medieval period invading Bedouins forced them to become nomadic. ▷ 2.15, 2.16, 2.17, 2.21

BETHLEHEM

City of the ancient Holy Land south of Jerusalem, home of King David and birthplace of JESUS. HADRIAN built a shrine to Adonis on the original site of the nativity in AD 135, but CONSTANTINE built the church of the Nativity there in 333 (it was rebuilt by JUSTINIAN I in the 6th century). ▷ 2.06

BINDUSARA

MAURYAN king of India (r.c.293–268 BC), father of ASHOKA. Bindusara campaigned in the Deccan as far south as Karnataka. ▷ 2.22

BITHYNIA

Ancient region of northwest Anatolia that, despite its strategic position, mostly maintained its independence from Achemenid, Greek and Macedonian rule until the 2nd century BC, when a HELLENISTIC Bithynian kingdom flourished, its capital at Nicomedia. In 74 BC the last ruler bequeathed the state to the Romans, who created a single province of BITHYNIA and PONTUS. Its prosperity continued until the early 2nd century AD. ▷ 2.09, 2.10, 2.13

BODH GAYA

Village in Bihar state, northern India, and the reputed site of the enlightenment of Siddhartha Gautama, the Buddha. ASHOKA built a shrine there in the 3rd century BC that was restored and rebuilt several times, notably in the 7th century AD (and in the 19th century). Bodh Gaya was an important monastic and pilgrimage center until it was abandoned in the 15th century. ▷ 2.22

BONAMPAK

MAYAN site of the late Classic period (AD 600–800), now in Chiapas province, southern Mexico. Discovered in 1946, the site includes several temples as well as some of the best-preserved Mayan frescoes. Showing scenes of war, they revised the old view of Mayan civilization as essentially peaceful. ▷ 2.28

BONONIA, BATTLE OF

Battle fought at the site of modern Bologna in the Po valley in 192 BC, in which the Romans finally conquered the GALLIC Boii, who, along with other Gallic tribes, had occupied the region for centuries. The Latin colony of Bononia was founded in 189 BC. ▷ 2.18

BOSPORUS, KINGDOM OF

Kingdom on the northern coast of the Black Sea from 438 BC to the 3rd century AD. Greek in origin, it was influenced by the local Scythian cultures. Although the kingdom never forgot its Greek roots, it became a loyal ally of ROME and was eventually absorbed by BARBARIAN tribes. ▷ 2.01, 2.02, 2.09, 2.10, 2.15

BOUDICCA

The wife of Prasutagus, a client king of the ICENI of East Anglia. Ill treatment of his family by imperial officials after his death prompted an uprising in AD 60–61. The Iceni, helped by the Trinovantes and led by Boudicca, sacked Camulodunum (Colchester), Londinium and Verulamium (St Albans), but were defeated by Suetonius Paulinus, the local Roman governor, and Boudicca took poison. ▷ 2.18

BRAHMINISM

Early form of HINDUISM that developed from VEDISM in the 2nd millennium BC. It focused on the sacrificial role of the Brahminic (priestly) caste and stressed the importance of the supreme power (absolute Self), known as Brahma. By about 500 BC Brahminism had ossified and was challenged by other forms, including BUDDHISM. Hinduism, which emerged in response to this challenge, placed relatively greater emphasis on other deities and devotional practices. ▷ 2.06

BRASIDAS

Spartan general who captured a number of important Athenian cities in the northern Aegean in the early part of the PELOPONNESIAN WAR, before being killed in 422 BC. ▷ 2.08

BRIGANTES

The largest Iron Age tribe in Britain, with an OPPIDUM at Isurium (Aldborough, north Yorkshire). Queen Cartimandua maintained amicable relations with Rome, but later conflicts resulted in Roman annexation in AD 71–79, the development of a Roman town at Isurium, villas in the countryside, and the exploitation of the local lead deposits by AD 81. ▷ 2.18

BRITANNIA

Name given to Britain as a Roman imperial province. Initially governed from London, it was divided into Upper (capital London) and Lower (York) in the early 3rd century AD, and was further subdivided under DIOCLETIAN. Britannia was prosperous and stable, with agriculture the main occupation, some metal extraction and craft production, and varying degrees of Romanization across the region. Attempts to conquer the whole island of Great Britain failed and Roman power rarely extended north of the Forth–Clyde isthmus. Britannia, in effect, became independent in 410 when the emperor HONORIUS instructed the BRITONS to arrange their own defenses. Most of the former province was settled by the ANGLO-SAXONS in the late 5th century AD. ▷ 2.03, 2.13, 2.15, 2.18

BRITONS, ANCIENT

The Iron Age cultural groups of Britain exhibited a variety of social organizations, though all were mainly dependent on agriculture and separated into tribal chief-doms with settlement hierarchies headed by various forms of enclosed settlements. Contacts with the continent were especially strong in the south and southeast, where cross-channel trade brought products such as Gallo-Belgic coinage and wine amphorae. ▷ 2.16

BRUTTIANS

An Italic people attested from the 4th century BC in the largely mountainous region of modern Calabria, southern Italy. They ousted the encroaching LUCANIANS and became independent in about 356 BC. In the 4th and 3rd centuries BC they harassed the Greek cities on the coast, and from the 3rd century had a stormy relationship with Rome, alternately becoming an ally and rebelling. ▷ 2.12

BRUTUS, MARCUS JUNIUS

(c.85–42 BC) Roman senator and politician who supported POMPEY the Great but was made governor of CISALPINE GAUL after JULIUS CAESAR's victory in the civil war. In 44 BC he was leader of the republican party and a principal conspirator, with Gaius Cassius Longinus, in the assassination of Caesar. He was defeated at Philippi by Octavian (AUGUSTUS) in 42 BC.

BUDDHISM

Religious philosophy that emerged in India in the 5th century BC, following the teaching of Siddhartha Gautama, the Buddha ("Enlightened One"), who lived and taught in MAGADHA, northern India. In its pure form Buddhism rejects belief in the gods, emphasizing instead the possibility of salvation through an enlightenment achieved by following Buddhist precepts (the Eightfold Path). Some forms of Buddhism, however, worship the Buddha as a god. In the 3rd century AD the tradition divided into two forms: MAHAYANA (Great Vehicle) and THERAVADA (Doctrine of the Elders). Buddhism was taken to China from the 1st century AD, and Japan in AD 552; it traveled to southeast Asia in about AD 400. It lost its hold in India to a Hindu revival (c.600–700), and to the Muslims after 1200. ▷ 2.06, 2.22, 2.23, 2.24

BURGUNDY, KINGDOM OF

The Burgundians were a Germanic peoples who crossed over the Rhine into the ROMAN EMPIRE in strength in AD 406. They formed a kingdom, first in northern GAUL, then in southwestern France, until they were absorbed into the kingdom of the FRANKS in 534. ▷ 2.15, 2.16, 2.17

BUSTA GALLORUM, BATTLE OF

Battle fought in Italy in AD 552 in which the eastern Roman forces, led by NARSES, defeated the OSTROGOTHS, securing imperial control of Italy south of the Po. ▷ 2.17

CAESAR, GAIUS JULIUS

(100–44 BC) Roman general and statesman. Born to a great patrician family, he rose to eminence through military distinction and astute political maneuvering during a troubled period in Roman history. A skilled orator known for his vanity, he was also prepared to take great risks – both personal and financial – to secure advancement. In 49 BC, after lucrative campaigns in GAUL, he invaded Italy and began a civil war as a means of ridding himself of enemies and competition. He eventually defeated POMPEY, his major opponent, and appointed himself dictator for life in 44 BC, so bringing about the final collapse of the ROMAN REPUBLIC.

His liasion with CLEOPATRA did little to increase his popularity. As dictator he introduced the Julian calendar, reorganized the eastern provinces, founded many colonies

and increased the number of patrician families, senators, priests and magistrates. Although he refused the title of *rex* (king), he aimed at deification and became increasingly unpopular with his fellow nobles, who eventually assassinated him in 44 BC. ▷ 2.03, 2.13, 2.18, 2.19

CALEDONIA, CALEDONII

The Roman terms for the Scottish Highlands beyond the river Forth, and its inhabitants. This hostile upland zone was never completely conquered by the Romans, though Agricola waged a campaign in 82–83 BC and won the BATTLE OF MONS GRAUPIUS. In AD 197 the Caledonii broke their treaty with Rome. They were suppressed in 209 by SEPTIMIUS SEVERUS, but rose up again in 210–11. ▷ 2.18

CALIGULA

See GAIUS CAESAR

CAMEL

One of two domesticated species: the two-humped Bactrian camel was native to central Asia and may have been used in central and southern Asia by 2000 BC; the single-humped dromedary or Arabian camel was domesticated earlier in the Middle East, but was not introduced to Egypt or the Sahara until about 100 BC – a development that made possible the emergence of trans-Saharan trade. ▷ 2.21

CANNAE, BATTLE OF

Remarkable victory for the CARTHAGINIAN general HANNIBAL (216 BC) against the Romans in southern Italy. The Romans had superior forces but were surrounded by the Carthaginian cavalry. Military historians describe the battle as a classic example of the use of an encircling tactic to defeat the compact Roman forces. ▷ 2.12

CAPPADOCIA

Large region in northeastern Asia Minor bordering on the Black Sea. Originally part of the Achemenid empire, it was partially Hellenized after ALEXANDER's conquests, then became a client kingdom of Rome. Officially made a province of the ROMAN EMPIRE in AD 17, its border marked the empire's eastern frontier. ▷ 2.09, 2.10, 2.13

CARACALLA

Emperor of Rome (r.AD 211–17) who was renowned for his exceptional cruelty. He succeeded SEPTIMIUS SEVERUS and murdered his brother Geta to become sole ruler of the empire. He also extended citizenship to all free inhabitants of the empire.

CARNUNTUM

Important site on the Danube, originally part of NORICUM, then added to PANNONIA in about AD 14. A Roman military base was established there, with a civil settlement some 5 kilometers (3 miles) to the west. MARCUS

AURELIUS wrote the second book of his *Meditations* here. The site was destroyed in the MARCOMANNIC WARS, then rebuilt. ▷ 2.14

CARRHAE

Ancient Mesopotamian city (also known as Haran) founded by the Assyrians. It was the site of a battle in 53 BC in which the Parthians, relying mainly on their archers, halted a Roman invasion led by MARCUS LICINIUS CRASSUS. ▷ 2.11, 2.13

CARTHAGE, CARTHAGINIANS

A Phoenician colony on the coast of northeast Tunisia, traditionally founded in 814–813 BC. Carthage enjoyed a good harbor, fertile hinterland and a strategic position in the Mediterranean, and soon planted colonies of its own along the north African and Spanish coasts. It fought the Greeks over Sicily for 300 years, made treaties with Rome in 508 and 348 BC that were favorable to Carthage's monopoly of maritime trade, and developed a large empire. Carthage and Rome eventually came into conflict over Sicily. The three PUNIC WARS (264–146 BC) ended in defeat by Rome and the city's complete destruction. Carthage was refounded as a Roman colony by JULIUS CAESAR, became the capital of Africa Proconsularis and by the 2nd century AD was second only to Rome and ALEXANDRIA. Held by the VANDALS in AD 439–533, it was captured by Muslim forces in 697. ▷ 2.12

CASSANDER

Son of Antipater who stabilized MACEDONIA after his father's death in 319 BC and was proclaimed "King of the Macedonians" in 305 BC. His death in 297 saw Macedonia racked by fresh power struggles. ▷ 2.09

CASTE SYSTEM

Social system most fully elaborated in early Hindu India, whereby all members of society are placed within ranked hereditary social groups. The original system allowed for four castes: the *brahmins* (priests) were the highest caste, followed in order by *kshatriyas* (warriors), *vaishyas* (tradesmen) and *shudras* (servants). Further groupings were later introduced. ▷ 2.06

CATO, MARCUS PORCIUS

"Cato the Censor" (234–149 BC) was best known as a leading Roman orator. He served in the army and government, and worked as a lawyer. A forthright man and champion of traditional Roman values, he was also a gifted writer. His output was encyclopedic in breadth but his only surviving work is *De Agri Cultura* (On agriculture).

CAUDINE FORKS

Battle (321 BC) in which the Romans, seeking control of southern Italy, were defeated by the Samnites. The Roman army was forced to pass "beneath the Samnite yoke", a humiliation unique in Roman history. ▷ 2.12

CELTIBERIANS

Graeco-Roman name for the peoples living around the Ebro valley in the eastern Meseta of Spain. Their culture was influenced by Celtic migrants in the 7th to 6th centuries BC and an important type of settlement was the hillfort (*castro*). After a series of wars with locals and CARTHAGINIANS (2nd to 1st centuries BC), Rome was victorious. ▷ 2.12, 2.18

CELTIC LANGUAGE

A branch of Indo-European, Celtic is divided into Insular Celtic (Goidelic – comprising Irish, Scots-Gaelic and Manx, and British – comprising Welsh, Cornish and Breton), and Continental Celtic, of which the best known is Gaulish, with many inscriptions dating from the 2nd to 1st centuries BC. Continental Celtic was effectively extinct by the early Middle Ages. Welsh and Breton are the most important surviving Celtic languages. Smaller communities of Scots and Irish-Gaelic speakers survive in remote areas. ▷ 2.14, 2.18

CELTS

An important group of proto-historic CELTIC-speaking peoples of central and western Europe and the British Isles. Their origins are probably in the Bronze Age Urnfield and Hallstatt cultures. From the 5nd century BC they were associated with the distinctive LA TÈNE style, which became widespread in central-western Europe and in Britain.

The Celts were organized into aristocratic chiefdoms. Tradition described them as fierce fighters and fine horsemen. They invaded the Classical world, settled in CISALPINE GAUL, sacked Rome in 390 BC, raided GREECE, crossed the HELLESPONT in 278 BC and settled in GALATIA in central Anatolia. The Celts worshipped a multitude of gods, they mostly associated with specific localities, such as springs and groves, and had a priestly class known as the druids. From 225 BC Rome gradually extended control over the Celtic territories in northern Italy, Spain and Provence (by the later 2nd century BC). At the same time the Celts in central Europe were being conquered by the GERMANS. In 58–52 BC JULIUS CAESAR subdued the Celtic groups in GAUL and from AD 43 those in Britain were also defeated. By the 2nd century AD only the Celts in Ireland and the Scottish highlands remained free. ▷ 2.05, 2.09, 2.10, 2.12, 2.18, 2.19

CERRO DE LAS MESAS

Archeological site that was part of the classic VERACRUZ GULF COAST CIVILIZATION, which reached its height between about AD 300 and 600. Its artifacts resemble those of surrounding civilizations of the period and indicate trading links with TEOTIHUACÁN, though links with the Olmecs are not clear. ▷ 2.27

CERROS

Late Preclassic period MAYAN city in eastern Yucatán, Mexico. A trading center surrounded by extensive canal systems, it was mainly built in the 1st century BC but collapsed not much more than a century later. ▷ 2.28

CHAERONEA

Ancient city of northern Boeotia in GREECE and the site of a battle in 338 BC at which PHILIP II OF MACEDON defeated the Athenians and Thebans, so winning control of Greece. A second battle (86 BC) saw the defeat of MITHRADATES VI of PONTUS by the Roman general, Sulla. ▷ 2.08

CHAERONEA, BATTLE OF

Decisive battle of 338 BC in which PHILIP II OF MACEDON crushed the combined armies of ATHENS and THEBES. It can be said to be the moment when the great age of the independent city-state came to an end. ▷ 2.18

CHALCEDON, COUNCIL OF

A major council of the early church held at the city of Chalcedon, near Constantinople, in AD 451. It proclaimed that JESUS was of two distinct natures – human and divine. Although many Christian groups refused to accept this, the Chalcedonian formula is still accepted by Christian churches of the West. ▷ 2.16

CHANDRAGUPTA I

Founder of the GUPTA dynasty in MAGADHA, northeast India (r.AD 320–35). He was a local chief who married into the nearby Licchavi tribe in 320 and by the time of his death he controlled a region that included much of modern Oudh and Bihar. ▷ 2.23

CHANDRAGUPTA I MAURYA

Founder of the MAURYAN DYNASTY of north India (r.321–c.293 BC). He conquered NANDA MAGADHA and came to control most of northern India. In about 305 he defeated SELEUCOS I to take over the Indus valley and part of Afghanistan. In c.293 he abdicated in favor of his son BINDUSARA. According to tradition, he became a Jain monk and starved himself to death in 286. ▷ 2.22, 2.23

CHANDRAGUPTA II

GUPTA emperor of India (r.AD 380–414) who brought the Gupta empire to its peak by conquering the Western SAKA kingdom in Gujarat and Malwa, western India. He made his capital at Ayodhya, supported learning and the arts, and maintained a prosperous and tolerant empire. ▷ 2.23

CHENGDU

City of southwestern China, now capital of Sichuan province. It rose to prominence under the QIN (3rd century BC) and has long been the key to communications between western and eastern China. In AD 221 it became capital of the kingdom of SHU, but fell to Wei in 263. An important trading center since 600, it became a major industrial center in the later 20th century. ▷ 2.25

CHERNOLES
Early Iron Age site (c.750–500 BC) in Moldova and a culture complex characterized by its distinctive pottery, which is found from Poland to the upper reaches of the river Don. This culture is sometimes identified with the ancestral Slavic peoples. ▷ 2.19

CHOLULA
Mesoamerican city, close to modern Mexico City. First occupied in about 500 BC, it later came under the influence of nearby TEOTIHUACÁN. During this period the largest pyramid in Mexico – 55 meters (170 feet) high – was built there. Its forces probably destroyed Teotihuacán in about AD 700, whereafter it became a TOLTEC, MIXTEC and then AZTEC center. It was destroyed by Cortes in 1519, and its inhabitants were massacred. ▷ 2.27

CHOSROES
See KHOSRU

CHRISTIANITY
Religion that developed in the eastern part of the ROMAN EMPIRE in the 1st century AD, that proclaimed the teacher and healer JESUS of Nazareth as the Son of God and savior of the world. Beginning as a Jewish sect, Christianity was given more of a Greek flavor and its beliefs were systematized. The faith spread to Asia Minor, GREECE and eventually to Rome itself, through ST PAUL, by the year AD 60.

Despite frequent persecution at the hands of the Romans, Christianity spread through the empire and was given a major boost by the conversion of the emperor CONSTANTINE in AD 312. It became the official faith of the empire in AD 391, and the Christian church, focused on the pope in Rome, became a force of enduring civilization in the face of BARBARIAN invasions. Conversion of the barbarian kings ensured that Christianity became the dominant religion of Europe, and despite doctrinal divisions (notably between the Orthodox and Catholic churches in 1054, and the Protestant and Catholic churches in the 16th century), it has survived and spread to become the world's largest religion in the 20th century. ▷ 2.06, 2.15, 2.17

CHRYSOSTOM, JOHN
One of the "fathers of the church" (c.AD 347–407), brought up in ANTIOCH. He was a popular preacher and writer on Christian life. Made patriarch of Constantinople in 398, he sought to reform the clergy and bring the court to adhere to strict standards of morality. He fell out with the emperor in 403 and was exiled.

CICERO
A famous Roman orator (106–43 BC) who held political posts and worked as a leading lawyer. His fortunes suffered various reversals during the upheavals of the 1st century BC.

He eventually fell out with the emperor AUGUSTUS and died in 43 BC, a victim of the proscriptions. ▷ 2.13

CILICIA
The eastern part of southern Asia Minor, the more fertile areas of which were settled by Greeks. Its coastline later proved a haven for pirates and it was absorbed as a province of Rome in 80 BC. Its most famous governor was the Roman statesman CICERO, its most famous citizen ST PAUL and its most famous romantic encounter was that between MARK ANTONY and CLEOPATRA at Tarsus. Cilicia later became part of the Byzantine empire. ▷ 2.09, 2.10, 2.13

CIMBRI
Germanic tribe whose migration in the late 2nd century BC from its homeland in Jutland threatened the borders of Roman Italy. The Cimbri defeated the Romans at ARAUSIO in 105 BC, but following a reorganization of the Roman army were themselves destroyed at Vercellae in 101 BC. ▷ 2.19

CLASSICAL PERIOD
The period in Greek history dating from 480 BC (the defeat of the Persians) until the death of ALEXANDER in 323 BC. The Classical period is normally seen as the height of Greek civilization. It includes the great years of Athenian democracy and empire (480–430 BC), the work of the historians HERODOTUS and THUCYDIDES, the major philosophers, SOCRATES, PLATO and ARISTOTLE, and the flourishing of Greek drama.

CLAUDIUS
(r.AD 41–54) Until he was unexpectedly proclaimed emperor of Rome by the Praetorians following the assassination of Caligula (AD 41), Claudius had held a low position in the imperial family. Hampered from childhood by a limp and speech defect (perhaps cerebral palsy), he led a retiring scholarly life, writing histories (in this he was advised by LIVY). As emperor he preserved the peace, enlarged the empire, and paid attention to the welfare of the populace, but he was thought over-influenced by his wives and freedmen. He was poisoned by his wife Agrippina, so that she could ensure the succession of NERO, her son by a previous marriage. ▷ 2.13, 2.14

CLEOPATRA
Last of the Ptolemies, Cleopatra (r.51–30 BC) used her charisma and astuteness to lure two Roman generals, JULIUS CAESAR and MARK ANTONY, into supporting her disintegrating kingdom. She had children by them both. Her stratagems failed when Mark Antony and Cleopatra's forces were defeated by Octavian (later the emperor AUGUSTUS) at ACTIUM in 31 BC, and she committed suicide. She has remained an object of fascination ever since. ▷ 2.13

CLOTHAR
Two Frankish kings of the 6th to 7th centuries AD. Clothar I (r.511–61) was the son of CLOVIS and ruled a third of the Frankish kingdom from Soissons; by 558 he had outlived his brothers to reunite his father's kingdom, conquer BURGUNDY and campaign in Spain. His grandson, Clothar II, was king of Neustria (r.584–629), but ruled the entire Frankish kingdom from 613. ▷ 2.17

CLOVIS
King of the FRANKS (r.AD 481–511) and founder of the Merovingian dynasty. A tribal chieftain, he fought against the Romans and drove them from GAUL in 486. In 493 he married a Burgundian princess and was baptized in about 503, following a victory against the ALEMANNI. A champion of Catholicism, Clovis united the Franks, made Paris his capital and defeated the VISIGOTHS in 507. ▷ 2.17

COBÁ
Classic period MAYAN regional capital in northeastern Yucatán, Mexico, and one of the largest Mayan cities at its peak in AD 400–800. A network of raised roads linked it to neighboring cities. Cobá was defeated by Chichén Itzá in about 900. In the 1970s it was the site of a major excavation. ▷ 2.28

COMMODUS, LUCIUS AURELIUS
Emperor of Rome (r.AD 180–92). Born in about AD 161, Commodus succeeded his father MARCUS AURELIUS in 180, survived an assassination attempt in 182 and from then on effectively left the running of government to a series of favorites. By 191 Commodus was apparently insane, occupying much of his time performing as a gladiator and otherwise abusing his position (this included renaming Rome as the Colonia Commodiana and executing many senators). Laetus had him strangled in 192 and his memory was condemned. ▷ 2.15

CONSTANTINE THE GREAT
(r.AD 306–37) Proclaimed emperor of Rome by his troops in AD 306, Constantine is known for his support of CHRISTIANITY. He defeated Maxentius, his rival for control of the western empire, in 312 with a smaller force. In response to a vision, he had sent his soldiers into battle with crosses on their shields and apparently believed his victory was aided by the Christian God. Constantine subsequently granted Christians toleration (EDICT OF MILAN, 313) and actively promoted Christianity during the remainder of his reign. In 324 he defeated Licinius, who controlled the eastern empire, to become the sole ruler of the ROMAN EMPIRE. In the same year he founded Constantinople on the site of Byzantium as a new capital. Constantine was baptized shortly before his death in 337, near Nicomedia. ▷ 2.04, 2.06, 2.15, 2.16

CONSTANTINIAN DYNASTY
Roman dynasty founded by CONSTANTINE THE GREAT after he won control of the western ROMAN EMPIRE in AD 306. Constantine legitimized and supported CHRISTIANITY. On his death in 337 the empire was divided between his three sons – Constantine II, Constantius and Constans. By 350, however, Constantius was the only survivor. Constantius was succeeded by his cousin JULIAN (361–63), the last of the dynasty, who attempted to restore PAGANISM but died fighting in PERSIA. ▷ 2.15

CONSTANTINOPLE, COUNCILS OF
Two ecumenical councils of the church, held to resolve Christian doctrine. The first (AD 381) was called by the emperor THEODOSIUS and confirmed the doctrine of the Trinity, reiterating the conclusions of the COUNCIL OF NICAEA (325). The second (553) is considered the fifth ecumenical council, convened by JUSTINIAN. It condemned the doctrine of Monophysitism.

COPÁN
Classic period MAYAN city, now in western Honduras. The site was settled by 1000 BC and the city was built from 200 BC, with an artificial acropolis topped by temple-pyramids and a large number of inscribed hieroglyphs. There is also a BALLCOURT. The city reached its peak in the 7th century AD under King Smoke Jaguar, but in 738 it was defeated by its neighbor, QUIRIGUA. By 900 the city had been abandoned. ▷ 2.28

COPTIC LANGUAGE
The Egyptian language written with GREEK letters. It was used in early Christian texts in Egypt and is still used in the ceremonies of the Coptic church. ▷ 2.14

CORINTHIAN LEAGUE
League of Greek cities established at Corinth in 338 BC by PHILIP II OF MACEDON as a means of perpetuating Macedonian control over GREECE. The league was sustained by ALEXANDER THE GREAT but broke up on his death. ▷ 2.08, 2.09

CRASSUS, MARCUS LICINIUS
Roman military commander and politician of the 1st century BC who defeated the rebel slave leader, Spartacus, and was a patron of JULIUS CAESAR. He was killed in battle in 53 BC against the Parthians near CARRHAE in northern Mesopotamia, in a disastrous attempt to emulate Caesar's military achievements. ▷ 2.13

CTESIPHON
Ancient city near Baghdad in modern Iraq that was the winter residence of the Parthian kings from about 100 BC, and was occupied by the Romans in the 1st century AD. It became the SASANIAN capital in AD 226 and was conquered by the Arabs in 63. It was

abandoned after the foundation of Baghdad in the following century; the ruined palace of KHOSRU I survives. ▷ 2.11, 2.15

CYNOSCEPHALAE, BATTLE OF
Major battle fought in 197 BC between Philip V of MACEDON and the Romans, which ended in the defeat of the Macedonians and the beginnings of Roman hegemony in GREECE. ▷ 2.10, 2.13

CYRENE
The leading Greek colony in Africa, founded from Thera in about 630 BC. Located in a fertile region near the coast (modern Shahat), Cyrene was prosperous and was noted for its agricultural products and horses. It came under Roman control in 96 BC and continued to exist until the Arab invasions of the 7th century AD. ▷ 2.21

CYRUS THE YOUNGER
Son of Darius II and Achemenid governor of Lydia and Phrygia (western Anatolia) in the late 5th century BC. In a bid for the Persian throne in 401 he assembled an army including more than 12,000 Greek mercenaries, but died in battle at Cunaxa in Babylonia. The campaign was described by XENOPHON, a leader of the Greek army. ▷ 2.08

DACIA
Located in central Europe north of the Danube, roughly equivalent to modern Romania, Dacia was a fertile area with good metal reserves. It became a powerful kingdom under Decebalus in the late 1st century AD. TRAJAN defeated the Dacians in the First (101–02) and Second Dacian Wars (105–06), which are commemorated on TRAJAN'S COLUMN. Under HADRIAN Dacia was divided into three provinces. Gothic invasions in the 3rd century drove out the Romans by AD 270. ▷ 2.03, 2.13, 2.14, 2.15, 2.18

DAKSHINAPATHA
Kingdom of ancient southern India that was conquered by the MAURYAN king BINDUSARA in the 3rd century BC. ▷ 2.22

DAO DE JING
The central text of Daoism, traditionally ascribed to LAO ZI (6th century BC), but composed in about 240 BC. It consists of about 40 short, allusive pieces comprising advice to a ruler or man of wisdom, emphasizing the mysterious energy (*qi*) unifying and informing all things, and the principles and virtue (*te*) by which union with this energy can be maintained – the principle of non-action being the most important. The principles of Daoism came to underlie the religious philosophy of much of east Asia. By the early centuries AD, Daoism had incorporated many indigenous beliefs in China and included worship of many deities (including Lao Zi himself) and sacred places. It also developed a distinctive form of monasticism. ▷ 2.06

DARIUS I
Achemenid king of PERSIA (r.521–486 BC). After securing his authority against a series of local revolts, he strengthened the satrap system of government. He continued the policy of restoring the Jewish state and contributed to the rebuilding of the Temple at Jerusalem. His campaign against the SCYTHIANS (513) led him into Thrace, where he crossed the Danube and, following a revolt of the Greek cities of Lydia in 499, he sent an expedition against the mainland Greeks in 490; it was turned back at MARATHON. He planned a second expedition, but died before it could go ahead. ▷ 2.07

DARIUS III
Achemenid king of PERSIA (r.336–330 BC). During his reign, ALEXANDER THE GREAT of MACEDON invaded, defeating Darius at Issus (333) and Gaugamela (331). Darius fled to BACTRIA but was murdered, bringing the Achemenid empire to an end. ▷ 2.09

DEAD SEA SCROLLS
Manuscripts discovered in 1947 in a cave at QUMRAN in the West Bank, near the Dead Sea. They contain fragments of the Old Testament and other biblical texts, and formed the library of the ESSENES Jewish community, which was destroyed in AD 68. They have revealed much about the diversity of the Jewish faith at the time of JESUS.

DECIUS
Roman emperor (r.AD 249–51) whose short reign was occupied with war against the Carpi and GOTHS, and the attempt to shore up the empire by reinvigorating the Roman state cults. Decius was defeated and killed in 251 in a battle with the Goths at Abrittus. ▷ 2.15, 2.19

DEKELEIA
Village in Attica that came to prominence during the PELOPONNESIAN WAR, when it was occupied by the Spartans (413 BC). The Spartans closed the Athenian silver mines and lured part of the slave population from ATHENS. ▷ 2.08

DELIAN LEAGUE
League of Aegean city-states formed under the leadership of ATHENS in 478 BC to continue hostilities against PERSIA. Its original meeting place was DELOS, but Athens assumed ever greater control of the league and its meetings were moved there in about 454 BC. By the 440s the league had effectively become an Athenian empire. ▷ 2.07, 2.08

DELOS
Aegean island and important cult center of Apollo and Artemis from the 8th century BC onwards. It was the headquarters of the DELIAN LEAGUE between 478 and 454 BC. In Roman times the island became a major slave-trading center. ▷ 2.07

DEMOCRACY, GREEK
Greek democracy had its roots in the people's assemblies of Dark Age Greece. In some city-states, predominantly in ATHENS in the 5th century BC, the assembly – which all male citizens had the right to attend – eventually became the center of political power, with the *demos* (the people) also taking turns to be magistrates and jurors. With its demands for intense commitment from citizens, Greek democracy would not have been possible without slave labor. ▷ 2.01, 2.07, 2.09

DEMOCRITOS
Greek philosopher from Abdera in Thrace famous for the theory (c.420 BC) that all matter was made up of atoms which moved through empty space to make different combinations, and thus the observable substances of the physical world. ▷ 2.08

DEMOSTHENES
The greatest of the Athenian orators (384–322 BC), he is remembered above all for his impassioned denunciations of the ambitions of PHILIP II OF MACEDON. He could do little to save his city, however, and ATHENS was defeated by Philip in 338 BC. Despite the defeat, Demosthenes remained a leading statesman in Athens until his death. ▷ 2.08

DEMOTIC LANGUAGE
The language used by the people of ancient Egypt. The word "demotic" also described the script used to write everyday documents. Demotic Egyptian was resilient enough to survive centuries of rule by GREECE and Rome. ▷ 2.14

DIADOCHI, WARS OF THE
General term for the wars that broke out at the death of ALEXANDER THE GREAT in 323 BC and lasted until the BATTLE OF IPSUS (301 BC), stabilizing the empire as a number of smaller states. Diadochi is Greek for "successors". ▷ 2.02, 2.09, 2.10

DIASPORA, JEWISH
Literally "scattering", the forcible dispersal of the Jews and by extension the communities that formed as a result. The exile into Babylon (587–537 BC) was the first such dispersal, and led to permanent Jewish settlements in Mesopotamia and Egypt. A second Diaspora occurred in the AD 130s: following the crushing of a Jewish revolt by the Romans, Jews were banished from much of JUDEA and from Jerusalem. They settled widely throughout the Middle East, north Africa, GREECE and southern Italy. Further dispersals of Jews took place in and after the Middle Ages. ▷ 2.06

DIOCLETIAN
Roman emperor from AD 284 to 305. After 50 years of debilitating civil war and BARBARIAN raids, Diocletian reorganized the empire so that power was shared between four imperial rulers (the TETRARCHY) and resources were organized more effectively in the service of defense. The emperor's status was elevated to that of a semi-divine figure closely associated with the traditional Roman gods. One result of this was the persecution of Christians. It was largely due to Diocletian that the empire survived into the 5th century. ▷ 2.14, 2.15

DIONYSIOS I, KING OF SYRACUSE
A talented general, Dionysios (430–367 BC) seized power in Syracuse in 405 BC and mobilized the city's power against the CARTHAGINIANS, who occupied western Sicily. Though he effectively organized resources and men from mainland Italy, he never dislodged the Carthaginians. He prided himself on his Greek heritage, even competing as a dramatist in ATHENS. ▷ 2.08

DUMNONII
A local tribe occupying Devon, Cornwall and part of Somerset, probably defeated by VESPASIAN. After 43 BC it became a self-governing *civitas* ("community") under the FLAVIAN dynasty, with a capital at Isca (Exeter). Romanization mainly affected Isca, while many continued to live in traditional enclosed farmsteads. ▷ 2.18

DURA EUROPOS
An ancient Mesopotamian city founded in about 300 BC by a SELEUCID general. In the late 2nd century BC the city was taken by the Parthians and became a center for trade between the Mediterranean and central Asia. In AD 165 it was seized by the Romans and built up as a frontier fortress, but in 256 it was taken and destroyed by the Sasanians. Archeological excavations of the site during the 1920s and 1930s provided considerable detail about the everyday life of the period. ▷ 2.11

EARLY INTERMEDIATE PERIOD
The period in South America between the Early Horizon and MIDDLE HORIZON periods, dating from 200 BC to AD 500. This period saw the first states in the Andean region, notably MOCHE and TIAHUANACO. ▷ 2.27

EASTER ISLAND
Remote island in the eastern Pacific Ocean, settled in about AD 300 by the Polynesians. By 1000 a great phase of building and artistic production had begun, including the island's great stone sculptures. A unique writing system, known as Rongorongo, was developed. The first Europeans arrived briefly in 1722, but, before the visit of Captain Cook in 1774, deforestation brought social collapse, civil war and severe population decline. ▷ 2.26

ECNOMUS, BATTLE OF MOUNT
A decisive victory, fought off the southern coast of Sicily, of the Roman fleet, led by Regulus, over the CARTHAGINIANS (256 BC) in the First PUNIC WAR. Regulus went on to invade north Africa but was captured. ▷ 2.12

EDESSA
HELLENISTIC city of northern Mesopotamia, taken by the Romans in the 1st century AD. In AD 260 it was seized by the SASANIANS under SHAPUR I, following a prolonged siege in which the Roman emperor VALERIAN was captured. An important Christian center within the Byzantine empire, it fell to the Arabs in 639. ▷ 2.11, 2.13, 2.15

EL BAUL
Ancient MAYAN site in the southern Guatemalan highlands dating from the late Preclassic and Classic periods (c.AD 100–800). Its monumental sculptures include the earliest example of the "long-count calendar", dated to AD 36. ▷ 2.28

EL MIRADOR
Ancient MAYAN site in central Yucatán, Mexico, and one of the earliest important Mayan centers. It flourished from 150 BC to AD 150, when it lost its pre-eminence to nearby TIKAL. It included the largest known pyramid of the Western Hemisphere, some 70 meters (230 feet) high. The site was rediscovered in 1926, but not excavated until the 1970s. ▷ 2.28

EL TAJÍN
Large Mesoamerican site in eastern Mexico, the chief ceremonial center of the late Classic period VERACRUZ civilization, mostly built between AD 600 and 900. The Pyramid of the Niches (with 365 niches in four storeys) is the oldest of its structures. The site includes at least three separate BALLCOURTS. El Tajín displays close cultural contacts with the Classic MAYA. ▷ 2.27

ELLORA
Religious site in Maharashtra state, western India. Cut into a cliff face are more than 30 temples of Hindu, Buddhist and Jain origin dating from AD 500 to 900. Covered in sculptures, the Hindu Kailasa temple (mid-8th century), dedicated to Shiva, is the finest of the group. ▷ 2.06

EPAMINONDAS
(c.420–362 BC) Outstanding general and leader of THEBES in the 370s BC. His victory at Leuctra in 371 broke the power of Sparta and made Thebes the leading Greek city-state. Theban power collapsed following his death at the BATTLE OF MANTINEA in 362.

EPHESUS
Important Ionian city on the coast of Asia Minor whose earlier remains include a great temple to its patron goddess Artemis (c.600 BC). It flourished in HELLENISTIC times and was adopted as the center of the Roman administration of the province of Asia. It

received a famous visit from ST PAUL. Ruins of the ancient city, many of them from late antiquity, remain in abundance. ▷ 2.06, 2.07, 2.08, 2.13, 2.14, 2.15

EPHTHALITE ("WHITE") HUNS

Group of central Asian peoples of uncertain origin, but probably from the eastern steppes. Their relationship with the HUNS, who invaded Europe under ATTILA, is uncertain. They conquered the eastern provinces of the SASANIAN empire in the AD 480s and in the early 6th century gained control of northwestern India, where they were known as the Hunas. They were driven out of India in 528, and from PERSIA in 557. By 600 they had been defeated in central Asia by the Turks. ▷ 2.11, 2.20, 2.23

EPICUROS

Greek philosopher (341–270 BC) who believed that the search for pleasure is the true end of life. By pleasure Epicuros did not mean luxury or decadence but peace of mind through friendship and intellectual pursuits. He believed that there was no life after death and that the gods had no role in a world that was physically self-sufficient. ▷ 2.09

ERATOSTHENES

Greek intellectual and scholar (c.285–194 BC) who was chief librarian at the famous library in ALEXANDRIA. Remembered as a poet, historian, literary critic, philosopher, geographer and mathematician, among his achievements was the most accurate measurement of the Earth's circumference. ▷ 2.10

ERMANARIC

OSTROGOTHIC king (d.c.AD 372) who ruled in the Ukraine region. He was killed – or committed suicide – when the HUNS invaded the region. ▷ 2.19

ESSENES

The smallest of the three Jewish sects of the last centuries BC, who lived a communal life apart from the rest of society. Their main center was probably at QUMRAN, where the DEAD SEA SCROLLS were found. The relationship between the teachings of the Essenes and those of JESUS remains controversial.

EUBOEA

Large Greek island running north–west to south–east alongside the east coast of central GREECE. Its prominence in Greek history dates from the 10th to 8th centuries BC, when it occupied an important position in the reviving Aegean trade. The settlement at Lefkandi (10th century BC) was the most advanced in Greece. The cities of Chalcis and Eretria established many colonies in the northern Aegean and pioneered Greek trade in the west in the 8th century BC, but exhausted themselves in the Lelantine War (late 8th century BC). The island later came under strong Athenian influence. ▷ 2.07

EUCLID

Greek mathematician (fl.300 BC) remembered for his *Elements*, a textbook of elementary mathematics, which remained the standard introduction to the subject for 2,000 years.

EURIPIDES

Major Athenian tragedian (c.480–407 BC) whose plays explore the full breadth of human emotions – from religious ecstasy (the *Bacchae*) to the desperation of a thwarted woman driven to infanticide (*Medea*), and the obsessive nature of lust (of Phaedra for her stepson in *Hippolytus*). Euripides was inventive and controversial, prepared to question the justice of war, even when ATHENS was in the midst of one, and ready to rewrite traditional myths so as to heighten their emotional impact. ▷ 2.08

EZANA

King of AXUM (r.c.AD 325–55) who conquered the kingdom of Kush and established Axum to include most of modern Ethiopia. In about 350 he was converted to CHRISTIANITY by FrSLumentius, a Syrian. He set up the Ethiopian church and resisted the attempts of the Roman emperor Constantine II to bring Axum under the influence of the Roman Catholic church. ▷ 2.21

FLAVIAN DYNASTY

Roman dynasty composed of the emperors VESPASIAN (r.AD 69–79), his elder son Titus (r.79–81) and younger son Domitian (r.81–96). ▷ 2.15

FORMER HAN

See HAN DYNASTY

FRANKS

Germanic tribal confederation settled in the eastern Rhineland in the 3rd century AD. They were divided into the Salian Franks and the Ripuarian Franks. The Salian Franks, under their leader CLOVIS, defeated the Romans in GAUL in 486. Thereafter he re-united the two groups and established a kingdom that included most of modern France and the Rhineland. ▷ 2.15, 2.16, 2.17, 2.19

FUNAN

The first kingdom of Cambodia. Founded in the 1st century AD, it grew to become a regional power by 400. Funan was heavily influenced by Hindu culture from India and flourished as a result of trade with India and China. Its capital was at Vyadhapura, near Banam. Funan was overthrown by Chen-la in the mid-6th century. ▷ 2.26

GAIUS CAESAR

Emperor of Rome (r.AD 37–41), often known as Caligula ("Little Boot"), who succeeded TIBERIUS. He had a reputation for extravagence, cruelty and megalomania, and he may have suffered from epilepsy. He was assassinated in 41.

GALATIA

A region in central Asia Minor that was settled by migrating Celtic tribes in the 260s BC; it retained a Celtic flavor throughout the imperial period. Galatia was also a Roman province from 25 BC, in much the same area. It was to these Galatians that ST PAUL addressed his epistle. ▷ 2.10, 2.13, 2.18

GALEN

(c.AD 130–c.201) One of the most important physicians of the ancient world. Originally from PERGAMON, Galen spent much of his life working in ROME. His work covered every area of medicine, but he is particularly remembered as a pioneer in physiology and anatomy, drawing careful conclusions through the dissection of animals. His intellectual authority, based on the 3 million words of his surviving work, dominated the later Western medical tradition.

GALERIUS

(AD 250s–311) Roman general who was appointed by the emperor DIOCLETIAN as a Caesar in 293, one of two subordinates of the emperor himself, to help coordinate the defense of the ROMAN EMPIRE. Galerius was responsible for a massive defeat of the Persians (AD 298), which brought lasting peace on the empire's eastern frontier. Initially a persecutor of the Christians, he announced a policy of toleration shortly before his death. ▷ 2.15

GALLA PLACIDIA

Roman empress (r.AD 388–450) who was the daughter of THEODOSIUS. After being held hostage by the VISIGOTHS, she married the Visigothic king Ataulf. After his death she became co-empress with Constantius, and later ruled as regent for her son, VALENTINIAN III.

GALLIA, GALLIAE

See GAUL

GALLIC EMPIRE

"Empire" declared in AD 260 by a usurper, POSTUMUS, on the northern frontier of GAUL. A former Roman commander, Postumus, had his own legions and the support of the local aristocracy, and at one point he claimed control over Gaul, Britain and France. He successfully defended the frontier against GERMAN tribes, but after his death his territory was reabsorbed into the empire (AD 274). ▷ 2.15

GANDHARA

SATRAPY in the remote far east of the Achemenid empire that was conquered by ALEXANDER THE GREAT and was the scene of one of his greatest victories (at Hydaspes in 326 BC). Ceded by the SELEUCIDS to the Indian MAURYAN empire in 303 BC, it was an important avenue for east–west trade. ▷ 2.10, 2.23

GAOZU (LIU BANG)

Emperor of China (r.206–195 BC) and the founder of the HAN DYNASTY. He was born a commoner, Liu Bang, but rebelled against QIN rule following the death of SHI HUANGDI. He won control of the kingdom of Han (western China) in 206 and unified China by 202 BC, firmly suppressing internal dissent. Gaozu, his posthumous title, meant "high progenitor". ▷ 2.24

GAUGAMELA, BATTLE OF

See ALEXANDER THE GREAT

GAUL

The fertile and prosperous area roughly equivalent to modern France. Occupied by Celtic and related tribes, the south was influenced by Greek colonization. Gaul gradually came under Roman control. The Mediterranean south formed Provincia (modern Provence) in 121 BC, and in 58–50 BC JULIUS CAESAR conquered the rest. AUGUSTUS divided it into four provinces – Narbonensis, Lugdunensis, AQUITANIA and BELGICA. It was seized by GERMAN peoples in the 5th century AD. ▷ 2.10, 2.12, 2.13, 2.14, 2.15, 2.16, 2.17, 2.18, 2.19

GAUL, CISALPINE

The prosperous region of northern Italy, comprising the Po plain and mountain fringes from the Apennines to the Alps, that was influenced and settled by CELTS from the mid-1st millennium BC. By 191 BC the region had fallen to Rome. It was heavily colonized and soon became a Roman province. ▷ 2.12, 2.13, 2.18

GAULS

See CELTS; GAUL

GEDROSIA

Desert area along the coast of the Arabian Sea, originally part of the Achemenid empire, then conquered by ALEXANDER and ceded by the SELEUCIDS to the Indian MAURYAN empire in 303 BC. ▷ 2.10

GEPIDS

A Germanic tribe that lived in the southern Baltic region during the early centuries AD and had moved to central Europe (modern Hungary) by AD 300. The Gepids attacked the ROMAN empire but were defeated at the Battle of Naissus in 296. They were instrumental in the defeat of the HUNS at the BATTLE OF NEDAO in 454. ▷ 2.15, 2.16, 2.17, 2.19

GERMANIA

The Roman name for the lands east of the Rhine occupied by "free" GERMANS, and for the imperial provinces (Germania Inferior, Germania Superior) on the west bank of the lower and middle Rhine. These were lost in the 5th century AD to Frankish and Alamannic peoples. ▷ 2.13

GERMANS

Tribes of the ancient world that originated in southern Scandinavia and moved into central Europe and Germany in the last centuries BC. The German language was distinct by about 500 BC; a thousand years later it had split into its distinctive northern, eastern and western forms. The German peoples included the GOTHS, LOMBARDS, FRANKS, ANGLO-SAXONS, Burgundians and Scandinavians. ▷ 2.19

GOSPELS

The accounts of the life of JESUS that form the first four books of the NEW TESTAMENT of the Bible, probably written by the evangelists Mark (the earliest), Matthew, Luke and John from AD 70 to 100, using oral reminiscences and perhaps a common lost written source, sometimes known as Q.

GOTHS

One of the ancient GERMAN peoples. According to legend they derived from southern Scandinavia and crossed to northern Germany, where they defeated the VANDALS. In the 2nd century AD they moved to the Black Sea region and began to raid the ROMAN empire. They divided into the OSTROGOTHS (eastern Goths, living in the Ukraine) and VISIGOTHS (western Goths, in modern Bulgaria). ▷ 2.19

GRACCHUS, TIBERIUS

(163–133 BC) Roman reformer. As tribune of the plebs in 133, he attempted to enact a land reform policy. He was opposed by the senatorial elite – many of whom had acquired large areas of public land illegally – who murdered him. Tiberius' brother GAIUS attempted to continue his work, but he too was murdered in 121 BC. ▷ 2.13

GREECE, ANCIENT

Greece is a mountainous country and the ancient Greeks were a hardy, independent people. Their first civilization, the Mycenaean, rested on agriculture but also extended trade networks. A Dark Age followed the collapse of the Mycenaeans (1100 BC), but by the 8th century BC a growing population saw the emergence of small city-states – urban centers dependent on their local territory. The city-state fostered sophisticated politics, marble temples, drama and philosophy. There were also shrines – Olympia and Delphi among them – that offered a cultural focus for all Greeks, including those who migrated through the Mediterranean.

After success in the PERSIAN WARS (490 and 480 BC) there were no limits to Greek self-confidence, and the 5th century BC saw the achievements of the CLASSICAL PERIOD. In the late 5th century BC, however, the PELOPONNESIAN WAR between ATHENS and Sparta (which Athens lost) heralded the decline of the city-state and Greece was crushed by Macedonian expansion in the late 4th century BC. Following ALEXANDER's

conquests, Greek culture spread throughout Asia and into Egypt in the HELLENISTIC PERIOD, and remained intact after absorption into the ROMAN EMPIRE. The Byzantine empire that emerged in the 6th century AD was still culturally a Greek state. ▷ 2.07, 2.08, 2.09, 2.10, 2.13, 2.14, 2.15, 2.16, 2.17

GREEK LANGUAGE

Greek is known to have been spoken by the Mycenaeans. By the 8th century BC there were numerous dialects, though these were mutually intelligible and the Greeks themselves spoke of being united by language. The first written Greek texts date from the 8th century BC. By the 3rd century BC a standardized Greek, *koine,* was used across the expanded Greek world.

GREGORY OF TOURS

(AD 538–93) Born into an aristocratic Romano-Gallic family, Gregory became – like many of his family before him – bishop of Tours. He is chiefly remembered for his history of the 6th century FRANKS. ▷ 2.17

GREGORY THE GREAT, POPE

Roman aristocrat and pope from AD 590 to 604, who founded the modern papacy. Breaking with the older eastern Christian centers, Gregory the Great invoked the supremacy of Rome and worked tirelessly to impose his authority on the church in the west. The conversion of the English was his most lasting achievement. ▷ 2.17

GULF COAST CIVILIZATIONS

The Mesoamerican cultural traditions that flourished in eastern Mexico in the first seven centuries AD (Classic period). Based on the styles found in urban centers, three such traditions have been identified, those of Cerro de las Mesas, Remojadas and VERACRUZ. All showed considerable exchange with the more dominant TEOTIHUACÁN, as well as Olmec and MAYAN influences. ▷ 2.27

GUPTA EMPIRE

Indian dynasty, rulers of the northeastern state of MAGADHA, who extended their sway across the north and east of the subcontinent from AD 320 until the mid-6th century. The influence of the dynasty was felt even more widely. It was founded by CHANDRAGUPTA I; other notable figures were his son SAMUDRAGUPTA and CHANDRAGUPTA II. Despite their shrinking empire, the dynasty continued to rule Magadha until 720. The Gupta period is considered a time of classic Hindu culture in India. ▷ 2.23

HADRIAN

Emperor of Rome from AD 117 to 138. Born in Spain, he became the ward of TRAJAN, his father's cousin, who adopted him as his successor. He spent much of his reign touring the provinces, notably building Rome's first artificial frontiers – the limes – a continuous palisade linking the frontiers of the Rhine and Danube, and HADRIAN'S WALL in northern England. He made an impact on the empire by these provincial tours, his frontier policy and his intellectual and reforming interests. Worn out and ill, he spent his last years in Rome and died in AD 138. He was buried at his great mausoleum, the present Castel Sant'Angelo, in the center of Rome. ▷ 2.11, 2.13, 2.15

HADRIAN'S WALL
The frontier wall between the Roman province of BRITANNIA and the unconquered tribes to the north, it runs 129 kilometers (80 miles) from Wallsend-on-Tyne to Bowness-on-Solway. Built for the emperor HADRIAN in about AD 122–26 (the eastern part in stone, and the western in turf), it had fortified gateways every Roman mile, observation towers in between and 12 forts, including Housesteads and Chesters. It was replaced in about 142 by the ANTONINE WALL further north, then came back into use during the 160s, until the garrison was finally removed in the 4th or early 5th century AD. ▷ 2.15

HAN DYNASTY
Dynasty of ancient China that came to power in 206 BC and ruled until AD 220 (with a brief interruption in AD 9–23, when the usurpur WANG MANG seized power). Before AD 9 the dynasty was based at Chang'an and is sometimes known as the Western or Former Han; in the period after the capital was moved to Luoyang in 23, it is known as the Eastern or Later Han. Established by GAOZU, the dynasty introduced many of the traditional forms of Chinese imperial rule, including the centralized education system and bureaucracy. ▷ 2.24

HANNIBAL
Among the greatest of generals, Hannibal led CARTHAGE's forces in the Second PUNIC WAR (218–202 BC), attempting to weaken Rome so that it no longer presented a threat to the CARTHAGINIAN empire. In spite of his military brilliance he underestimated Rome's strength. He surprised the Romans by invading Italy from the north, across the Alps, but despite the astounding victories at the rivers of Ticinus and Trebia, at Lake Trasimenus and at CANNAE, Hannibal was eventually bottled up in southern Italy. With the Carthaginians under pressure in Spain and north Africa, he returned to Carthage in 205 BC and was defeated by the Romans under SCIPIO AFRICANUS at the Battle of Zama (202 BC). Enemies at home forced him into exile in the east. In 183–182 BC Rome persuaded Prusias I of BITHYNIA to surrender him, but Hannibal avoided this by taking poison. ▷ 2.02, 2.12

HASMONEANS
See MACCABEES

HECATAEUS
Geographer from Miletus who wrote an account of the Mediterranean and its peoples in about 500 BC. His critical approach to the stories he was told foreshadows the more sophisticated work of the historian HERODOTUS, who acknowledged his debt to Hecataeus. ▷ 2.18

HELLENIC LEAGUE
An alliance of THEBES and ATHENS that was established after clever Athenian diplomacy in 340 BC, in the vain hope of defending GREECE against PHILIP II OF MACEDON. The combined Greek armies were defeated at the BATTLE OF CHAERONEA in 338 BC. ▷ 2.01, 2.02, 2.08

HELLENISTIC PERIOD
Period in Greek history dating from the death of ALEXANDER THE GREAT (323 BC) to the conquest of Egypt by Rome (30 BC), and a time when Greek culture spread across Asia and into Egypt as a result of Alexander's conquests. Kingdoms rather than city-states formed the centers of power, but it was a time of vigorous intellectual activity in the sciences, mathematics and astronomy (above all in ALEXANDRIA) and in philosophy (EPICURUS and the STOICS in ATHENS). In the event, the Hellenistic kingdoms were unable to offer a coordinated response to the expansion of Roman power, and the Greek world became part of the ROMAN EMPIRE. ▷ 2.10

HELLESPONT
The first part of the straits at the entrance to the Black Sea, control of which was essential for exporting the resources of the sea to the Mediterranean world. It is the site of a famous bridge that was constructed by XERXES of PERSIA to convey his troops from Asia to Europe in 480 BC. ▷ 2.07

HERACLEA, BATTLE OF
A battle fought in 280 BC in southern Italy between the Romans and King PYRRHUS of Epirus (319–272 BC), who was supporting the Hellenic Tarentines against Rome. Pyrrhus won, but suffered crippling losses, giving rise to the term "Pyrrhic victory". ▷ 2.12

HEROD THE GREAT
The son of a local Judaean ruler, Herod was used by the Romans as a client king of JUDAEA (r.40–4 BC) and the surrounding area. For much of his reign he was a trusted king who utilized his wealth flamboyantly in a number of building projects (most notably in the rebuilding of the Temple at Jerusalem), as well as in lavish benefactions in the Greek world. The last years of his reign were marked by increasing unrest, which resulted in full Roman control of Judaea on his death. As he was the Herod of the Nativity stories, the date of his death has helped to date the birth of JESUS to about 4 BC. ▷ 2.13

HERODOTOS
Greek historian (c.484–c.425 BC) best known for his history of the PERSIAN WARS, as much a survey of the known world as a narrative account of the wars themselves. He was the first chronicler of the past to test his sources critically and is seen as the father of history. Throughout his historical work, Herodotos stresses the moral supremacy of the Greeks over their opponents on the grounds that Greeks lived in free states, while the Persians lived under a tyranny. ▷ 2.07, 2.08

HIMYARITE KINGDOM
Kingdom of southern Arabia from the 2nd to 6th centuries AD. The Himyars were a tribe within the kingdom of Saba, and they maintained Sabean culture in their kingdom. The capital was at San'a. The kingdom was destroyed by an invasion from the Ethiopian kingdom of AXUM in the 520s. ▷ 2.21

HIPPARCHOS OF BITHYNIA
Important Greek astronomer of the second half of the 2nd century BC, who used Babylonian records and his own careful observations to predict the movements of the stars and eclipses. In the course of his work he invented trigonometry. He was an important influence on the astronomer CLAUDIUS PTOLEMY. ▷ 2.11

HIPPO REGIUS
Ancient city on the north coast of Africa, near modern Annaba, Algeria, founded by the CARTHAGINIANS in the 4th century BC. It was later the capital of the kingdom of NUMIDIA. From the 2nd century BC it was a Roman colony. During the Christian era it became a bishopric and St AUGUSTINE was bishop there from AD 395 to 430. The city was taken by the VANDALS in the 430s and later flourished under the Arabs.

HIPPOCRATES
Greek physician of the 5th century BC, from the island of Cos. A highly influential figure in medical history, he is associated with the idea that the patient must be treated as a whole, and that the physician must put the needs of the patient first. He also stressed the importance of diet.

HISPANIA, HISPANIAE
Roman provinces of the Iberian peninsula. Two provinces were formed in 197 BC from territory conquered during the Second PUNIC WAR – Hispania Citerior and Ulterior. Both were gradually extended inland in campaigns against native peoples, and were renamed TARRACONENSIS and Baetica respectively after AUGUSTUS completed the conquest of Iberia in 19 BC. ▷ 2.15

HOHOKAM CULTURE
An early culture of southern Arizona in southwestern North America, that flourished from c.AD 300 or earlier. Beginning as hunter-

gatherers who also grew maize, they had developed a full farming way of life by AD 800 and built a complex system of canals to irrigate the land. Cotton was also developed as a major crop. BALLCOURTS have been discovered at some of their ritual centers, including Snaketown, suggesting the influence of Mesoamerica. The Hohokam culture collapsed during the early 15th century. ▷ 2.04

HONORIUS
Roman emperor who ruled the western empire from AD 395 to 423. While he secluded himself at RAVENNA, Rome was sacked by the VISIGOTHS under ALARIC (AD 410) and a massive BARBARIAN invasion of GAUL (406–07) led to the beginning of the disintegration of the empire. ▷ 2.16

HSIEN-PI (XIANBI)
TUNGUSIC nomadic people from Manchuria who threatened the northeastern border of China in the 3rd century AD, and overran the northern plains in the following century. The TOBA were a branch of the Hsien-pi. ▷ 2.24, 2.25

HSIUNG-NU
See XIONGNU

HUARI (WARI)
Site in the highlands of PERU around which an empire emerged in about AD 500 to dominate the region from Cuzco to the coast throughout the MIDDLE HORIZON PERIOD. The site was abandoned by about 1000. The Huari built roads and well-planned cities (notably Pikillacta), features that were later adopted by the INCAS. ▷ 2.27

HUARPA CULTURE
Site in the Peruvian highlands around which a small state was created during the EARLY INTERMEDIATE PERIOD (200 BC–AD 500). The Huarpa developed terracing and irrigation canals. ▷ 2.27

HUNS
TURKIC nomadic pastoralist peoples from central Asia, who moved westward into Hungary in about AD 372, causing many Germanic tribes in eastern Europe to flee to the ROMAN EMPIRE. They forced the Roman emperor THEODOSIUS to pay them tribute in 432. In the 440s the HUNS, under ATTILA, invaded the Balkans, followed in 451 by GAUL and Italy. After Attila's death in 453 they were destroyed by a confederation of Germanic tribes at the BATTLE OF NEDAO in PANNONIA. ▷ 2.16, 2.17, 2.19, 2.20, 2.23

IAZYGIANS
Sarmatian tribe that threatened the Danube region and the northern borders of the ROMAN EMPIRE from the 1st century AD. DIOCLETIAN successfully campaigned against them at the end of the 3rd century.

IBERIANS
Ancient inhabitants of southeast Spain who are of unknown origin and spoke a non-Indo-European language. By the mid-1st millennium BC they were in the early stages of state formation, but further development was halted after conquest by the CARTHAGINIANS. They lost their distinctive identity under Roman rule. ▷ 2.11, 2.15, 2.18

ICENI
British tribe in Norfolk and Suffolk that made a treaty with CLAUDIUS but subsequently rebelled in AD 60–61 under BOUDICCA. After its defeat a *civitatis* ("community") was established at the capital of Venta (Caistor-by-Norwich). The wealth of this area is expressed in gold and silver hoards, such as those from Mildenhall and Thetford. ▷ 2.18

ILLYRIANS
Large group of related Indo-European peoples found in Classical times, east of the Adriatic. They harassed MACEDONIA and Epirus, sided with POMPEY during the civil war, and were only slowly brought under effective Roman control. By 11 BC they were incorporated in the Roman province of Illyricum, which was later divided into the provinces of Dalmatia and PANNONIA. ▷ 2.01, 2.02, 2.07, 2.08, 2.12, 2.18

INDO-SCYTHIANS
See YUE QI

IPSUS, BATTLE OF
Decisive battle fought in central Phrygia in 301 BC, at which ANTIGONOS, contender for ALEXANDER THE GREAT's empire, was defeated and killed by SELEUCOS. It marked the end of any attempt to maintain Alexander's empire intact. ▷ 2.09, 2.10

IRANIAN LANGUAGES
Group of languages within the Indo-European family. It includes Avestan and Old Persian (the languages of ancient Iran), as well as the languages of many of the historic nomadic peoples of central Asia, including Parthian, Soghdian and Saka (also known as Khotanese). Modern Persian has an Iranian basis, as have the languages of Afghanistan, Kurdistan and Tajikistan. ▷ 2.20

ISSUS RIVER, BATTLE OF
See ALEXANDER THE GREAT

JAINISM
A religion of India founded in the 6th century BC by Mahavira as an offshoot of Vedic Hinduism. Its central tenet is the release from the material world through austerity, and a strict code of *ahimsa* (non-violence) to all living creatures. Jainism rivaled BUDDHISM in the early centuries BC, but declined after 100 BC. Its influence has remained strong in India; it affected Mahatma Gandhi, among others. ▷ 2.06

JEBEL BARKAL
Archeological site in Sudan, the burial site of the kings of Mero from 590 BC to AD 330. The tombs were built in the form of steep pyramids; many other signs of Egyptian influence were discovered there. ▷ 2.21

JENNE-JENO
Ancient town on the upper Niger, now in Mali, west Africa. The site was occupied from AD 400 or earlier. Its walls, the first to be built in sub-Saharan Africa, were erected in 400–800, and a distinctive style of terracotta pottery developed there. It flourished as a center for trade and agriculture until the 14th century, when the site was abandoned in favor of the nearby city of Jenne. ▷ 2.21

JEROME, ST
(c.AD 347–420) Outstanding biblical scholar responsible for the translation of the GREEK and Hebrew texts of the Old and NEW TESTAMENTS into an authoritative LATIN version (the VULGATE BIBLE). A troubled and abrasive figure, Jerome found it difficult to reconcile his love of the classics with his Christian faith, but his own learning survives in his works on monasticism and celibacy. ▷ 2.06

JESUS OF NAZARETH
Teacher and healer (c.6 BC–AD 30) of JUDEA, believed by Christians to be the Christ or Son of God. He preached a form of messianic Judaism, but was crucified on the charge of blasphemy against the Jewish faith. His followers believed in his resurrection and a sect grew up in which he was the Savior. Initially limited to Jews, this sect – known as the Christians – was broadened to accept Greeks and other non-Jews by ST PAUL, who proclaimed the message throughout the Roman world. The life and teachings of Jesus were set down in the four GOSPELS between AD 70 and 100. ▷ 2.06

JIN
Wealthy and powerful kingdom of northern China that emerged in the Springs and Autumns period (8th–6th centuries BC) and flourished in the early part of the Warring States period (from 480 BC). It gradually weakened and split up in about 400 BC to form the nucleus of Wei, ZHAO and HAN. ▷ 2.24

JIN DYNASTY
Chinese dynasty ruling from AD 265 to 420. Its founder, WUDI, ruler of the northern kingdom of Wei, conquered the southern kingdom of Wu, briefly uniting China under his rule. His successors lost control of Wei after 280, but the dynasty retained its control in the south. ▷ 2.24, 2.25

JUAN-JUAN
A confederation of nomadic peoples of east Asia, dominated by the Mongols, who succeeded the XIONGNU to control Manchuria

in AD 400–553, frequently threatening northern China. Following the collapse of the confederation at the hands of the Blue Turks, part of the Juan-juan known as the AVARS moved into eastern Europe. ▷ 2.20

JUDAS MACCABEUS

See MACCABEES

JUDEA

A kingdom of southern Palestine that gained its independence briefly from the SELEUCIDS in the 160s BC, and again from 140 BC. Judea became a Roman province in the 40s BC under a client king, later King HEROD (r.37–4 BC). Judea came under Roman rule in AD 6 and was ruled alternately by Herod's descendants and by Roman officials. The province was renamed Syria Palestina after the Jewish revolt of the AD 120s.

JUGURTHA

King of NUMIDIA who reigned from 118 to 104 BC and the grandson of MASSINISSA. From 112 Jugurtha tried to maintain the independence of Numidia from Roman rule, but he was captured in 105 and executed the following year.

JULIAN

(AD 331–63) After some highly successful campaigns on the northern borders of the ROMAN EMPIRE, Julian succeeded his cousin Constantius as emperor in 361. The last of the pagan Roman emperors, he attempted, without success, to stem the advance of CHRISTIANITY. He was killed campaigning in PERSIA. ▷ 2.15

JUNAGADH

Town in Gujarat state, west India, with Buddhist and Hindu remains which date from the 3rd century BC. It was the capital of Gujarat in the early centuries AD. A large-scale irrigation project was carried out there by ASHOKA in the mid-3rd century BC and a rock outside the town bears an inscription by him. ▷ 2.22, 2.23

JUSTINIAN

(AD 482–565) Ruler of the eastern ROMAN EMPIRE from 527. One of the dominating figures of late antiquity, Justinian attempted the reconquest of the western empire, with some success, in north Africa, southern Spain and Italy. Counted among Justinian's major achievements was the codification of Roman law and the construction in Constantinople of Hagia Sophia – one of the great buildings of antiquity. He hoped to create a united Christian church but his attempts to enforce doctrinal unity simply led to greater fragmentation among Christian groups in the east. Justinian's wife Theodora, a former circus artiste, often played an influential role, particularly in his religious policies. ▷ 2.17

JUTES

Germanic tribe from Jutland, one of the three main groups to invade Britain in the 5th century AD. Little is known of their history prior to the invasion. The Jutes mainly settled in Kent and the Isle of Wight. ▷ 2.16

KALINGA

Ancient kingdom of eastern India, now in northern Andhra Pradesh state. It was conquered by MAGADHA in about 340 BC, but seceded before being reconquered by ASHOKA in 261 BC. Following the collapse of the MAUYRAN EMPIRE Kalinga regained independence and its prosperity was based on flourishing trade with southeast Asia. It was conquered again by the GUPTAS, and finally disappeared in 1324 at the hands of the Delhi sultanate. ▷ 2.22

KAMINALIJUYÚ

Ancient Mesoamerican site, close to Guatemala City. It was first inhabited in about 1500 BC and flourished from 300 BC. Under the influence of TEOTIHUACÁN, it was one of the largest MAYAN cities of the Classic period, with more than 200 mounds and pyramids. The site was abandoned by AD 1000. ▷ 2.28

KANISHKA

King of the KUSHAN state of central Asia (r.c.AD 100–30). Ruled from Peshawar, his kingdom encompassed northern India, Afghanistan and part of central Asia. Remembered as a patron of BUDDHISM, his empire provided early contacts that led to the introduction of Buddhism to China. He was also in contact with the ROMAN EMPIRE, and the Gandhara style of art, which fused Hellenistic and Indian traditions, flourished under his rule. During his reign a Buddhist council was held in Kashmir that led to the formation of MAHAYANA BUDDHISM. ▷ 2.23

KARMA

In Hinduism, the law that governs the effects of actions on the subsequent condition of the soul, especially with regard to the process of reincarnation. The doctrine of *karma* developed in the 5th century BC.

KEYHOLE TOMBS (KOFUN)

Monumental tombs of the YAMATO period monarchs of Japan (3rd to 7th centuries AD). Named after their distinctive shape (also known as "square-front, round-back tombs"), the largest examples were built on the Yamato plain. The tomb of the emperor Nintoku, at Mozu in central Honshu, is up to 500 meters (1600 feet) in length, and consists of a mound surrounded by a triple moat. ▷ 2.25

KHARAVELA

King of KALINGA in east India (r.c.AD 50). He was a follower of JAINISM but campaigned successfully both in the Deccan and in southern India. ▷ 2.22

KHOSRU (CHOSROES) I ANUSHIRVAN

SASANIAN emperor of PERSIA (r.AD 531–79), known as "of immortal soul" and as "the just". He extended Sasanian power in BACTRIA, Sogdiana, the Middle East and the Yemen, and reformed the empire, reorganizing taxation and the bureaucracy and maintaining a mainly professional army. He encouraged the arts and welcomed many Greek scholars to Persia. The palace at CTESIPHON is said to date from the period of his reign. ▷ 2.11

KHOSRU II

SASANIAN emperor of PERSIA (r.AD 591–628) who campaigned successfully against the eastern ROMAN EMPIRE in Mesopotamia from 602, taking Damascus in 613, ALEXANDRIA in 616 and CHALCEDON in 617. His conquests were reversed in 622–27 by the eastern Roman emperor, Heraclius, despite an expedition to besiege Constantinople in 626. Following final defeat at Nineveh, Khosru was assassinated. His reign is remembered as a time of courtly splendor and administrative centralization, but his war with the eastern ROMAN EMPIRE fatally weakened Persia on the eve of the Arab invasions. ▷ 2.11

KHOTAN

City now in Xinjiang province, western China, one of the oasis cities on the SILK Route, and the site of the first introduction of BUDDHISM to China in the 3rd century BC. It was the scene of a battle in AD 90 when the Chinese defeated the Kushans. The city's main period of prosperity came during the Islamic era, from the mid-8th century. ▷ 2.23

KO HUNG

Chinese philosopher, alchemist and theorist of Daoism (AD 253–333) who developed the Daoist search for the elixir of life in his work, *He Who Holds to Simplicity.* His work incorporated Confucian ethics and criticized the individualism of earlier Daoists.

KOFUN PERIOD

Name given to the early YAMATO period of Japanese history (AD 300–550), named after its distinctive "old tombs" (*kofun*) and especially the huge KEYHOLE TOMBS. During this period the first states and confederations emerged in Japan, and Shinto shrines, such as those at Ise, were built.

KUJALA KADPHISES

Founder of the KUSHAN state (r.c.AD 25–75) in BACTRIA. He invaded north India and conquered the Western Sakas in about 50. ▷ 2.23

KURGAN

Distinctive barrow of the STEPPE peoples of southern Russia and eastern Europe, usually the burial site of a chieftain or group of notables. The earliest *kurgans* date from the 4th millennium BC, and distinctive culture areas can be traced as far west as the Danube and Adriatic regions. The practice continued through the Catacomb grave cultures of the Bronze Age into historical times, among the Scythians and Sarmatians. ▷ 2.20

KUSHAN EMPIRE

Central Asian empire, established by a sub-group of the YUE QI nomads, that was based in BACTRIA and founded by KUJALA KADPHISES in the 1st century AD. The empire grew by 100 to incorporate most of modern Afghanistan, Pakistan and much of northern India as far east as Varanasi, as well as Turkmenistan and Uzbekistan. BUDDHIST in faith and eclectic in culture, the Kushans contributed to a mixing of Greek, Roman, Persian, Indian and Chinese influences throughout the region. The empire declined in the 4th century. ▷ 2.10, 2.11, 2.20, 2.21, 2.22, 2.23

LA TÈNE CULTURE

A Swiss lakeside deposit of votive metalwork at La Tène that has given its name to an archeological culture, and to the later Iron Age period in Europe, dating from about 450 until the Roman conquest. The La Tène style first developed in the area from the Marne to the upper Danube, and was used on fine bronze vessels, armor, horse gear and jewelry for the aristocracy. It is characterized by elegant, stylized curvilinear animal and vegetable forms, with elements from Scythian animal designs and the Hallstatt geometric tradition. La Tène cultural material soon appeared over a larger area, including parts of Britain. ▷ 2.18

LAO ZI

Chinese philosopher (fl.6th century BC), traditionally the author of the DAO DE JING (now known to have been compiled in the 3rd century BC) and founder of Daoism. Little is known about his life for certain, but many legends survive, including stories of his meeting in old age with his younger contemporary, Confucius. ▷ 2.06

LAPITA CULTURE

A cultural tradition of the western Pacific, named after an archeological site in New Caledonia, where a distinctive style of pottery decoration was discovered in the 1950s. It arose in the Bismarck archipelago in about 1600 BC and spread through the island chains of MELANESIA, reaching Fiji, Samoa and Tonga by 1000 BC. The Lapita culture is considered ancestral to the Polynesian identity and can be used to trace the migration routes of the Polynesians. ▷ 2.26

LATER HAN

See HAN DYNASTY

LATIN LANGUAGE AND ALPHABET

Belonging to the Italic group of Indo-European languages (including Faliscan, Umbrian and Oscan), Latin is first attested by inscriptions from Latium dating to the early 1st millenium BC. The alphabet is based on a southern Etruscan type, which is itself adapted from a Greek model. As Rome extended its territory, Latin spread as the main language of Italy and many other parts of the ROMAN EMPIRE. Classical Latin is best defined by the Latin literature of about 90 BC to about AD 120. Vulgar Latin was the spoken language of the mainly illiterate population, and its regional dialects developed into the ROMANCE LANGUAGES. ▷ 2.14, 2.17, 2.18

LAURION

The Laurion silver mines in southern Attica were among the most productive in the Greek world, and made a vital contribution to ATHENS' prosperity. The Athenian navy, which defeated the Persians, was built largely out of their proceeds. The mines were owned by the state, leased out to citizens and mined by slaves, whose working conditions were appalling and life expectancy short. ▷ 2.07

LEONIDAS OF SPARTA

King of Sparta (r.490–480 BC) who was responsible for the defense of the pass at THERMOPYLAE against the invading Persian army of XERXES. He and his 300 companions died heroically after they were outflanked by the Persians. ▷ 2.07

LEPTIS MAGNA

Phoenician trading station founded in about 600 BC on the coast of Tripolitania, north Africa. The continued prosperity of the city derived largely from the fertile hinterland, which by the late republic was producing considerable quantities of olive oil. The city was embellished with fine municipal buildings, built by the emperor SEPTIMIUS SEVERUS (who was born there), and many Roman remains are visible. It fell into decline from the 4th century AD. ▷ 2.21

LICCHAVIS

Tribe of northern India in modern Bihar state that maintained a distinct identity from the 6th century BC to the 4th century AD, when they established a dynasty in NEPALA. Unlike other states of the region, they maintained a republican form of government. ▷ 2.23

LIU BANG

See GAOZU

LIVY

Roman historian (59 BC–AD 17) who formed part of the circle of AUGUSTUS and encouraged the young CLAUDIUS to become a historian. He spent 40 years writing his own monumental history of Rome, from its origins to 9 BC, in 142 books (of which 35 have survived) – the *Ab Urbe Condita*. ▷ 2.13

LOMBARDS

Ancient Germanic peoples, one of the SUEVI tribes, who lived in northwest Germany in the 1st century AD. In 400 they lived in modern Austria and in the mid-6th century they settled PANNONIA. In 568, led by Alboin, they invaded northern Italy, setting up a Lombard kingdom that flourished in the 7th and 8th centuries.

LONG WALLS OF WEI, ZHAO AND YAN

Walls built in the north and west of China by three of the leading kingdoms in the Warring States period, in the 4th and 3rd centuries BC, to protect China from nomadic incursion (and, in the case of Wei, from invasion by QIN). Mainly built of earth, the northern walls were about 100 kilometers (60 miles) further north than the line of the later Great Wall of China. ▷ 2.24

LUCANIA, LUCANIANS

Roughly equal to modern Basilicata, southern Italy, this mountainous zone was said to be occupied by a group of tribes, including the Oenotrians, Chones, and Ausonians. Greek colonization began along the coast in about 700 BC, and between about 420 and 390 BC the Oscan Lucani took control of the region (except for the Greek cities). Urban sites developed in about the 4th century BC, which may have been organized in a league. The area was generally hostile to Rome, but came under its control by the late republic and prospered under the empire. ▷ 2.12

LUOLANG

Ancient name for Pyongyang, capital of a HAN Chinese colony (also known as Nangnang) founded in about 108 BC on the site of an earlier Korean town. It was capital of the Korean Koguryo kingdom from AD 313, and later of Koryo. ▷ 2.24, 2.25

LUSITANIA, LUSITANIANS

A Celticized region of western Iberia that was inhabited by various groups, including the Lusitani, Vettones and Celtici. The Lusitani were attacked by Rome and finally fell to JULIUS CAESAR in 61 BC. The region formed part of Hispania Ulterior and in 27 BC became part of the Augustan province of Hispania Lusitania. It was an important source of metals and its fish sauce was widely exported. By AD 411 Lusitania had come under BARBARIAN control. ▷ 2.12, 2.13, 2.18

LYSIMACHOS

General of ALEXANDER THE GREAT who built up a large kingdom after his death in 323 BC. It eventually included Thrace (the province allocated to Lysimachos by Alexander), MACEDONIA and parts of Asia Minor. Lysimachos was defeated and killed by SELEUCOS in 281 BC and his kingdom disintegrated. ▷ 2.09, 2.10

MACCABEES

Priestly Jewish family who led a revolt against the SELEUCID dynasty in the mid-2nd century BC. From 166 it was led by Judas Maccabeus, who occupied Jerusalem in 164 and rededicated the Temple, but was killed in 161. The conflict continued until the late 140s BC, after which JUDEA became an independent kingdom ruled by the Maccabees (or Hasmonean) family until civil war in 63 BC led to Roman intervention by POMPEY. The family continued to resist the Romans until 30 BC, when Hyrcanus II was put to death. ▷ 2.10

MACEDON, MACEDONIA
Macedonia occupies the strategically important area between the Greek peninsula and the Balkans. Ruled by the Teminid dynasty from about 650 BC, Macedonia was converted into a powerful and prosperous state by PHILIP II (r.360–336 BC), who laid the economic and military foundations for the success of his son, ALEXANDER THE GREAT. Macedonia survived as a kingdom into HELLENISTIC times, but was eventually defeated by Rome at the BATTLE OF CYNOSCEPHALAE (197 BC) and later broken up (148 BC). It is not clear whether the Macedonians spoke a GREEK dialect or a language independent of Greek, but they had absorbed many Greek influences by the 4th century BC and Alexander's conquests spread Greco-Macedonian culture far into Asia. ▷ 2.07, 2.08, 2.09, 2.10, 2.12, 2.13

MACEDONIAN WAR, FIRST
Conflict between Philip V of MACEDON and ROME in 214–205 BC, and the first time Rome directly intervened in the Greek peninsula. Rome had been roused by Philip's alliance with HANNIBAL. The war ended in stalemate but warfare was to be renewed in 201 BC and Philip was comprehensively defeated at CYNOSCEPHALAE in 197 BC. ▷ 2.10

MAGADHA
Kingdom of the lower Ganges valley and by about 700 BC one of the 16 *mahajanapadas*, ("great realms"), with a capital at PATALIPUTRA. Under King Bimbisara (c.543–491 BC) Magadha became the dominant power in India, annexing neighboring kingdoms such as Anga and Kosala. From the 4th to 2nd centuries BC it was the center of the NANDA and MAURYAN empires. ▷ 2.22, 2.23

MAGNESIA, BATTLE OF
Important battle fought in 190 BC, the climax of the war between the SELEUCID king ANTIOCHUS III and ROME. Antiochus was defeated and forced to cede the west coast of Asia Minor to Rome's ally, PERGAMON. ▷ 2.10, 2.13

MAHABHARATA
Indian religious and literary epic poem comprising more than 90,000 couplets. Compiled from earlier sources by about AD 400, it tells the story of a princely feud said to have occurred before 1000 BC and offers insights into the proper conduct of kings and warriors, and the correct behavior for those seeking rebirth. Part of the text, known as the *Bhagavad Gita*, comprises the most important Hindu text and describes advice given by the god Krishna to a prince, Arjuna, as he prepares for battle.

MAHAYANA BUDDHISM
Literally meaning "greater vehicle", the tradition of BUDDHISM mainly practiced in China, Japan and Tibet. This tradition taught that the Buddha himself was the temporary earthly manifestation of a transcendent quality, and that the goal of Buddhists should be to achieve the status of *bodhisatva* – one who has postponed his enlightenment while working for the salvation of all. ▷ 2.06

MAIDEN CASTLE
One of the largest hillforts in Britain, near Dorchester, southern England. Begun in the early Iron Age, the hillfort was later extended to fortify the entire hill and rebuilt until the hilltop was defended by four massive concentric sets of ramparts and ditches. By 50 BC the site had become the tribal capital of the Durotriges, with coinage and imported Gallo-Roman luxuries. Excavation has revealed evidence of its sack by VESPASIAN's legion, including piles of slingshot and a war cemetery. The population was moved to the site of Durnovaria (Dorchester) and the hillfort was abandoned.

MAKKURA
Ancient kingdom of Africa centered on the Nile in the modern Sudan. Arising in the 6th century AD, it was converted to CHRISTIANITY in about 550 and conquered its northern neighbor Nobatia in the 8th century. It was overthrown by the Arabs in 1317. ▷ 2.21

MANCHING
Large Celtic oppidum in Bavaria, southern Germany, on low-lying ground on the southern bank of the Danube. By the 2nd century BC it had earth ramparts 7 kilometers (4.5 miles) long, containing a complex of regularly laid out houses with workshops supplying a wide range of crafts. Manching fell to the Romans in 50 BC. The site was excavated from 1955. ▷ 2.18

MANETHO
Egyptian priest (fl.c.305–285 BC) who composed an important history of Egypt in Greek. His division of the Egyptian pharaohs into dynasties has survived; though confusing in parts, it has proved of great value to historians.

MANI
Persian philosopher (c.AD 216–76) and founder of MANICHAEISM. He was of Zoroastrian background but the religion he preached from 242 incorporated aspects of BUDDHISM and CHRISTIANITY. He successfully sought converts throughout the SASANIAN empire until 272, when his followers were persecuted. He was executed for heresy in 276. ▷ 2.11

MANICHAEISM
The religion preached by MANI, combining elements of ZOROASTRIANISM, BUDDHISM and CHRISTIANITY, in the 3rd century AD in PERSIA. Following Mani's death in 276, the religion spread throughout the ROMAN empire (especially north Africa), where it became a powerful Christian heresy by the 4th century, proscribed by the emperor JUSTINIAN. Manichaeans preached the fundamental conflict between the spiritual, good realm of God, and the material, evil realm of Satan. The term was generally used for any similar dualist heresy in the Middle Ages, but a truly Manichaean sect survived in central Asia until the 13th century. ▷ 2.06

MANTINEIA, BATTLE OF
Battle of 418 BC fought in the central Peloponnese during the PELOPONNESIAN WAR. The SPARTANS crushed a combined force of Athenians, Argives and Mantineians, and in doing so ensured their control of the Peloponnese for another 30 years. One of the largest hoplite battles known, it involved perhaps 20,000 infantry. ▷ 2.08

MARATHON, BATTLE OF
Famous Athenian victory in 490 BC over the Persians on the plain of Marathon in northern Attica, that effectively marked the defeat of DARIUS I's invasion of GREECE. Outnumbered, the Athenians stretched their lines and enveloped the Persian army. Some 192 Greeks and an estimated 6,400 Persians died. The victory helped create the myth of Athenian pre-eminence among the Greeks, though the "run" with the good news from Marathon to ATHENS – the inspiration for the modern marathon – is probably fictional.

MARCOMANNI
GERMAN tribe that forms part of the SUEVI group. In the 1st century BC they migrated from central Germany into Bohemia and were trading partners of the Romans. In AD 167 they invaded the ROMAN empire but were expelled from Italy by MARCUS AURELIUS. ▷ 2.15, 2.19

MARCOMANNIC WARS
Wars fought by Rome in AD 166–73 and 177–80 against the MARCOMANNI, a west GERMAN (Suevic) tribe which had migrated from Saxony and Thuringia (c.100 BC) and finally settled in Bohemia, establishing a powerful kingdom there. The wars began when they invaded PANNONIA and DACIA in 166. The most dangerous period for Rome was when MARCUS AURELIUS was defeated in 170 and the Marcomanni and Quadi of Slovakia crossed the Danube, swept over the Julian Alps and besieged AQUILEIA. Rome fought back and the Marcomanni were

defeated as they tried to recross the Danube with their booty. The wars continued until 180, and were depicted on the column of MARCUS AURELIUS in Rome. ▷ 2.15

MARDONIUS

Persian general and son-in-law of DARIUS I. He played an important part in settling the Ionian revolt and restoring PERSIA's prestige in Thrace in the 490s BC. Chosen by XERXES to be his leading general for the invasion of 480 BC, Mardonius was left in charge of the campaign of 479 BC but was defeated and killed at the BATTLE OF PLATAEA. ▷ 2.07

MARIUS, GAIUS

(c.157–86 BC) Roman politician and soldier responsible for perfecting Rome's legionary army. Beginning in 104 Marius reformed the Roman army and turned it into a professional force. His reforms immediately proved their worth when he defeated the TEUTONES at Aquae Sextiae and the CIMBRI at Vercellae in 102 and 101 BC, both peoples who had previously inflicted serious defeats on Roman armies. He came into conflict with Sulla in 88 BC over command of an expedition to the east and was forced into exile. Returning in 87, he was elected consul but died shortly afterwards. ▷ 2.13, 2.19

MASADA

Small plateau, 457 meters (1,500 feet) high, on the Dead Sea. Accessible only by a steep path, it was the site of King HEROD's most spectacular fortress residences, including two lavishly decorated palaces, a garrison-block, baths and storerooms. In the ZEALOT rebellion against Rome it was the last stronghold to be taken, falling in AD 73 or 74, after a six-month seige by Flavius Silva. Most of the 960 defenders were reported to have commited suicide rather than surrender. ▷ 2.13

MASSINISSA

King of NUMIDIA, north Africa (r.c.202–148 BC), who fought in Spain in 212 for the Carthaginians against Rome. He changed sides in 204; in return the Romans helped him gain the throne. He built a strong Numidian state in the early 2nd century and forcibly developed agriculture there among the previously pastoralist BERBERS. ▷ 2.12

MATHURA

Ancient city of central India, now in Uttar Pradesh state. It is the traditional birthplace of the Hindu god Krishna and one of the seven holy cities of Hinduism. It was the center of a school of Hindu arts and culture from the 2nd century BC, notably in the KUSHAN and GUPTA periods. Most of the Hindu remains were destroyed by Muslims from the 16th century. ▷ 2.22, 2.23

MAURETANIA

Area of north Africa whose name means "land of the moors". Its population mainly consisted of the Moorish branch of the BERBER group. Much of the region was mountainous or rocky, but the lowland zones were fertile and its chief exports were wine, precious woods and purple dye. Phoenician trading stations were established along the coast in the 8th and 7th centuries BC. Kingdoms were formed by the late 3rd century BC, and were gradually amalgamated. In 33 BC Mauretania passed to Roman control, and in c.AD 44 CLAUDIUS constituted two Mauretanian provinces. ▷ 2.13, 2.21

MAURICE

Eastern Roman emperor (r.AD 582–602) who, despite inheriting a virtually bankrupt empire that was threatened by BARBARIANS, successfully kept its borders intact. Maurice benefited from peace with the Persians, which allowed him to concentrate on other enemies, such as the AVARS. His armies mutinied in 602 and Maurice was murdered by the mutineers' leader, Phocas. ▷ 2.17

MAURYAN DYNASTY

The first dynasty to build an empire extending across most of the Indian subcontinent. It was founded by CHANDRAGUPTA I MAURYA (r.321–c.293 BC), who took over MAGADHA and built an empire that reached beyond the Indus into Afghanistan, claiming part of ALEXANDER's easterly conquests. Its capital was PATALIPUTRA. His successors BINDUSARA and ASHOKA extended the empire to the south. It began to decline in the late 3rd century BC, and the dynasty finally collapsed c.185 BC. ▷ 2.22

MAUSOLEUM

The burial place of MAUSOLOS of Caria at Halikarnassos, one of the Seven Wonders of the Ancient World, completed in about 350 BC. A gargantuan structure complete with a central platform, colonnades and a pyramid, it was typical of the more extravagant approach to rulers' tombs seen in the HELLENISTIC PERIOD. ▷ 2.08

MAUSOLOS

Ruler of Caria (377–353 BC), Mausolus enjoyed a semi-independent role within the Persian empire and had extensive contacts with the Greek world, annexing neighboring islands such as Rhodes and Cos in the 350s BC. He instigated the building of the MAUSOLEUM as his tomb. ▷ 2.08

MAXIMIAN

Roman emperor (r.AD 286–305) who ruled as the western "Augustus" after DIOCLETIAN divided the empire into two. He abdicated with Diocletian in 305, but subsequently became embroiled in a civil war for the succession and committed suicide in 310.

MAYAN CIVILIZATION

Ancient Mesoamerican civilization centered on the Yucatán peninsula of modern Mexico, Guatemala and Honduras. The Maya people settled the region by about 1000 BC; the so-called Preclassic period continued to AD 250, by which time the first Mayan cities – such as TIKAL – were established. In the Early Classic period (AD 300–600) Tikal and the other cities of the central lowlands were dominant, and in the Late Classic period (600–800) Mayan civilization reached its peak, based on a large number of small, independent city-states. In the Postclassic period the center of gravity shifted to the north, as CHICHÉN ITZÁ, influenced by the Toltecs, became dominant, while environmental crisis caused civilization to decline in the south. The Maya were gradually conquered by the Spanish; the last state fell in 1697. ▷ 2.28

MELANESIA, ANCIENT

Region of the Pacific northeast of Australia, south of the Equator, comprising New Guinea, the Solomon Islands, New Hebrides, New Caledonia, the Bismarck archipelago and Fiji. Melanesia was the home of the LAPITA culture (which was to develop into the Polynesian culture) in about 1600 BC, though other pottery traditions, including that of Mangaasi on Vanuatu, also flourished from 700 BC. ▷ 2.26

MENCIUS (MENGZI)

Chinese philosopher (371–289 BC) who traveled throughout China promoting the teachings of Confucius to the kings of the various Warring States. His teaching is known from his writings, *The Book of Mencius*. His reputation languished until the 11th century AD, when his work was republished as one of the *Four Books* of Confucianism.

METAURUS RIVER, BATTLE OF

Battle fought in 207 BC in Umbria between Roman forces and the younger brother of HANNIBAL, Hasdrubal, who was bringing reinforcements to Hannibal from Spain and GAUL. Hasdrubal was defeated and killed, so ending CARTHAGE's last hope of victory in Italy. ▷ 2.12

MEXICO, VALLEY OF

One of the centers of ancient civilization in Mesoamerica, known to the indigenous population as Anahuac. About 80 x 60 kilometers (50 x 40 miles), the valley was fertile and agriculturally productive by 200 BC, when the city of TEOTIHUACÁN was founded. It later became the center of the Toltec and Aztec civilizations. ▷ 2.27

MICRONESIA

The western Pacific north of the equator, comprising the Caroline, Marshall, Mariana and Gilbert islands, as well as Nauru. The archeology of this region is incomplete, but it appears that it was settled in the 1st millennium BC from the south, west and southeast. Most Micronesians speak Malayo-Polynesian languages. A remarkable ceremonial center was built at Nan Madol on the island of Pohnpei (Caroline Islands) from the 9th century AD; it was probably no longer in use by the 16th century. ▷ 2.26

MIDDLE HORIZON PERIOD
Period in South America from AD 500 to 1000, distinguished by the spread of the HUARI culture around the region. The period culminated with the collapse of both the Huari and TIAHUANACO empires, marking the start of the Late Intermediate period. ▷ 2.27

MILAN, EDICT OF
Edict issued in AD 313 by CONSTANTINE THE GREAT and his co-emperor Licinius, granting toleration of all religious sects throughout the ROMAN EMPIRE. The main beneficiary was CHRISTIANITY, which, in addition to toleration, gained the financial and moral support of the emperor. ▷ 2.15

MILVIAN BRIDGE, BATTLE OF
Major battle fought north of Rome in AD 312, in which CONSTANTINE THE GREAT defeated Maxentius, his rival for the western empire, and assumed control of the west. Later legends told of the support, through a vision of a cross, of God. ▷ 2.15

MIN-YUE
Ancient state of the AUSTRO-ASIATIC YUE peoples of southeast China, now in Fujian province. It flourished from the 4th century BC and was conquered by the HAN DYNASTY in the late 2nd century BC. ▷ 2.02, 2.03, 2.24

MITHRADATES VI
(r.120–63 BC) The greatest HELLENISTIC king of PONTUS in Asia Minor, and Rome's most dangerous enemy in the 1st century BC. He extended his control to include the Crimea, CAPPADOCCIA and Paphlagonia, and finally annexed BITHYNIA. Rome intervened and three Mithridatic wars were fought between 89 and 66 BC. Sulla won the first for Rome and Mithridates was allowed to retire to Pontus. The second war (c.83–81 BC) was inconclusive. Mithridates invaded Bithynia in 74 or 73 BC, beginning the third war, which was won by POMPEY. Mithridates retired to the Crimea but refused to give up the war against Rome. He was planning an invasion of Italy when his son Pharnaces led a revolt against him, and he took his own life in 63 BC. ▷ 2.10, 2.13

MITHRAISM
Religion of the late ROMAN EMPIRE that originated in PERSIA as an offshoot of ZOROASTRIANISM. By the 5th century BC Mithra had become the main Persian deity, and the cult expanded throughout the Roman world in the 1st century AD. Mithraism emphasized the cosmic conflict between light and darkness, and took the form of a mystery religion centered around the rite of bull sacrifice. It had declined by AD 400. ▷ 2.06

MOCHE
Ancient culture of coastal PERU, named after a site with vast ceremonial structures and royal graves. The Pyramid of the Sun was the largest adobe structure in the ancient Americas (it was partly destroyed by the Spaniards in the 16th century). The site was in occupation from about 100 BC and the state's influence was widely felt in the area from about AD 200. It declined in about 500. Mochica pottery showed a high degree of skill and character, deriving in style from the Chavín culture. ▷ 2.27

MONGOLIAN LANGUAGES
Group of languages, including Kalmyk, Buryat and Khalka (also known as Mongolian), spoken in eastern Russia, Mongolia and northwest China. They became distinct from the TURKIC languages early in the 1st millennium AD.

MONS GRAUPIUS, BATTLE OF
Fought in the difficult terrain of north Scotland in 83 BC between the local CALEDONII and the Romans under Agricola. Although Agricola won the battle, he did not succeed in conquering the Caledonii. ▷ 2.18

MONTÉ ALBÁN
Zapotec ceremonial center and political capital built on several hills in the Oaxaca valley, central Mexico, from about 500 BC. The earliest structures include a temple platform with a series of figurative sculptures of defeated enemies and hieroglyphic inscriptions. The city reached the height of its grandeur in about AD 100–700. ▷ 2.27

MUSEUM
A place of the Muses, or one where the arts sponsored by them were practiced. The most celebrated museum was in ALEXANDRIA. Founded by the Ptolemies, it was not primarily concerned with the collection of objects but supported scholars who carried out original research, particularly on earlier GREEK literary texts.

MYLAE, BATTLE OF
In the First PUNIC WAR (264–241 BC) the Romans saw the need to wrest command of the sea from CARTHAGE and in 260 BC built a fleet of 100 quinqueremes, fitted with a rotatable boarding bridge. The Roman fleet under Duilius defeated Carthage in this naval battle at Mylae (modern Milazzo, Sicily). ▷ 2.12

NABATEA
Ancient kingdom of the Middle East, now in Jordan. With its capital at PETRA, the Nabatean kingdom was established during the late 4th century BC, and by 85 BC controlled the northern Red Sea coast, Damascus and the Lebanon. Following the conquests of POMPEY in the Levant in 63 BC, Nabatea became an ally of the Romans; the kingdom was

annexed by TRAJAN in AD 106, becoming the Roman province of Arabia. The Nabateans used a consonantal script that was ancestral to Arabic. ▷ 2.10

NAN-YUE
Ancient state of southern China and north Vietnam inhabited by the AUSTRO-ASIATIC YUE peoples. Nan-yue flourished between 206 and 113 BC, after which it was incorporated within the HAN empire. ▷ 2.24

NANDA DYNASTY
Dynasty that ruled in MAGADHA, in ancient India, founded by Mahapadma in about 364 BC. Under Nanda rule Magadha began a period of expansion, and the dynasty controlled a vast army. It was overthrown by CHANDRAGUPTA I, founder of the MAURYA dynasty, in 321 BC. ▷ 2.01, 2.02, 2.22

NAQSH-I RUSTAM
Archeological site in southern PERSIA, the site of the tombs of many of the early Achemenid kings, as well as several Sasanian sculptures, including a carving depicting the capture of the Roman emperor VALERIAN in AD 260. ▷ 2.11

NARSES
(AD 480–573) Armenian eunuch, general and adviser to the eastern Roman emperor JUSTINIAN. As commander of the imperial bodyguard, Narses played a major part in suppressing the Nika riots of 532, which nearly overthrew Justinian. He was later responsible for completing the conquest of the OSTROGOTHIC kingdom of Italy between 551 and 562. ▷ 2.17

NAZCA
Ancient culture of coastal PERU that flourished from 200 BC to AD 600, during the EARLY INTERMEDIATE period. The desert-based Nazca culture produced fine textiles and pottery, but is distinguished for its geometric patterns (geoglyphs) formed by clearing areas of desert of their stones. The significance of these patterns is controversial, but they appear to have been ritual walkways associated with the cult of the rain-god. The Nazca culture declined with the rise of TIAHUANACO. ▷ 2.02, 2.03, 2.04, 2.27

NEARCHOS
Naval commander who performed the remarkable feat of sailing ALEXANDER THE GREAT's fleet from the Indus river to the mouth of the Persian Gulf, without the loss of a single ship, in 325 BC. He later wrote his memoirs of the voyage and of Alexander's earlier Indian campaigns. ▷ 2.09

NEDAO, BATTLE OF
Battle fought in AD 454 in modern Hungary at which the Huns were defeated by a coalition of GERMAN tribes. The Hunnish empire abruptly collapsed. ▷ 2.16

NEO-PLATONISM
Development of PLATO's philosophy, notably by PLOTINUS (AD 205–70). Plotinus argued that there was a single supreme force that was the source of all existence and values. It was possible for human beings to grasp the essence of this force through reasoned reflection on its nature. Christian thinkers, notably AUGUSTINE, equated Plotinus' supreme force with the Christian God. ▷ 2.15

NEPALA
Ancient kingdom of Nepal, first referred to in the Vedic texts. It was the birthplace of Siddhartha Gautama, the Buddha, in the 6th century BC. The kingdom was extended by the LICCHAVI dynasty from the 4th century AD. In the 10th century the Malla dynasty introduced thoroughgoing Hinduism and established contact with China and India.

NEPOS, JULIUS
Roman emperor of the west from AD 474 to 475. He recognized Visigothic sovereignty in Spain and southern GAUL. Deposed by the general Orestes, who placed his son ROMULUS AUGUSTULUS on the throne, Nepos fled to Dalmatia. He continued to be recognized as the western emperor by Zeno, the emperor of the east, until his murder in 480. ▷ 2.16

NERO
Roman emperor (r.AD 54–68) and the stepson and successor of CLAUDIUS. In his early years in power he was dominated by his mother Agrippina, whom he had murdered in 59. He took delight in the arts, particularly music, and the THEATER, and became increasingly extravagant and unpopular. In AD 64 Rome suffered a devastating fire, which Nero used as an excuse to begin persecution of the young Christian church in Rome. Serious plotting against him began in 68, and he killed himself.

NEW TESTAMENT
The Christian part of the Bible, comprising 27 books written in GREEK: the four GOSPELS, the Acts of the Apostles, letters of ST PAUL and other apostles to the early churches, and the Revelation of St John. The canonical version of the complete New Testament was assembled in AD 367 by St Athanasius.

NICAEA, COUNCIL OF
Ecumenical council of the Christian church, called (and presided over) by the emperor CONSTANTINE in AD 325. It resolved the conflict between the Arians and the Orthodox view over whether the Son and the Father were "of one substance", and produced the Nicene creed as a statement of the faith.

NOK CULTURE
Early Iron Age farming culture of the Benue plateau region, modern Nigeria, from about 600 BC to AD 400. Nok craftsmen produced striking terracotta sculptures of human heads, animal figurines, fine pottery and iron artifacts, though little is known of Nok culture or social organization. ▷ 2.21

NOMADISM
Way of life typified by the lack of permanent settlement and usually cyclical movement from place to place. Hunter-gatherers are usually nomadic, but most nomads are pastoralists, moving in search of new grazing for their herds. Those who have permanent homes but leave them periodically are said to be semi-nomadic; those who move seasonally are said to practice transhumant pastoralism. Nomadism has been typical of the Eurasian steppes and of north Africa. The sudden arrival of large groups of nomads frequently caused severe alarm to more settled societies. Nomadism arose in the 8th century BC, and continued as an important force in world history until the 18th century AD. ▷ 2.20

NORICUM
A predominantly Celtic region in the eastern Alps, whose main tribe was the Taurisci. It is a fertile area with iron reserves. In the early 2nd century BC Noricum was the name of a Celtic federal state. It was incorporated into the ROMAN EMPIRE in 16 BC and became the province of Noricum. In the 5th century AD the region was occupied by Germanic peoples. ▷ 2.13

NORTHERN ZHOU
Minor dynasty based at Chang'an that ruled northern China from AD 557 until its overthrow by the SUI DYNASTY in 581. ▷ 2.25

NUMANTIA, SIEGE OF
A CELTIBERIAN walled city by the 4th century BC, Numantia was the last Celtiberian stronghold to resist Rome. After an eight-month seige, the 4,000 inhabitants surrendered in 133 BC to the Romans under SCIPIO AFRICANUS. The city was then destroyed and the survivors were sold into slavery. ▷ 2.18

NUMIDIA
Originally the country of the Numidiae, African nomads to the west and south of CARTHAGE. Numidia sided with Rome during the Third PUNIC WAR, but supported POMPEY in 47–46 BC and the indigenous dynasty was overthrown. Eastern Numidia was established as the Roman province of Africa Nova in 46 BC. The African provinces were rearranged under AUGUSTUS and again under SEPTIMIUS SEVERUS, who created the province of Numidia in AD 197–98. Numidian bears, leopards and lions were supplied for shows in Roman amphitheaters. ▷ 2.12, 2.21

OCTAVIAN
See AUGUSTUS

ODOACER
Germanic king of Italy (r.AD 476–93). As leader of the German mercenaries he deposed the last Roman emperor, ROMULUS AUGUSTULUS, in 476. He maintained the existing Roman institutions. His rule was not recognized by the eastern emperor Zeno, who, in 488 sent THEODORIC to depose him. Odoacer agreed in 493 to share his authority with Theodoric, who then assassinated him. ▷ 2.16, 2.17

OPPIDUM
A large, complex type of settlement, generally fortified, that developed across Celtic Europe in the 2nd and 1st centuries BC. They were central areas involved in long-distance trade, specialized craft production, sometimes minting of coinage, and tribal administration. JULIUS CAESAR found that each Gaulish tribe had several oppida, though not all were of equal importance. Oppida were superseded by planned Romanized towns. ▷ 2.18

OSTIA
The port of Rome, at the mouth of the Tiber river in central Italy. The earliest remains at the site date to the late 4th century BC. Most of what is visible has been dated to the 2nd and 3rd century AD. About 75 percent of the inner city was uncovered in excavations between 1938 and 1942, and the findings confirm Ostia's important role in Rome's commerce, communications and naval history. Great storehouses and port facilities were built during the empire. There were also lavish civic buildings reflecting the relative wealth of much of the population, and seaside villas along the coast. Ostia was abandoned in the 5th century AD. ▷ 2.14

OSTROGOTHS
Major group of Gothic tribes, settled in the Ukraine region in the late 4th century AD, when they were defeated by the HUNS. In the mid-5th century they were living in PANNONIA and then invaded Italy, where their king THEODORIC set up a kingdom in 493. The kingdom was destroyed by the eastern Roman emperor JUSTINIAN between 535 and 562. ▷ 2.16, 2.17, 2.19

OVID
Roman poet (43 BC–AD 17) who turned from public life to poetry, becoming the leading poet in Rome. In 8 BC Ovid was banished (for his erotic poem, The Art of Love, and an undisclosed indiscretion) to a wretched outpost of the empire – Tomis on the Black Sea – where he eventually died. His works include the Metamorphoses. ▷ 2.13

PACAL
MAYAN king of PALENQUE (r.AD 615–83), whose magnificent pyramid-tomb was excavated in 1949. It included a jade mask and breastplate.

PAGANISM
Literally, the religion of the countryside, but used by extension to describe any polytheistic

religion, including the official faiths of the Classical world, in contrast to CHRISTIANITY.

PALENQUE
Ancient MAYAN city in Chiapas, southern Mexico, that flourished in the second half of the Classic period (AD 300–800). Its monuments are among the most remarkable of the region, notably the Temple of the Inscriptions (where PACAL's tomb was found) and the Great Palace. Palenque was one of the first Mayan sites to be rediscovered (by a Spanish soldier) in 1786. ▷ 2.28

PALLAVA DYNASTY
Indian dynasty originating in the north, who established a capital at Kanchipuram (Tamil Nadu state) and came to hold sway in the south. They rose to prominence in the 4th century AD. They were defeated by the GUPTAS in about 360, but continued to rule until the late 9th century, when they fell to the Chola dynasty. At the height of their dynasty architecture flourished, notably in the temples of Mahabalipuram and Mamallapuram. ▷ 2.23

PALMYRA
Syrian trading town based on a desert oasis, Palmyra grew rich from trade between east and west during the Roman period. In the AD 260s it declared its independence, first under Odaenathus and then under his wife, ZENOBIA, but was reconquered by VALERIAN in 272. ▷ 2.14, 2.15

PAMA-NYUNGAN LANGUAGES
The main language group of the Aboriginal inhabitants of Australia, spoken throughout the continent, except the northwest. ▷ 2.26

PAMPA GRANDE
Archeological site in the Lambayeque valley of PERU to which the capital of the Mochica state was moved after MOCHE itself was abandoned in about AD 500. ▷ 2.27

PAMPHYLIA
Region of central-southern Asia Minor settled by the Greeks from the 8th century BC, but later (AD 43) linked with Lycia as a province of the ROMAN EMPIRE. It enjoyed great prosperity under Roman rule. ▷ 2.13

PANNONIA, PANNONIAE
The Pannonii were an ILLYRIAN group with Celtic influences, south and west of the Danube. From the late 2nd century BC they were in conflict with Rome, invaded Istria in 14 BC and were ruthlessly suppressed by TIBERIUS. The Roman province of Pannonia was established in AD 9. In 106 AD it was divided into Pannonia Superior and Pannonia Inferior, and further subdivided under DIOCLETIAN. In the 4th century AD Pannonia suffered BARBARIAN invasions and finally fell to Radagaisus and the OSTROGOTHS in AD 405. ▷ 2.13, 2.15, 2.18

PAPACY
See ROME, BISHOP OF

PARACAS CULTURE
A farming and fishing culture of the Early Horizon period on the south Peruvian coast (c.650–150 BC), within the area of Chavín influence. It is mostly known from Paracas tomb sites, which contain distinctive painted ceramics and mummified human remains, fine decorated textiles and other objects preserved in dry conditions.

PARNI
Ancient nomadic IRANIAN-speaking peoples from the eastern Caspian who entered the former Persian empire in the early 3rd century BC. In 238 BC they founded the semi-independent Parthian kingdom under the ARSACID dynasty and assimilated with the native Parthian peoples. ▷ 2.09, 2.10, 2.11

PARTHENON
Major temple to Athene the Maiden (Greek Parthenos) built on the Athenian Acropolis in the 430s BC and renowned for the splendor of its marble, the ingeniousness of its design (achieved through sloping its columns slightly inwards) and its sculptured reliefs. ▷ 2.07

PATALIPUTRA
Ancient city of northern India, on the site of Patna in Bihar state, founded in the 5th century BC as the capital of MAGADHA; it was also the MAURYAN capital. The city was sacked by the Bactrian Greeks in 185 BC, but revived to become the GUPTA capital in the 4th century AD. It was abandoned three centuries later but was rebuilt by the Mughals. ▷ 2.10, 2.22

PATRIARCHS
The five senior bishops of the Christian church, all of whom exercised authority over a wide area. The patriarchal sees were Rome, Constantinople, ANTIOCH, ALEXANDRIA and Jerusalem, and their pre-eminence over other bishoprics was confirmed by JUSTINIAN in the 6th century AD. ▷ 2.17

PATRICK, ST
Romano-British aristocrat and Christian evangelist (c.AD 385–461), probably born in Wales. Few firm facts are known of his life. He is said to have introduced CHRISTIANITY to Ireland after he was taken there as a young man by pirates and escaped to GAUL. He studied at a monastery in Auxerre before being sent as bishop to Ireland in 432. He made his first converts at the ancient royal center of TARA. In the mid-440s he set up the archbishopric at ARMAGH.

PAUL, ST
Major figure of the early Christian church who combined a relentless missionary zeal (which took him to Christian communities throughout the eastern Mediterranean) with

an effective theology based on faith in the risen Christ. His letters offer important insights into the early Christian communities. He probably died a martyr in Rome in about AD 65. ▷ 2.06

PAZYRYK
Archeological site on the Altai Mountains, Russia. Among its 40 burials is that of a nomadic Scythian chieftain, together with a dismantled wagon, rich grave-goods and human sacrifices, dating from about 600 BC. The goods include bronze mirrors and SILK from China. The bodies, preserved in the permafrost, display extensive tattooing. ▷ 2.20

PELOPONNESIAN WAR
Major struggle between Sparta and ATHENS, and their allies, that lasted from 431 until 404 BC, when Athens was defeated. Neither side had any effective means of destroying the other, but Athens was weakened by the massive losses of the Sicilian expedition (415–413 BC) and Sparta was strengthened by Persian support. Sparta's final naval victory at AEGOSPOTAMI (405 BC) broke Athens' link with its Black Sea grain supplies and led to its surrender. ▷ 2.08

PERGAMON
Important stronghold in western Asia Minor that became capital of the ATTALID dynasty (241–133 BC) and a showpiece of HELLENISTIC art and architecture. The city's name was extended to that of the surrounding Attalid kingdom. Attalus III bequeathed his kingdom to Rome and Pergamon remained prosperous in Roman times. ▷ 2.10, 2.13, 2.18

PERICLES
Major statesman of ATHENS in the 5th century BC (r.490–429 BC). Pericles masterminded the coming of DEMOCRACY (461 BC) and retained a leading role as one of the city's generals for 30 years. He was associated in particular with the glorification of the city, not only in his famous funeral speeches, but in buildings such as the PARTHENON. ▷ 2.07, 2.08

PERSIA, ANCIENT
Region east of the Fertile Crescent and south of the Caspian, and home of several major civilizations of the Classical world. It was named by the Greeks after the Parsua tribe of southwestern Iran, who inhabited Persis (the modern region of Fars). The Persians were descendants of Indo-Iranian nomads who had occupied the region in the 8th century BC. They conquered Babylon in 539 BC under Cyrus, founder of the Achemenid dynasty, who built an empire across the Middle East. It was overthrown by ALEXANDER THE GREAT, but a new Persian empire was built, first by the Parthians and then the SASANIANS (from AD 224). The Sasanians were defeated by the Byzantines in the 620s, and the region was overrun by the Arabs in the following decades. ▷ 2.11

PERSIAN WARS
The Persians invaded GREECE twice. The first invasion, a punitive expedition against ATHENS in 490 BC, was defeated at MARATHON. The second, in 480 BC, was an all-out attempt at conquest by XERXES, who led a massive invasion force into Greece. After initial victories and the burning of Athens, the Persians were defeated at sea at SALAMIS (480) and Mycale (479), and on land at PLATAEA (479). The victory brought a surge of self-confidence to the Greeks and above all to Athens. ▷ 2.07

PERU, ANCIENT
Center of ancient South American civilization. Peru's first cultures alternated between the desert- and river-valley-based cultures of the coastal regions and those of the Andes. The history of the region is divided into the following periods: the Initial period (1800–800 BC); the Early Horizon period (800–200 BC), dominated by the Chavín culture; the EARLY INTERMEDIATE PERIOD (200 BC–AD 500), during which the MOCHE state flourished; the MIDDLE HORIZON PERIOD (AD 500–1000), dominated by the HUARI and by TIAHUANACO; the Late Intermediate period (1000–1470), the time of Sícan and Chimú, and finally, the Late Horizon period (1470–1530), during which the Inca empire controlled Peru and much of western South America. ▷ 2.27

PETÉN
Highland and forested region of northern Guatemala, south of the Yucatán peninsula, and home of the Mayan city-states of the Classic period, such as TIKAL. It was the last part of the Maya region to be conquered by the Spaniards. ▷ 2.28

PETER, ST
Traditionally the first apostle or follower of JESUS and the founder and first bishop of the church of Rome (d.c.AD 64). A former fisher-man, he was depicted in the GOSPELS as the leader of the Twelve Disciples. After the crucifixion he emerged as the leading figure in the group of surviving followers, credited with miracles and with defending the Christian faith, though his reluctance to open the faith to non-Jews was criticized by ST PAUL. He traveled to Rome in about AD 55, where he headed the nascent church and was martyred in NERO's reign. The NEW TESTAMENT books, traditionally said to be his epistles, are widely considered not to have been written by him.

PETRA
Ancient desert city, now in Jordan, and the capital of the Nabatean kingdom from the 4th century BC until AD 106, when the Romans occupied it. Petra became a center for overland trade with the east until the Islamic period. Its tombs, with elaborate facades, are carved into the rock of a narrow gorge.

PHARISEES
The largest of the three main Jewish sects, it came to prominence in the 2nd century BC. The Pharisees sought to maintain the oral Jewish tradition, as well as placing great stress on the strict interpretation of the scriptures and the Law. The Pharisees were criticized by JESUS, but they continued to dominate Jewish thought until the destruction of the Temple in AD 70.

PHAROS LIGHTHOUSE
Famous lighthouse constructed by Sosistratos of Cnidus on the island of Pharos, off ALEXANDRIA, in about 300–280 BC. More than 100 meters (328 feet) high, it was one of the Seven Wonders of the Ancient World and survived until the 12th century AD. ▷ 2.10

PHARSALUS, BATTLE OF
The final confrontation between JULIUS CAESAR and POMPEY. Fought in 48 BC at Pharsalus in Thessaly, GREECE, Pompey was defeated and escaped to Egypt, where he was murdered. ▷ 2.13

PHEIDIAS
Greek sculptor of the second half of the 5th century BC, considered one of the greatest sculptors of the ancient world. Pheidias was responsible for the massive statues of Athena in the PARTHENON and of Zeus at Olympia. He was probably responsible for overseeing the sculptured reliefs of the Parthenon. ▷ 2.08

PHILIP II OF MACEDON
Ruler of MACEDON (r.359–336 BC) who united and expanded his kingdom to make it the dominant power in the Greek world, with control of much of northern GREECE. His secret lay in his brilliantly trained and well-led army, one of whose most crushing victories was over the Athenians and Thebans at CHAERONEA in 338 BC. Philip laid the political and military foundations for the conquests of his son, ALEXANDER. ▷ 2.08, 2.09

PHRAATES
Name given to five Parthian kings of PERSIA. Phraates I (r.c.191–176 BC) began a policy of expansion in the north. Phraates II (r.138–128 BC) definitively defeated the SELEUCIDS, but faced nomadic invasions in the east. Phraates III (r.70–57 BC) and Phraates IV (r.c.37–2 BC) intrigued with the Romans for control of Armenia. Phraates V (r.2 BC–AD 4) confirmed Roman control over that area.

PHRYGIAN LANGUAGE
Ancient language related to GREEK that (written in Greek characters) survived as one of the local languages of the ROMAN EMPIRE. ▷ 2.14

PICTS
The name Pictae or "painted people" was first used by the Romans in AD 297 for the Celtic peoples to the north of the ANTONINE WALL in Scotland. They lost their independence when they were defeated in the 9th century AD by Kenneth MacAlpin of Dalriada. ▷ 2.15

PILATE, PONTIUS
Roman governor of JUDAEA (r.AD 26–36). Appointed by TIBERIUS, his actions were frequently provocative to Jewish religious feeling, and he was dismissed for his handling of an anti-Roman demonstration in Samaria. He is best known for his ambiguous role in the crucifixion of JESUS and was venerated as a saint by the Coptic church of Egypt.

PLATAEA, BATTLE OF
The final decisive land battle of the PERSIAN WARS of 480–479 BC. After a series of maneuvers on the borders of Attica, the Persians were tempted to attack a Greek army which seemed in disarray, but which, under Spartan leadership, rallied to defeat them. The Persian commander MARDONIUS was killed. ▷ 2.07

PLATO
(c.429–347 BC) Athenian by birth, Plato was one of the great Greek philosophers. Much of his writings survive in the form of dialogues, in which a group of characters follows a discussion through to its conclusion. Plato believed that ideas such as goodness and justice existed as real – if invisible – entities, to be understood through reasoned thought on their nature. In the *Republic* he argued that effective government could be based on such understandings. Plato founded the ACADEMY, a school for philosophers which survived for centuries after his death. ▷ 2.08

PLAUTUS
Comic playwright, probably from Umbria, whose plays, written between about 250 and 184 BC, are the earliest LATIN works to have survived intact. He was strongly influenced by contemporary Greek drama. ▷ 2.13

PLOTINUS
Neoplatonist philosopher (AD 205–70) who lived and traveled in GREECE and PERSIA before settling in Rome at the age of 40 to teach philosophy. He was at the center of an intellectual circle, and from the age of 50 wrote a series of philosophical essays, the *Enneads*. ▷ 2.15

POLYCLITOS
A Greek sculptor from Argos of the late 5th century BC who believed that the parts of the human body related to each other in mathematical ratios. His sculpture of a spear holder, which survives only in copies, was supposed to provide a model of the correct proportions. ▷ 2.08

POLYNESIA
The largest of the three divisions of Oceania, in the central and southern Pacific. It consists

of the Hawaii islands, Samoa, Tonga, Tahiti and EASTER ISLAND; New Zealand is also considered part of Polynesia. Polynesia was settled from MELANESIA between 1000 BC and AD 1000. Its languages are a branch of AUSTRONESIAN. ▷ 2.26

POMPEII
The early history of settlement at this site in southern Campania is unclear. Originally an Etruscan settlement, it was occupied by the Oscan-speaking Samnites in the 5th century BC. In 80 BC Sulla imposed a colony of Roman citizens and LATIN replaced Oscan as the official language. The city flourished through the late republic and early empire, but suffered a severe earthquake in AD 62 and was destroyed by the eruption of Vesuvius in AD 79. Preserved under layers of pumice, large-scale excavations of the site after the late 1700s revealed in poignant detail evidence of Roman daily life. ▷ 2.13

POMPEY
(106–48 BC) Roman military commander and skilled politician. His greatest military achievements were his eastern campaigns (66–62 BC), in which he defeated MITHRIDATES VI, founded colonies, annexed Syria and turned JUDEA into a client kingdom. By this and other means he accrued great wealth and both official and unofficial power. He engaged in lengthy and complex rivalry against CRASSUS and JULIUS CAESAR for the leadership of Rome. He was finally defeated by Caesar in 48 BC at PHARSALUS in GREECE, and fled to Egypt, where he was murdered. ▷ 2.13

PONTUS
Mountainous region on the south edge of the Black Sea, east of BITHYNIA, with fertile valleys, fine timber and mineral reserves. Greek colonies were established on the coast, but had relatively little effect on the interior. The kingdom of Pontus reached its largest extent under MITHRIDATES VI, who challenged Roman power in Asia Minor. In 63 BC POMPEY organized Pontus as a province, but it drifted out of Roman control under MARK ANTONY and was gradually brought back into the empire under AUGUSTUS. ▷ 2.10, 2.13

POSTUMUS
Roman general responsible for guarding the Rhine from BARBARIAN attacks, who seized power for himself in AD 260 and established a GALLIC EMPIRE, which at its height controlled GAUL, Britain and Spain. He was killed in 269 and his territory was regained for the ROMAN empire in 274. ▷ 2.15

POTEIDAIA
One of the most important of the colonies of Corinth established in about 600 BC to exploit trade with MACEDONIA. It became an uneasy subject of the Athenian empire and the help that was given by Sparta, in support of Corinth when Poteidaia revolted from ATHENS in 432, was one of the factors leading to the PELOPONNESIAN WAR. ▷ 2.08

PRAXITELES
Influential Athenian sculptor of the mid-4th century BC whose masterpiece, a statue of the goddess Aphrodite, broke with convention by its show of nudity. Rejected by the more conservative cities of GREECE, it was displayed in a circular shrine in the city of Cnidus. ▷ 2.08

PROCOPIUS
(c.AD 499–566) Important historian who was responsible for a detailed history of the campaigns of JUSTINIAN in Africa and Italy. He also completed a notorious "secret history" of Justinian's reign, and a study of the emperor's building projects. ▷ 2.17

PTOLEMAIC EGYPT
From 305 BC until its annexation by Rome in 30 BC, Egypt was ruled by the Greek Ptolemaic dynasty. Their capital at ALEXANDRIA was maintained separately from the rest of Egypt, though there were Greek enclaves along the Nile. The country was heavily exploited to sustain the high living and cultural interests of the Ptolemies. At their peak in the 3rd century BC the Ptolemies dominated the eastern Mediterranean, but after 168 BC they relied increasingly on Roman support. The last Ptolemy, CLEOPATRA, was reduced to manipulating her lovers, JULIUS CAESAR and MARK ANTONY, in the vain hope of keeping her country independent. ▷ 2.09, 2.10

PTOLEMY, CLAUDIUS
Alexandrian astronomer, geographer and mathematician of the mid-2nd century AD. His *Almagest* brought together the findings of earlier astronomers, notably HIPPARCHOS, and consolidated and extended them to form a coherent astronomical system that was to remain influential for more than 1,000 years. ▷ 2.15

PTOLEMY I
General of ALEXANDER THE GREAT who on Alexander's death seized the Egyptian part of his empire and declared himself king (r.305–284 BC). He set up his capital at ALEXANDRIA and successfully established a GREEK-speaking administration, though it was heavily exploitative of the native peoples. He also annexed Cyprus and some Aegean islands. ▷ 2.09, 2.10

PTOLEMY IV
Ruler of Egypt from 244 to 205 BC. During his reign PTOLEMAIC control of Egypt began to disintegrate, with THEBES coming to enjoy virtual independence. Ptolemy was eventually murdered by his courtiers and the loss of Ptolemaic possessions in the Aegean followed soon afterwards. ▷ 2.10

PUNIC WARS
Fought between 264 and 146 BC, the Punic wars ended with the defeat of the CARTHAGINIAN empire by Rome. "Punic" derived from "Poeni", the Roman name for the Carthaginians. The First Punic War (264–41) erupted after Rome became ruler of Magna Graecia (a Greek territory in southern Italy and Sicily), where Carthage also had territory; the action was mostly confined to Sicily. In 241 an exhausted Carthage made peace with Rome, losing its territories in Sicily, Corsica and Sardinia.

In 219 HANNIBAL took SAGUNTUM in Spain, provoking the Second Punic War (218–201 BC), famous for the campaigns of Hannibal and SCIPIO AFRICANUS. After Hannibal's victory at CANNAE (216), much of southern Italy rebelled against Rome. He remained invincible but failed to widen the area of revolt sufficiently. With the other armies occupied in Spain and north Africa, Carthage could not supply him with enough reinforcements. Scipio Africanus eventually took the war to north Africa, won over the Numidian princes and defeated Hannibal at Zama in 202 BC. Carthage sued for peace once more, losing its empire in Spain. Rome still saw Carthage as a threat and initiated the Third Punic War (149–146 BC), which ended in a Roman victory, the destruction of the city and the enslavement of its people. Carthage's territory became the Roman province of Africa. ▷ 2.10, 2.12, 2.13, 2.21

PUSHYAMITRA SHUNGA
Indian ruler, a soldier who assasinated the last MAURYAN king of MAGAHDA in 185 BC and founded the SUNGA dynasty. ▷ 2.22

PYDNA, BATTLE OF
Decisive battle (168 BC) between the Romans and Perseus of MACEDONIA (son of Philip V) in northwest GREECE. The Macedonians were heavily defeated and their country was divided into four republics (in 148 BC it was annexed as a province), which represented a turning point in the Roman annexation of Greece. ▷ 2.10, 2.13

PYRRHUS
Ambitious king of Epirus (r.297–272 BC) who restored the strength of his kingdom and is remembered for his campaigns against the Romans (280–275 BC) in support of the Greek colonies in Italy. He won several battles, but his losses were so great that the term "Pyrrhic victory" was coined to describe them. He eventually withdrew to GREECE, but died on campaign in the Peloponnese. ▷ 2.12

PYTHEAS OF MASSILIA
Greek navigator of the late 4th century BC whose most famous voyage took him through the Straits of Gibraltar to explore the coasts of western Europe, circumnavigating Britain, perhaps reaching Norway and sailing into Arctic waters. ▷ 2.09, 2.19

PYU

Ancient Tibeto-Burmese peoples of the Irrawaddy valley of Burma, who dominated the region from the 3rd century BC. By the early centuries AD they had come into contact with Indian and Chinese culture and were followers of THERAVADA BUDDHISM. They controlled some 20 small kingdoms in southern Burma. Their chief city, Sri Ksetra, was abandoned in the 6th century, and they were overrun by the Burmese in the 9th century AD. ▷ 2.26

QATABAN

Ancient kingdom of the southern Arabian peninsula that flourished in the second half of the 1st millennium BC, one of the so-called "incense kingdoms", which relied on trade in aromatic gums for their prosperity. Its capital was at Miswah. Qataban was gradually superseded by the HIMYARITE KINGDOM, and was finally conquered in the 1st century AD. ▷ 2.01, 2.02

QIN DYNASTY

Dynasty that ruled China between 221 and 206 BC, traditionally considered the first to unite the country, and from which China derives its name. The Qin originated in the west of the country, but in the late 4th and 3rd centuries BC conquered the competing kingdoms. Zheng (r.246–210 BC) completed the unification of the country and took the title SHI HUANGDI, the "First Emperor". Under his rule from the capital at XIANYANG (near Xi'an in modern Shaanxi province), an administrative centralization was carried out and he sought to obliterate many traces of the past. He also built a series of border ramparts to resist nomad attack from the north. These are generally seen as the origins of the later Great Wall. Soon after his death civil war destroyed the dynasty. ▷ 2.24

QUIRIGUA

Classic period Mayan city in the southern area, now in Honduras. It has notable carved *stelae* (stone monuments), including the largest monolithic monument of the MAYA, the portrait of an unidentified ruler. Quirigua challenged the power of the nearby COPÁN in the 8th century BC. ▷ 2.28

QUMRAN

Ancient village near the Dead Sea, in the modern West Bank. From the 2nd century BC it was home to an ESSENE community and was destroyed several times by the Romans, prior to its abandonment in AD 68. It was here that the DEAD SEA SCROLLS were discovered in 1947.

RAETIA (RHAETIA)

Roman province in Europe, now southwest Germany, Austria and Switzerland. It was conquered by Rome in 15 BC and was the hub of strategic communications routes to the north and east. ▷ 2.13

RAMAYANA

Classical Indian epic composed in SANSKRIT in the 3rd century BC, from earlier legends and Vedic sacred material. Said to be the work of a single author – the poet Valmiki – it contains up to 40,000 couplets and tells the story of Rama and the princess Sita, who eventually gain the throne of Ayodhya. Like the MAHABHARATA, the Ramayana has been immensely influential in Indian culture. ▷ 2.23

RAVENNA

City on the Adriatic (northern Italy) chosen as a capital of the western ROMAN EMPIRE by HONORIUS in AD 402, because of its good sea communications with Constantinople and easily defendable position in marshland. ODOACER and the Ostrogothic king THEODORIC also made it their capital (late 5th century). Rivalry between Arian OSTROGOTHS and native Latin Christians led to the building of its magnificent churches and their mosaics. Ravenna was retaken by JUSTINIAN's general, BELISARIUS, in 540. ▷ 2.16, 2.17

RECUAY CULTURE

Ancient culture of northern highland PERU that flourished in the EARLY INTERMEDIATE PERIOD (200 BC–AD 500). It is typified by distinctive resist-painted ceramics. Recuay inherited much of the dominance of Chavín, and influenced the contemporary MOCHE culture on the coast. ▷ 2.27

REMOJADAS

Classic period civilization of the VERACRUZ lowlands of the Gulf Coast of Mexico that flourished from AD 1 to 700. Distinctive clay models – including "laughing figures" – and larger sculptures have been found in its burial mounds. They reveal the influence of both the MAYAN and TEOTIHUACÁN cultures. ▷ 2.27

RHAPTA

Ancient trading port in east Africa, possibly in the Rufiji delta or Zanzibar channel, that is mentioned by Greco-Roman writers of the early centuries AD. It exported ivory, tortoise-shell and coconut oil, and imported weapons and iron tools from the Mediterranean. ▷ 2.21

ROMAN EMPIRE

From 27 BC Rome and its territories were ruled by a series of emperors, beginning with AUGUSTUS. By the 2nd century AD the empire covered about 13 million square kilometers (5 million square miles), with an estimated population of 55 million. Rome's main aims were to maintain peace within the empire and to extract money and other resources, mostly through taxation. The empire was administered as a series of provinces. Local elites became increasingly important and were given various administrative posts: by the 3rd century AD they had become highly Romanized. In the 3rd and 4th centuries the empire declined through internal conflict and external threat, the latter coming especially from the Germanic peoples, including the VISIGOTHS, FRANKS, VANDALS and OSTROGOTHS. From the late 3rd century it became usual for the eastern and western halves of the empire to be ruled separately. The western empire was occupied by Germanic peoples in the 5th century. The eastern empire survived and was gradually transformed into the medieval Byzantine empire. ▷ 2.13, 2.14, 2.16, 2.19

BISHOPS OF ROME TO AD 600

Peter	to c.64	Fabian	236–50	Celestine I	422–32
Linus	c.67–76/79	Cornelius	251–53	Sixtus III	432–40
Anacletus	76–88 or 79–91	Lucius I	253–54	Leo I	440–61
		Stephen I	254–57	Hilary	461–68
Clement I	88–97 or 92–101	Sixtus II	257–58	Simplicius	468–83
		Dionysius	259–68	Felix II	483–92
Evaristus	c.97–c.107	Felix I	274	Gelasius I	492–96
Alexander I	105–15 or 109–19	Eutychian	275–83	Anastasius II	496–98
		Gaius	283–96	Symmachus	498–514
Sixtus I	c.115–c.125	Marcellinus	291/296–304	Hormisdas	514–23
Telesphorus	c.125–c.136	Marcellus I	308–09	John I	523–26
Hyginus	c.136–c.140	Eusebius	309/310	Felix III	526–30
Pius I	c.140–55	Miltiades	311–14	Boniface II	530–32
Anicetus	c.155–c.166	Sylvester I	314–35	John II	533–35
Soter	c.166–c.175	Mark	336	Agapetus I	535–36
Eleutherius	c.175–89	Julius I	337–52	Silverius	536–37
Victor I	c.189–99	Liberius	352–66	Vigilius	537–55
Zephyrinus	c.199–217	Damasus I	366–84	Pelagius I	556–61
Calixtus I (Callistus)	217–22	Siricius	384–99	John III	561–74
		Anastasius I	399–401	Benedict I	575–79
Urban I	222–30	Innocent I	401–17	Pelagius II	579–90
Pontian	230–35	Zosimus	417–18	Gregory I	590–604
Anterus	235–36	Boniface I	418–22		

ROMAN REPUBLIC
The period in Rome's history between 509 BC, when the ruling Tarquinian dynasty was expelled, and the beginning of the ROMAN EMPIRE under AUGUSTUS in 27 BC. Republican Rome was governed by officials called magistrates (consuls, censors, etc.), who were elected by the Roman people, and the Senate, an assembly of ex-magistrates. The republic saw the dramatic expansion of Rome's territories both in and beyond Italy, and the successful waging of war against various powerful opponents, notably the Samnites, GAULS and CARTHAGINIANS. The later republic was a time of political corruption and power struggles between the leading generals and families, and growing popular discontent. The republic finally collapsed into civil war and was replaced by the monarchical government of AUGUSTUS in 27 BC. ▷ 2.12

ROMANCE LANGUAGES
A group of related European languages descended from LATIN, including French, Italian, Spanish, Catalan, Portuguese and Romanian. In the regions where these are spoken, the language developed from the vernacular Latin during the ROMAN EMPIRE and was influenced, but not destroyed, by the languages of the invading Germanic peoples.

ROME, BISHOP OF
By tradition (though not accepted beyond the Roman Catholic church) the head of the Christian church, also known as the pope. The first bishop of Rome, from AD 55, was ST PETER. The primacy of the bishopric is based on Christ's appointment of him as the foundation of the church. The position rose to prominence during the period of BARBARIAN invasion, when it preserved the tradition of Roman imperialism and civilization.

ROME, SACKS OF
Rome was first sacked by the GAULS in 390 BC: a Roman garrison held out on the Capitoline Hill and the Gauls were persuaded to leave by a payment of tribute. The most famous sack of Rome took place in AD 410, after the Romans refused to make concessions to the Visigothic leader, ALARIC. Rome was not seriously damaged, and though by this time it was no longer capital of the empire, it was a serious blow to Roman prestige. Rome was sacked a third time by the VANDALS in 455, after a marriage treaty involving the Vandal king Gaiseric's son had been broken by Rome. The seizure of Sicily, Rome's oldest province, by the Vandals soon followed. ▷ 2.12, 2.16, 2.18

ROMULUS
See AUGUSTULUS, ROMULUS

ROSETTA STONE
Granite stone discovered at Rosetta in 1799 that contains a PTOLEMAIC decree (of 196 BC) in three scripts – hieroglyphic, DEMOTIC and GREEK. The Rosetta Stone provided vital clues in the decipherment of hieroglyphics by the French scholar Champollion in 1822.

ROYAL ROAD
Road from the Achemenid winter capital of Susa to Sardis in Lydia. It covered some 2,200 kilometers (1,500 miles) and 111 relay stations along the route provided couriers with overnight accommodation and fresh horses. The journey took three months on foot, but the fastest couriers could cover it in a week.

SACBE
Mesoamerican causeway, named after the Mayan word for "white road". Typically up to 1 meter (3 feet) high and 5 meters (16 feet) wide, they are made of stone plastered with lime; some run up to 100 kilometers (60 miles). Many *sacbes* have been found around COBÁ. ▷ 2.28

SADDUCEES
One of the main strands of Jewish thought of the early 2nd century BC. Unlike the PHARISEES, the Sadducees accepted only the scriptures as a source of authority, and were monastic and conservative in their approach. They died out after the destruction of the Temple at Jerusalem in AD 70.

SAGUNTUM
North of modern Valencia, Spain, this was a citadel of the Edetai, who were allied to Rome. HANNIBAL beseiged Saguntum, thereby precipitating the Second PUNIC WAR. Captured by the Romans by 212 BC, the city became a Roman *municipium* (township) by the Augustan period. It survived until the mid-5th century AD, as attested by finds from its harbor of Grau Vell. ▷ 2.12

SALAMIS, BATTLE OF
Crucial naval battle between the Greek (predominantly Athenian) and Persian navies during the Persian invasion of GREECE in 480. Desperate after the sacking of ATHENS, the Greeks lured the Persian fleet into the channel between the island of Salamis and the mainland, and inflicted heavy casualties. Their victory prevented Persian forces from invading the Peloponnese and completing the conquest of Greece. ▷ 2.07

SAMNITE WARS
Series of wars fought between Rome and the powerful Samnites for control of central Italy. The First Samnite War (343–341 BC) gave Rome control of Campania. The Second Samnite War (327–304 BC) saw the Romans defeated at CAUDINE FORKS (321), but the Samnites could not follow up their victory. The Third Samnite War (298–290 BC) drew in the GAULS, Umbrians and Etruscans against Rome. The Romans defeated this coalition at Sentinum in 295 and had conquered most of peninsular Italy by 290. The Samnites were forced to become Roman "allies". ▷ 2.12

SAMUDRAGUPTA
Indian emperor of the GUPTA dynasty (r.AD 335–80). He consolidated the Gupta empire and then, building from his base near Delhi, extended it in the west by defeating the KUSHANS, as well as extending southward. He is said to have defeated or killed more than 20 other monarchs. His reign is considered a high point in Hindu Indian culture and society, and he is personally remembered as a poet and musician. ▷ 2.23

SANSKRIT
The classical literary language of India, still used for sacred or learned purposes. Vedic Sanskrit, one of the oldest surviving Indo-European languages, was used from about 1500 BC to 200 BC; classical Sanskrit was used from about 500 BC, developed first as a court language, then adapted for literary and religious purposes.

SASAN
Persian ruler of the 2nd century AD who gave his named to the SASANIAN DYNASTY founded by his grandson ARDASHIR I. Little is known about his life, but he was probably a prince in Persis (modern Fars). ▷ 2.11

SASANIAN DYNASTY
Dynasty ruling PERSIA, founded in AD 224 by ARDASHIR I, and destroyed by the Arab invasions of the 630s. The capital was at CTESIPHON. Under the Sasanians, Persia reached the peak of its ancient glory, rivaling that of Rome; they revived Achemenid traditions and made ZOROASTRIANISM their state religion. Notable monarchs include SHAPUR I (r.240–72), SHAPUR II (r.309–79), KHOSRU I (r.531–79) and KHOSRU II (r.591–628). ▷ 2.11

SATAVAHANIHARA
Ancient kingdom of western and central India from the 1st century BC to the 3rd century AD, with its capital at Pratisthana. It was the first state of the Deccan to build an empire in the south. Its greatest ruler was Gautamiputra (r.AD 106–30). ▷ 2.22, 2.23

SATRAPY
Unit of provincial government of Achemenid PERSIA, created by DARIUS I. The satrap was a royal appointee.

SAXON SHORE
Military command consisting of a chain of ten late Roman forts in southeast Britain, built to defend the province against Germanic pirates. The command also covered two other forts on the coast of GAUL. ▷ 2.15

SCIPIO AFRICANUS
(236–185 BC) Roman general who played a key role in the Second PUNIC WAR (218–01 BC) against CARTHAGE. After conquering Carthaginian Spain he took the battle to north Africa, won over the Numidian princes and defeated HANNIBAL at Zama in 202 BC. His

EMPERORS OF ROME

JULIO-CLAUDIAN DYNASTY

Augustus	27 BC–AD 14
Tiberius	14–37
Gaius (Caligula)	37–41
Claudius	41–54
Nero	54–68
Galba	68–69
Otho, Vitellius	69

FLAVIAN, NERVO-TRAJANIC AND ANTONINE DYNASTIES

Vespasian	69–79
Titus	79–81
Domitian	82–96
Nerva	96–98
Trajan (**97–98** with Nerva)	97–117
Hadrian	117–38
Antoninus Pius	138–61
Marcus Aurelius	161–80
(**161–69** with Lucius Verus)	
Commodus	180–92

SEVERAN DYNASTY

Pertinax	193
Didius Julianus	193
Septimius Severus	193–211
Caracalla (**211–12** with Geta)	211–17
Macrinus	217–18
Elagabalus	218–22
Alexander Severus	222–35

PERIOD OF POLITICAL ANARCHY AND DISORDER

The many usurpers are not listed

Maximinus	235–38
Gordian I and II (in Africa)	238
Balbinus and Pupienus (in Italy)	238
Gordian III	238–44
Philip	244–49
Decius	249–51
Trebonianus Gallus	251–53
Aemilianus	253
Valerian	253–60
Gallienus	253–68
(**253–60** with Valerian)	
Claudius II	268–70
Quintillus	270
Aurelian	270–75
Tacitus	275–76
Probus	276–82
Carus	282–83
Carinus and Numerian	283–84

DIVISION OF THE EMPIRE

Diocletian (sole ruler) **284–87**

West		East	
Maximian	287–305	Diocletian	284–305
Constantius	305–06	Galerius	305–11
Severus	306–07	Maximinus	309–13
Maxentius	306–12		
Constantine	306–24	Licinius Augustus	308–24
Constantine (sole ruler) **324–37**			
Constantine II	337–40	Constantius II	337–61
Constans	340–50		
Magnentius (usurper)	350–53		
Gallus Caesar	355–61		
Julian Caesar	355–61		
Julian (sole ruler) **361–63**			
Jovian (sole ruler) **363–64**			
Valentinian	364–65	Valens	364–78
Gratian	375–83	Theodosius	379–95
Theodosius (sole ruler) **394–95**			
Valentinian II (Italy, Illyricum)	375–92		
Maximus (usurper)	383–88		
Eugenius (usurper)	392–94		
Honorius	395–423	Arcadius	395–408
Constantius III	421	Theodosius II	408–50
Iohannes (usurper)	423–25		
Valentinian III	425–55	Marcian	450–57
Petronius Maximus	455		
Avitus	455–56	Leo	457–74
Majorian	457–61		
Libius Severus	461–65		
Anthemius	476–72		
Olybrius	472		
Glycerius	473		
Julius Nepos	473–75	Zeno	474–91
Romulus Augustulus	475–76		
		Anastasius	491–518
		Justin	518–27
		Justinian	527–65
		Justin II	565–78
		Tiberius II Constantine	578–82
		Maurice	582–602
		Phocas	602–10
		Heraclius	610–41

success bred enmity, however, and in 184 he faced accusations of embezzlement and bribe-taking in Asia. He avoided trial by going into voluntary exile in Campania, where he died in 183 BC. ▷ 2.12

SEGESTA

Native city of the Elymi in western Sicily. It agreed to support the Athenian invasion of Sicily in 415 BC, in the hope of strengthening itself against its rival, the Greek city of Selinus. Soon afterwards, however, the CARTHAGINIANS sacked Selinus, but the Segestans had to pay the price of coming under Carthaginian control themselves (409 BC). ▷ 2.08

SELEUCID KINGDOM

Kingdom carved by SELEUCOS I from the Asian possessions left by ALEXANDER THE GREAT. It originally stretched from the west coast of Asia Minor to the borders of India. A mass of different peoples and cultures, its history, perhaps inevitably, was one of gradual disintegration. Its last territory, Syria, and capital, ANTIOCH, succumbed to Rome in 64 BC. ▷ 2.09, 2.10, 2.11

SELEUCOS I

The founding king (r.312–281 BC) of the SELEUCID KINGDOM. Using Babylonia as a base, Seleucos gradually fought his way to control much of Asia, fighting against or making coalitions with rival successors to ALEXANDER's empire as occasion demanded. He founded Seleucia-on-the-Tigris, his first capital, and ANTIOCH, his western capital (300 BC). ▷ 2.09, 2.10

SENTINUM, BATTLE OF

See SAMNITE WARS

SEVERAN DYNASTY

Dynasty composed of the five Roman emperors, SEPTIMIUS SEVERUS (r.AD 193–211), CARACALLA (r.211–17), Macrinus (218), Elagabalus (r.218–22) and Alexander Severus (r.222–35). ▷ 2.15

SEVERUS, SEPTIMIUS

Proclaimed emperor of Rome in PANNONIA in AD 193, following the murder of Helvius Pertinax, he then marched on Italy to remove Didius Julianus. Severus then defeated Pescennius Niger, who had been proclaimed emperor in Syria. He campaigned successfully in Parthia, Africa and, with his son CARACALLA, in northern Britain. He died of gout at York in AD 211. ▷ 2.15

SHABAKA

King of Kush (r.712–698 BC) who conquered the whole of Egypt and made his capital at THEBES. He adopted the traditional style of the king of Egypt, setting up the 25th Dynasty of Egypt and initiating the Late period of Egyptian civilization. ▷ 2.21

SHANG YANG

The Wei-born prime minister of the QIN state in western China (d.338 BC), responsible for replacing an ancient aristocratic society with a centralized, militaristic state. In doing so, he laid the foundations for the future dominance of Qin, and of the forms of imperial government in China. ▷ 2.24

SHAPUR I

SASANIAN king of PERSIA (r.AD 240–72), the son of ARDASHIR I. He consolidated Sasanian power in Armenia and Mesopotamia, and in 260 defeated and captured the Roman emperor VALERIAN at EDESSA – an event celebrated in rock carvings throughout the empire. He supported the teachings of MANI. ▷ 2.11

SHAPUR II

SASANIAN king of PERSIA (r.AD 309–79). He came to the throne as an infant and, after assuming his full royal power at the age of 16, campaigned successfully in central Asia, taking Sasanian cultural influence as far as China. He campaigned against the Romans, but almost lost CTESIPHON to JULIAN in 363. He recovered Armenia and initially persecuted the Christian community there to force it to convert to ZOROASTRIANISM, though he later tolerated CHRISTIANITY. ▷ 2.11

SHI HUANGDI (FIRST EMPEROR)

The "First Emperor" of China (r.221–210 BC), formerly known as king Zheng of QIN (r.246–221). By defeating the states of Chu and Qi in 221 and 223, he unified the country for the first time. Establishing a centralized, bureaucratic empire, he laid the foundations for the Chinese empire, even though his dynasty did not long survive his death. He created a single Chinese script and system of weights and measures, and improved the communications systems. He also burned the works of many earlier scholars, including Confucius. His tomb at XIANYANG, near Xi'an in modern Shaanxi province, was discovered in 1974, guarded by a unique "terracotta army" of 6,000 life-sized soldiers, as well as hundreds of sacrificed horses and elaborate grave goods. ▷ 2.02, 2.24

SHU

Kingdom in the Sichuan basin of western China following the fall of the HAN in the AD 220s, with its capital at CHENGDU. It was conquered by Wei in 263. ▷ 2.24, 2.25

SHUNGA DYNASTY

Dynasty ruling the northern Indian kingdom of MAGADHA from 185 to 73 BC, founded by PUSHYAMITRA SHUNGA. ▷ 2.22

SILK

Fiber produced in the cocoons of moth caterpillars (silkworms). The manufacture of silk textiles, which began in China by 3000 BC (and remained a Chinese secret until AD 550), involved the care of silkworms and the cultivation of their food source, mulberry trees. The light, lustrous fabric was highly valued in antiquity. The silk trade began in the 1st millennium BC by caravan along the trans-Eurasian "Silk Route" from China, through the Gobi region, across the Pamir mountains into central Asia, and from there to the Middle East.

SIMA QIAN

Chinese scholar (c.145–85 BC) known as the "father of Chinese history", who was also the chief astronomer and expert of the calendar at the court of the HAN emperor, Wu. He developed his father's project of writing a definitive history of the whole of China, despite three years of imprisonment and castration for offending the emperor. His completed work, *Shih Chi*, ran to 130 chapters and included annals and genealogies of China's early kingdoms. ▷ 2.24

SKANDAGUPTA

The last king of the GUPTA dynasty of India (r.c.AD 455–67) to assert the power of the dynasty. His main achievement was the defeat of the EPHTHALITE HUNS in about 460. ▷ 2.23

SLAVIC (SLAVONIC) LANGUAGES

Part of the Indo-European group of languages, which includes Russian, Ukrainian and Belorussian (East Slavic); Polish, Czech and Slovak (West Slavic), and Serbo-Croat, Macedonian, Croatian, Slovenian and Bulgarian (South Slavic). Its common ancestral form, known as Proto-Slavic, was widely used in the 1st century BC, but the individual Slavic languages emerged during the 1st millennium AD. ▷ 2.19

SLAVS

A linguistic group that emerged as settled farmers in eastern Europe and the Balkans by the 5th century AD. The Slavs have little ethnic unity. In the Middle Ages a Slavic empire was built up in Moravia. ▷ 2.19

SOCIAL WAR

The Social or Italic War (91–87 BC) was fought between Rome and the *socii* – Rome's allies in Italy. The system of alliance devised by Rome was clever – the native communities were theoretically independent, but in practice merely subjects who supplied troops for Roman campaigns. The system became increasingly exploitive and the *socii* rose against Rome when denied citizenship. Rome was only able to defeat the rebellion by granting citizenship to those *socii* who returned to their allegiance. ▷ 2.13

SOCRATES

Athenian philosopher (469–399 BC), one of the most influential and perplexing figures of antiquity. Socrates devoted himself to finding the nature of goodness, which he believed provided the key to happiness. He unsettled many through his continuous questioning of conventional wisdom, and his proclamation that it was the wise man who understood that he knew nothing. Eventually put to death for corrupting the young, he was a hero to PLATO, who reproduced or developed many of the teachings of Socrates in his own work. ▷ 2.08

SOISSONS, BATTLE OF
Important battle (AD 486) in the rise to power of CLOVIS, king of the FRANKS. Clovis defeated Syagrius, one of the last Roman generals to hold power in the disintegrating empire, and was then free to overawe the less powerful chieftains of GAUL, thus achieving a unified Frankish kingdom. ▷ 2.17

SOPHOCLES
Important Athenian tragic dramatist who was active from 468 to 406 BC. Sophocles is remembered for the intensity of his tragedies, in which flawed personalities are confronted by appalling choices. He was the first dramatist to portray women (Antigone, Electra) trapped within their emotions and instincts, though his most celebrated character was a king, Oedipus, who gouged out his eyes after he learned that he had murdered his father and married his mother. ▷ 2.08

SPARTAN LEAGUE
A loose organization of Sparta and its allies formed in the late 6th century BC. Members followed a common foreign policy, though Sparta was the dominant member throughout, and the league's power collapsed as Sparta's did. It was dissolved in 366 BC. ▷ 2.07

SPHAKTERIA, BATTLE OF
Climax of Athenian success in the PELOPONNESIAN WAR of 425 BC, when a Spartan force on the island of Sphacteria was forced into surrender. Sparta was so humiliated that it eventually sought peace (421 BC), though the war resumed in 418 BC. ▷ 2.08

STEPPE NOMADS
Collective term for the peoples who inhabited the steppes of Eurasia from Classical times, made up mainly of loose confederations of tribes which could build and usurp huge empires very quickly, and which periodically threatened settled civilizations from Rome to China. The steppe nomads relied on herds of horses and lost their effectiveness when they were unable to find sufficient grazing for them. There were three main groups of Eurasian nomads: the IRANIAN-speaking (including the Scythians, Sarmatians and Kushans); the TURKIC-speaking (including the HUNS) and MONGOLIAN-speaking (including the JUAN-JUAN). ▷ 2.20

STILICHO
Half-German generalissimo and effectively ruler of the western ROMAN EMPIRE during the infancy of the emperor HONORIUS (from AD 395). Stilicho attempted, without much success, to quell a mass of BARBARIAN invaders. He was eventually charged with treason and executed in 408 by Honorius' advisers. ▷ 2.16

STIRRUP
Foot support for the rider of a horse. Stirrups gave a rider greater balance, and made it possible to fight effectively from the saddle. The use of stirrups was probably pioneered by STEPPE NOMADS in the early centuries BC, though there is a suggestion that stirrups may have existed in Assyria in 850 BC. The first stirrups were seen in India before 100 BC. They were not known in China until the 5th century AD, the same time they were introduced into Europe by the HUNS. The adoption of stirrups allowed the development of the knight fighting from horseback in medieval Europe, a change that was pioneered by Charles Martel in the Frankish kingdom in the 730s.

STOICS
Group of philosophers whose discussions (led by ZENO of Citium) took place in a stoa at ATHENS from 313 BC. The Stoics believed in one united world order moving onwards to an unknown purpose. Human beings had to learn how to understand and accept their own role within this order, having the freedom to live a good life, but always subject to greater powers. The Romans, and later the Christians, found Stoicism appealing. ▷ 2.09

STUPA
A decorated hemispherical stone mound surrounded by a paved walkway, distinctive of BUDDHISM, and built to house relics. The first *stupas* were built in northern India from the 3rd century BC, and represented the first form of religious architecture in the subcontinent. The form spread throughout the Buddhist world (in China and Japan it was modified into the pagoda form). The terraced temple of Borobudur in Java is also based on the *stupa* form. ▷ 2.06

SUEVI
Group of Germanic peoples that included the ALEMANNI, the MARCOMANNI and the LOMBARDS. In the 1st century AD they inhabited the east Elbe region, but invaded the ROMAN EMPIRE in the early 5th century. By 450 the Suevi controlled much of the Iberian peninsula, before being ousted by the VISIGOTHS. ▷ 2.16, 2.17, 2.19

SUI DYNASTY
Chinese dynasty (AD 589–618) founded by SUI WENDI, who unified China and introduced new bureaucratic controls to ensure the country's prosperity. His son Yang (r.604–18) continued to build the prestige of his father's empire, beginning the Grand Canal and the rebuilding of the Great Wall.

He campaigned in Korea in the 610s, but a popular revolt forced him to abdicate and the Tang dynasty was set up. ▷ 2.25

SUI WENDI (YANG JIAN)
Emperor of China (r.AD 589–618) and founder of the SUI DYNASTY. A soldier, he married a princess of the NORTHERN ZHOU and then overthrew the dynasty in 581. He campaigned against the Chen in the south, unifying the country for the first time in 350 years. He also campaigned effectively in Turkestan and Mongolia, and attempted to extend the power of China to the south. From 601 he became increasingly absorbed in public Buddhist observances, following the model of ASHOKA. ▷ 2.25

SUN TZU
Chinese writer (c.500 BC) whose volume, *The Art of War*, was the first major Chinese work on strategy. He emphasized the importance of political considerations to the military strategist and his work profoundly influenced later Chinese military thinking.

SUREN
Ancient kingdom of eastern Iran, Afghanistan and the Indus valley established by the Parthian Suren family in the 1st century BC, but conquered by the KUSHANS in about AD 50. ▷ 2.10, 2.11

SUTTON HOO
Aristocratic, pagan ANGLO-SAXON cemetery in Suffolk, England, dating from the late 6th to late 7th centuries AD. It is best known for its royal burial of a clinker-built ship, complete with opulent grave goods drawn from many parts of the then-known world. Other ships and aristocratic burials have since been discovered on the site, but none of such opulence.

SYPHAX
Numidian leader of the late 3rd century BC who tried to exploit the rivalry of the Romans and Carthaginians to his advantage. He was eventually defeated by the Romans after he allied with the Carthaginians, and died in Italy in 201 BC. ▷ 2.12

TABGATCH
See TOBA

TACITUS
Roman historian, born in about AD 56 in GAUL. He moved to Rome by AD 75 and held some political offices there, but was mainly occupied with writing. His works include *Agricola* (AD 98), a biography of Agricola (his father-in-law and governor of Britain for seven years), and the *Germania* (AD 98), a description of the Germanic tribes. The surviving books of his *Histories* (c.AD 109–10) and *Annals* (c.AD 120) record the events of AD 69–70 and the reigns of TIBERIUS, GAIUS (Caligula), CLAUDIUS and NERO. ▷ 2.13

TARA
Located in County Meath, Ireland, Tara was the original residence of the high kings of Ireland. There are many archeological remains of the early historic period – mainly forts and burial mounds. The site was most important as a political center from the 3rd to the 6th centuries AD. ▷ 2.18

TARRACONENSIS
The largest early imperial province in Spain, originally the province of HISPANIA Citerior (197 BC), renowned for its fine wine, fish sauce and silver mines. It was taken by the VISIGOTHS in about AD 475. ▷ 2.13

TARUGA
Early Iron Age site of the NOK CULTURE in the Benue region, Nigeria, with evidence of iron metallurgy (smelting furnaces) dating to the 5th century BC, and possibly as early as 800 BC. ▷ 2.21

TAXILA
City in the upper Indus valley, north Pakistan, and the capital of GANDHARA. It was conquered by the Persians in about 500 BC, when the region became the easternmost province of the Achemenid empire. The irregular layout of the site suggests that it was not a planned settlement, but expanded as its commercial importance increased on the strategic caravan route between India and Iran, via the Khyber Pass. ▷ 2.10, 2.22

TEN THOUSAND
Greek mercenary force raised by the Spartan commander Lysander, in support of a rebellion by the Persian, Cyrus, against his brother the king (401 BC). The rebellion was a failure but the ensuing Greek retreat of the "Ten Thousand" was immortalized by the historian XENOPHON. ▷ 2.08

TEOTIHUACÁN
Ancient city of Mesoamerica, close to modern Mexico City. First occupied in about 200 BC, by AD 500 it had became one of the world's largest cities, with a cultural and economic influence that was felt deep into the Maya region. Laid out on a strict grid, its monuments include the vast Pyramids of the Sun and Moon, as well as hundreds of other temples. There are no written records of its civilization, but its gods were worshiped by later Mesoamerican cultures, including the Toltecs and Aztecs. The city was sacked in about 700 and was excavated during the 1960s. ▷ 2.27, 2.28

TETRARCHY
Name given to the system of government introduced by DIOCLETIAN in the late 3rd century AD, in which rulership of the ROMAN EMPIRE was shared between four emperors. The empire was divided into eastern and western halves, each under a senior emperor, or "Augustus". Each Augustus ruled with the assistance of a junior colleague, or "Caesar", designated the successor to the Augustus. The system was intended to provide effective defense and bring stability to the imperial succession, but it quickly broke down after Diocletian's abdication in 305. ▷ 2.15

TEUTOBURGERWALD, BATTLE OF
Battle in AD 9, in which a Roman army under Varus was destroyed on the march by GERMANS under ARMINIUS, losing three legions and ending Roman attempts to conquer Germany. Recent finds of Roman military equipment have located the battlefield – about 16 kilometers (10 miles) north of the modern city of Osnabrück. ▷ 2.13, 2.19

TEUTONES
One of the ancient GERMAN tribes from Jutland in the late 2nd century BC. They invaded the ROMAN EMPIRE with the CIMBRI and were finally defeated at Vercellae in 101 BC. Their name was sometimes applied to the entire group of Germanic peoples. ▷ 2.19

THASOS
Island in the north Aegean known for its fertility and mineral wealth. Settled by the Greeks in about 650 BC, Thasos became prosperous and often extended its power onto the mainland of Thrace. A member of the DELIAN LEAGUE, it was occupied by ATHENS when it rebelled (465 BC). Later subdued by PHILIP II OF MACEDON, the island regained its prosperity in Roman times. ▷ 2.07

THEATER
The Greek theatron was originally the sitting place for an audience, though the word came to include the stage and buildings which formed the backdrop to it. Rudimentary at first, by the 4th century BC theaters were grandly built in stone or marble (as at Epidauros), and spread to the Roman world.

THEBES (GREECE)
Ancient settlement in southeastern Boeotia, an important Mycenaean center and the legendary birthplace of Heracles. The city re-emerged in the 6th century BC and for much of its history was preoccupied with maintaining control of the rich plain of Boeotia against the ambitions of ATHENS and Sparta. A stunning victory over Sparta at Leuctra in 371 BC saw Thebes become the most powerful state in GREECE for a short period, but after 360 BC it was of little importance. ▷ 2.08, 2.21

THEMISTOCLES
(c.524–459 BC) Athenian politician who was remembered for his skills in diplomacy and generalship. He was instrumental in building the Piraeus, the harbor in ATHENS, constructing a new navy from the city's silver resources, and masterminding the victory at SALAMIS. His later career was less fortunate. He was exiled from Athens and entered the service of the Persians before he died. ▷ 2.07

THEODORIC
King of Italy (r.AD 493–526), the OSTROGOTH Theodoric occupied the vacuum left by the collapse of the western empire. He tolerated Roman culture and his reign was a stable and effective one, though his Arian beliefs meant that Roman and Ostrogothic cultures remained distinct. He extended his kingdom to include parts of France and Spain. ▷ 2.17

THEODOSIAN DYNASTY
Dynasty founded by THEODOSIUS I. After his death in AD 395 it was divided, with one son, Arcadius, taking the east of the empire and another, HONORIUS, the west. Honorius saw only disintegration and withdrawal, but under Arcadius' successor, his son Theodosius II (emperor from AD 408 to 450), Constantinople was consolidated as the effective capital of the remaining empire. ▷ 2.16

THEODOSIUS I
Roman emperor from AD 379 to 395. Rising to power through his own abilities, Theodosius emerged as emperor in the east (AD 379) and, after campaigns in Italy, in the west (AD 387). He was the last emperor to rule the empire as a single unit. A devout Christian heavily influenced by AMBROSE, bishop of Milan, he ruthlessly imposed orthodox CHRISTIANITY on the empire. During his reign Gothic tribes were allowed to settle within Roman territory in return for providing armed support. ▷ 2.15, 2.16

THERAVADA BUDDHISM
The "Doctrine of the Elders", one of the major divisions of BUDDHISM, and the form most prevalent in Sri Lanka and southeast Asia. Theravada Buddhism was promoted by ASHOKA in the 3rd century BC, under whose influence it spread southward; it was taken to southeast Asia in the 11 to 14th centuries AD. It tends to be conservative and orthodox; the goal of the adherent is to achieve individual enlightenment. There is a strong monastic tradition. ▷ 2.06

THERMOPYLAE, BATTLE OF
Battle fought at the pass of Thermopylae by the Greeks, under the leadership of LEONIDAS and his force of Spartans, against the invading Persian army of 480 BC. Eventually the Persians crossed through the mountains behind the pass, but the Spartans fought heroically to the death, buying time for the rest of the Greek army to escape. ▷ 2.07

THREE KINGDOMS (CHINA)
The period of Chinese history between AD 220 and 265, following the collapse of the HAN DYNASTY. During these years, China was divided into the kingdoms of Wu, Wei and SHU. The Three Kingdoms period was briefly followed by the JIN DYNASTY. The period saw many Indian cultural influences enter China and is remembered in Chinese chivalry and folklore. ▷ 2.25

THREE KINGDOMS (KOREA)
Early period of Korean history (1st century BC to 7th century AD) in which the Korean peninsula was divided between the kingdoms of Koguryo, Silla and Paekche. ▷ 2.25

THUCYDIDES
(c.455–c.396 BC) One of the leading Greek historians, remembered for his detailed history of the PELOPONNESIAN WAR, written while the war was still being fought. Showing no illusions about the brutalities of war and power politics, Thucydides' work stands out for its colorful narratives and the powerful speeches he put in the mouths of its main characters. ▷ 2.08

TIAHUANACO (TIWANAKU)
Former city and religious center in the Andes, near Lake Titicaca, Bolivia. The site was occupied in the early centuries BC, but the Tiahuanaco state was formed in about AD 100. Its cultural influence spread throughout the Andean region. The site was abandoned in about 1000. Tiahuanaco is notable for its monolithic architecture, notably the Gateway of the Sun, carved with hieroglyphs and gods, and an intricate system of raised, irrigated fields capable of feeding its population of up to 50,000, despite an altitude of 4,000 meters (13,000 feet). ▷ 2.27

TIBERIUS
(r.AD 14–37) Born in 42 BC, he became the stepson of Octavian (AUGUSTUS) in 38 BC. After a successful military career, he was proclaimed emperor on Augustus' death in AD 14. A generally competent ruler, Tiberius became unpopular due to his unappealing manner, family jealousy and unscrupulous use of treason laws to destroy his political enemies – real or imagined. He retired to Campania in AD 27 and then to Capri, where he died in AD 37. The rumors of Tiberius indulging in vice on Capri are unsubstantiated. ▷ 2.04, 2.13

TIGRANES I
Armenian ruler (r.c.100–56 BC) who created a short-lived empire, which stretched from Parthia in the east to Syria and the Levant in the west, incorporating much of the decaying SELEUCID KINGDOM in the process (83 BC). Such expansion aroused Roman concern and Tigranes was forced back into Armenia by POMPEY. ▷ 2.10

TIKAL
Classic period MAYAN lowland city, now in northwestern Guatemala. Tikal came to prominence in the 5th century AD, when it had trading contacts throughout Mesoamerica, reaching as far as TEOTIHUACÁN. It contained five temple-pyramids and several palaces. It was excavated in the 1950s and 1960s. ▷ 2.28

TIWANAKU
See TIAHUANACO

TOBA (TABGATCH)
TURKIC-speaking nomadic people from Mongolia who invaded northern China in the 4th century AD. ▷ 2.25

TOBA WEI KINGDOM
Kingdom established in north China by the TOBA people in AD 439. The capital was initially at Pingcheng in the far north, but in 494 it was moved to Luoyang. The state endured until 534, when it split into eastern and western halves. ▷ 2.25

TOTILA
OSTROGOTHIC king (r.AD 541–52) who reconquered much of central and southern Italy, including Rome, from the eastern ROMAN EMPIRE. He died in battle, and the Romans regained the initiative once more. ▷ 2.17

TRAJAN
Roman emperor from AD 98 to 117. Born in AD 53 to a high-ranking family in Spain, he became emperor of Rome after the death of Nerva. Noted for his fair and considerate conduct, Trajan was respected by the senate, was reasonable in his dealings with the provinces, beloved by his troops – in whom he took a personal interest – and concerned with the welfare of the Roman people. He undertook a number of building projects to beautify and improve the facilities of Rome, including the construction of a new harbor at OSTIA, the Via Traiana and the new forum and basilica. He conquered DACIA (AD 101–02, 105–06), removing a potential threat to the empire's Danube frontier, but his conquests in Armenia and Parthia (115–17) were given up by his successor HADRIAN as being undefendable. ▷ 2.11, 2.13, 2.14, 2.15

TRAJAN'S COLUMN
Dedicated in AD 113 as part of TRAJAN'S forum at Rome, this 29-meter (95-foot) high marble column on a square sculpted base celebrated the emperor's military achievements. The detailed spiral reliefs on the shaft of the column, depicting Trajan's Dacian wars (AD 101–02, 105–06), were probably added after his death as a form of commemoration. ▷ 2.13

TRIREME
The standard Greek warship that was used most effectively by the Athenians in the 5th century BC (as at the BATTLE OF SALAMIS). Rowed by three banks of coordinated oarsmen, the galley was designed to ram its opponents at speed. Meticulous training and high morale were essential for its successful use. ▷ 2.07

TÚ-YÜ-HUN
TURKIC-speaking nomadic people of central Asia who threatened northwestern China in the 4th to 6th centuries AD. ▷ 2.25

TUNGUSIC
Language group spoken in eastern Siberia and northern Manchuria. Its speakers include the Tung-nu and the Manchus.

TURKIC LANGUAGES
Group of languages forming a subdivision of the ALTAIC languages, today including Turkish, Uzbeg, Azerbaijani, Tatar and Uighur, but historically also including many languages of the nomads of the east Asian steppes. ▷ 2.20

TURKISH KHANATES
The TURKIC-speaking confederation of tribes that established its authority over much of the central and east Asian steppes in the 6th century AD. ▷ 2.20

TWELVE TABLES
Tradition records that the Laws of the Twelve Tables – the basis of Roman law – were compiled in about 450 BC. Although the tradition cannot be confirmed, it is probable that they underlay the colonial charters of the late 4th century BC and were revised from the early 3rd century BC. ▷ 2.12

UAXACTÚN
Former MAYAN city of PETÉN in northern Guatemala, north of TIKAL. Although a minor site historically, it has yielded sufficient pottery remains to enable archeologists to construct a sequence of types of Mayan pottery. Important Preclassic discoveries were made at Uaxacún in the 1980s. The city flourished in the Classic period and declined in about AD 1000. ▷ 2.28

ULFILAS, BISHOP
(c.AD 311–83) Born into a Christian family and captured by the GOTHS, Ulfilas took on the mission of converting the Goths to Arian CHRISTIANITY, and translated the Bible into Gothic. The Arian Goths were shunned by orthodox Christians, which helps to explain the reluctance of the empire to come to terms with them. ▷ 2.15

UPANISHADS
Sacred texts of Hinduism and the final stage of the Vedas. There are more than 100 separate works, the most important of which were written from about 800 to 400 BC; the last date from AD 300 or later. They deal with speculative and philosophical issues in prose and verse, and stress the importance of Brahman, the doctrine of pure being.

VAKATAKA
Indian dynasty in the Deccan, said to have been founded by Vindhyasakti in about AD 260. From about 400 they were allied with the GUPTAS, but they took advantage of the Hunas invasions in the late 5th century to seize an empire in central India. The last known Vakataka king was Prithvishena II (c.470). ▷ 2.23

VALENS
Eastern Roman emperor from AD 364 to 378 and the brother of the western emperor, Valentinian I. He supported ARIANISM and began the persecution of orthodox Christians. He campaigned successfully against the VISIGOTHS but then allowed them into the empire in 376. He was killed at the BATTLE OF ADRIANOPLE. ▷ 2.15, 2.16

VALENTINIAN III
Western Roman emperor (r.AD 425–55) who presided over the final period of a determined defense of the empire by his military chief, AETIUS. Valentinian himself killed AETIUS in 454, fearing his political ambitions. The following year Valentinian was killed in a revenge attack by one of Aetius' retainers. Following Valentinian's death the western ROMAN EMPIRE lost all political stability and began its final disintegration. ▷ 2.16

VALERIAN
Roman emperor of senatorial origin who shared power with his son, Gallienus, between AD 253 and 260, at the height of the 3rd-century crisis. His main concern was to restore Roman control in the east, but he was captured, humiliated and killed by the Persian ruler SHAPUR I in 260. ▷ 2.11, 2.15

VANDALS
Germanic peoples who crossed over the Rhine in AD 406 and spread remorselessly through GAUL, Spain and eventually (under their impressive leader Gaiseric) into the rich Roman provinces of north Africa (429). They sacked Rome in 455, but were eventually conquered by JUSTINIAN's general, BELISARIUS, in 533. ▷ 2.15, 2.16, 2.17, 2.19

VANGA
Ancient kingdom of east Bengal, one of the *mahajanapadas* ("great realms") of the 6th century BC. It formed part of the MAURYAN empire and was later conquered by the GUPTAS. ▷ 2.22, 2.23

VANGIONES
GERMAN tribe that inhabited the west bank of the Rhine in the 5th century AD, and whose chief center was at modern Worms (known as Civitas Vangionum). The city was disputed by the Romans and Burgundians, and sacked by the HUNS (as Roman allies) in 436. It was rebuilt by the Merovingian kings. ▷ 2.16

VEII
The most southerly of the great Etruscan cities, 16 kilometers (10 miles) north of Rome, that was famous in antiquity for its terracotta statuary. In 396 BC the city was destroyed following a long siege by Rome, but a small settlement survived. Excavation has revealed extensive Villanovan cemeteries and the imposing extra-urban sanctuary of Portonaccio. ▷ 2.12

VENETI
The name given to two different groups in antiquity: a Celtic group in Brittany and part of Normandy which had strong links to southwest England (they were finally subdued by Rome in a naval battle of 56 BC), and a group that inhabited the fertile country around the head of the Adriatic; cultivated traders and horse-breeders, they were friendly to Rome and were probably granted full Roman citizenship in 49 BC. ▷ 2.18

VERACRUZ
Ancient civilization of the Gulf Coast of eastern Mexico of the Classic period (AD 1–700); its major center was at EL TAJÍN. It incorporated the remains of Olmec civilization and it was probably in Veracruz that the "long-count" calendar was devised, in the late 1st century BC. Veracruz was also deeply influenced by TEOTIHUACÁN. The BALLCOURT was a distinctive feature of Veracruz culture. ▷ 2.27

VERCINGETORIX
The son of a Gallic nobleman, he raised a coalition of peoples of central GAUL against JULIUS CAESAR in 52 BC. Caesar finally defeated Vercingetorix by successfully beseiging him at ALESIA, thereby effectively completing the Roman conquest of Gaul. Vercingetorix surrendered and was executed after Caesar's triumph of 46 BC. ▷ 2.18

VERGINA
A site in MACEDONIA that is now confirmed as the ancient capital of the Macedonian Teminid dynasty and the burial place of their kings. The most spectacular find has been the tomb, body and associated grave goods of PHILIP II. ▷ 2.08

VESPASIAN
Emperor of Rome from AD 69 to 79 and the founder of the FLAVIAN DYNASTY. Vespasian served as a soldier in Britain, Germany and Judaea, and asserted his claim to the throne by force. He sought to restore the finances of the state and celebrated the start of a new age of peace (despite completing the destruction of Jerusalem during a Jewish rebellion). He was succeeded by Titus.

VIJAYA
According to legend Vijaya was a prince of the 5th century BC, Bengali by origin, who was banished from his father's kingdom in Gujarat. He first colonized the island of Ceylon and established a dynasty on the west coast in 483 BC. The third king of the Vijaya dynasty established the kingdom of ANURADHAPURA and his descendants continued to rule there until AD 65. ▷ 2.22

VIMA KADPHISES
Kushan king from about AD 75 to 100 who conquered much of northern India. ▷ 2.23

VIRGIL
Roman poet (70–19 BC) from Mantua who was in the circle of AUGUSTUS. Most famous for his epic poem the *Aeneid*, which claims a Trojan origin for the Roman people, he also wrote the *Eclogues* and the *Georgics*, both celebrations of country life. ▷ 2.13

VISIGOTHS
Distinct group of GOTHS (probably western Goths) that emerged in the 4th century AD. They were admitted to the ROMAN EMPIRE in 376 as refugees from the HUNS. Badly treated, they rebelled in 378, defeating and killing the emperor VALENS in 378 at ADRIANOPLE. In search of land in the empire for themselves, they ravaged their way through GREECE and Italy (sacking Rome under ALARIC in 410), and were eventually settled in Aquitaine as foederati in 418. By 480 they had taken over southern GAUL and most of Spain. ▷ 2.04, 2.05, 2.15, 2.16, 2.17, 2.19

VITRUVIUS POLLIO, MARCUS
Roman military architect who served JULIUS CAESAR and AUGUSTUS. He is best known for his treatise, *De Architectura*, which was addressed to Augustus and stressed the intellectual and technical demands of the profession. ▷ 2.13

VOTADINI
Celtic tribe inhabiting the Scottish lowlands in the Roman period. Their capital was at Traprain Law, but they moved to Edinburgh in about AD 500, when they established the kingdom of Gododdin.

VOUILLÉ, BATTLE OF
Decisive battle in western France (AD 507) between the FRANKS, led by CLOVIS, and the VISIGOTHS. As a result, the Franks established their domination over present-day France and confined the Visigoths to the Iberian peninsula. The battle also ensured the victory of Catholicism over ARIANISM in the Frankish kingdoms. ▷ 2.17

VULGATE BIBLE
Translation by ST JEROME (AD 347–420) of the Old Testament and NEW TESTAMENT from Hebrew and GREEK into LATIN. The first accessible and reliable text of the Bible for the ordinary (Latin-speaking) reader in western Europe, it represents one of the great achievements of early Christian scholarship.

WANG MANG
Chinese nobleman, also known as "the usurper", who overthrew the western HAN DYNASTY in AD 6 and became regent for the child he had made emperor. Three years later Wang Mang claimed the throne himself, as the first of the Xin dynasty. He attempted to introduce land reform, without success. Rebellions occurred after devastating floods and famine in northern China and the Han were restored in AD 23. ▷ 2.24

WUDI (SIMA YEN)
First emperor of the short-lived JIN DYNASTY of China (r.AD 265–89), who came to power as a soldier in the northern kingdom of Wei and usurped its throne in 265. He attempted to reduce the power of the aristocracy, but was unable to protect China from BARBARIAN invasions. His title, Wudi, meant "martial emperor". ▷ 2.25

XENOPHON
(c.428–354 BC) Aristocratic Greek historian, soldier and politician. Originally from ATHENS, in his varied career he also served with a Spartan army. Xenophon is remembered for his vivid account of the March of the TEN THOUSAND and the *Hellenica*, an outline of Greek history from 411 to 362 BC and one of the few sources for the period, even if not now seen as a reliable one. ▷ 2.08

XERXES I
Son of DARIUS I and king of PERSIA from 486 to 465 BC. Xerxes is remembered in European history for his meticulously planned invasion of GREECE in 480 BC, which ended in failure. The expedition was probably only a minor incident during his reign, which was one of comparative stability. ▷ 2.07, 2.09

XIANYANG
The site in China, some 60 kilometers (40 miles) from Xi'an in modern Shaanxi province, of the tomb of the first QIN emperor, SHI HUANGDI. The tomb contained a terracotta army of 6,000 life-sized models of soldiers and horses. ▷ 2.24

XIAO GONG
King of QIN from 361 to 338 BC and – in partnership with his minister SHANG YANG – initiator of Qin's rise to dominance in China. Their reforms of administration, military service and trade strengthened Qin in both peace and wartime. ▷ 2.24

XIONGNU (HSIUNG-NU)
TURKIC-speaking nomadic peoples of the east Asian steppes. From 300 BC they repeatedly threatened northern China, prompting the Chinese to begin building a system of defensive walls. Raids continued until the late 2nd century BC, after which the Xiongnu split in two. The Xiongnu were permitted to settle inside the wall and their generals claimed to control northern China briefly in the 4th century AD, but from the 5th century the Xiongu disappeared. Xiongnu graves have revealed goods from Iran and GREECE. ▷ 2.20, 2.24, 2.25

YAMATO PERIOD
Period of Japanese history (AD 300–710) in which the authority of the emperor was first established and the distinctive Japanese culture began to emerge. During this period vast KEYHOLE TOMBS were built for the emperors, indicative of a hierarchical society.

From about AD 600 political centralization began, following the model of China; by 700 the state had established its authority over most of Japan. The capital was at ASUKA. BUDDHISM was introduced from Korea in 552, and ambassadors were sent to China in the 7th century.

YAXCHILÁN
Late Classic MAYAN city of the central area (now in Mexico). It is a river-based center, and its first *stelae* (stone monuments) date from about AD 300; the last date from the early 9th century. ▷ 2.28

YAYOI CULTURE
The Bronze and Iron Age culture of Japan (300 BC–AD 300), marked by the spread of wet-rice cultivation and the establishment of the first petty states. The potter's wheel was also known. Yayoi culture, a development of Jomon culture, was first established in Kyushu, Shikoku and southern Honshu, and gradually spread northward. It is named after the district of Tokyo where its artifacts were discovered. ▷ 2.25

YEAR OF FOUR EMPERORS
After NERO's suicide in AD 68 civil war erupted over the succession. Galba (r.68–69), Otho (r.69) and Vitellius (r.69) all reigned briefly, until stability was restored by VESPASIAN (r.69–79). ▷ 2.13

YUE
Vietnamese-speaking tribes in northern Vietnam and southern China who formed the kingdoms of NAN-YUE and MIN-YUE in the late 1st millennium BC. ▷ 2.24

YUE QI (INDO-SCYTHIANS)
IRANIAN-speaking nomads of central Asia and the Gansu region around the time of JESUS. Driven from their homelands by the XIONGNU in the early 2nd century BC, they moved to BACTRIA and eventually formed the KUSHAN empire. The Yue Qi were influential in the spread of BUDDHISM from India to China. ▷ 2.20, 2.23, 2.24

ZEALOT
Jewish faction, deriving from the revolt of the MACCABEES in the 2nd century BC, that fought to establish an independent Jewish kingdom according to the Torah. The Zealots became an organized force during the reign of HEROD (r.37–4 BC) and led a rebellion against a Roman census in AD 6. They were known as *sicarii* ("dagger-men") for their policy of assassination. After their revolt of AD 66–73, which led to the destruction of the Temple of Jerusalem by the Romans, the Zealots were much weakened.

ZENO
(335–263 BC) Greek philosopher who arrived in ATHENS in 313 BC and founded Stoicism (so-called because his discussions were held

under a stoa, an open-air colonnade). Followed by the STOICS, it was a highly influential philosophy not only for the Greeks, but for Romans and Christians as well. ▷ 2.09

ZENOBIA
Formidable queen of the Syrian trading city of PALMYRA. Zenobia established an independent empire, which extended as far as Egypt and Asia Minor, during a crisis in the ROMAN EMPIRE in the AD 260s. At first tolerated by the Romans as a bulwark against PERSIA, she was subdued by the emperor AURELIAN in 272, though her life was spared. ▷ 2.15

ZHANG QIAN
Chinese explorer (d.114 BC) who was the first to travel to central Asia (from 138) and bring back a reliable account of his journeys. On his first journey he visited the YUE QI and was held for ten years by the XIONGNU. His second journey took him to BACTRIA and Soghdiana, and brought China in contact with HELLENISTIC civilization.

ZHAO
Northern Chinese kingdom and one of the strongest states of the Warring States period. In 307 BC it introduced new cavalry techniques, imported from the nomads of the north, to China. However, it was conquered by QIN in 228 BC. ▷ 2.24

ZHENG (FIRST EMPEROR)
See SHI HUANGDI

ZHONGSHAN
Small northern Chinese kingdom of the Warring States period, conquered by ZHAO in 296 BC. ▷ 2.24

ZHOU, NORTHERN
See NORTHERN ZHOU

ZOROASTRIANISM
Ancient religion that emerged in PERSIA in the 6th century BC, founded by the prophet Zoroaster (c.630–c.550 BC), about whose life little definite is known. Its holy books are the *Avesta* and the *Zend Avesta*. Zoroastrianism sees the world in terms of a cosmic struggle between the forces of good (and light), led by AHURA MAZDA, and those of evil (and dark). Its ceremonies often show particular veneration for fire. Zoroastrianism was the religion of Achemenid, Parthian and SASANIAN Persia. Through its offshoot, MITHRAISM, it influenced the ROMAN EMPIRE and CHRISTIANITY in particular. It is still practiced in Iran and elsewhere; Indian adherents are known as Parsis. ▷ 2.06, 2.11

Text, timelines and maps
The authors and publishers readily acknowledge the work of a large number of scholars and published works, on which they have drawn in the preparation of this atlas. Many of these works remain in print, and can be used as reliable secondary reading on the many topics covered in this atlas. Among them are the following:

al Faruqi, Ismail Ragi (ed) *Historical Atlas of the Religions of the World* (New York and London 1974)
Allchin, B and R *The Birth of Indian Civilization: India and Pakistan before 500 BC* (London, 2nd ed 1994)
Bahn, Paul G (ed) *Cambridge Illustrated History of Archaeology* (Cambridge and New York 1996)
Baines, John and Malek, Jaromir *Atlas of Ancient Egypt* (Oxford and New York, 1980)
Barraclough, G (ed) *The Times Atlas of World History* (4th ed , London 1993 and New York 1994)
Beek, MA *Atlas of Mesopotamia* (London 1962)
Blunden, Caroline and Elvin, Mark *Cultural Atlas of China* (London and New York, 1986)
Boardman, J *The Greeks Overseas* (London 1964)
Bolton, Geoffrey (ed) *The Oxford History of Australia* (Oxford and Melbourne 1994)
Bonsall, C *The Mesolithic in Europe* (Edinburgh 1989)
Chadwick, Henry and Evans, Gillian R (eds) *Atlas of the Christian Church* (London and New York, 1987)
Champion, T, Gamble, C, Shennan, S and Whittle, A *Prehistoric Europe* (London 1984)
Chang, KC *The Archaeology of Ancient China* (Yale 1977)
Chard, CS *Northeast Asia in Prehistory* (Madison, USA 1974)
Coe, Michael, Snow, Dean and Benson, Elizabeth *Atlas of Ancient America* (London and New York, 1986)
Coe, Michael *Mexico: from the Olmecs to the Aztecs* (London and New York 4th ed 1994)
Cohn-Sherbok, D *Atlas of Jewish History* (London and New York 1994)
Coles, JM and Harding, AF *The Bronze Age in Europe* (London 1979)
Connah, G *African Civilizations: Precolonial cities and states in tropical Africa* (Cambridge and New York 1987)
Cook, JM *The Persian Empire* (London 1983)
Cornell, Tim and Matthews, John *Atlas of the Roman World* (London and New York, 1982)
Cotterell, A *East Asia* (London 1993, New York 1995)
Crawford, M *The Roman Republic* (London 1978, Cambridge, Mass 1993)

Cunliffe, Barry (ed) *The Oxford Illustrated Prehistory of Europe* (Oxford and New York 1994)
Davies, JK *Democracy and Classical Greece* (London 2nd ed 1993)
Davis, Norman *Europe: a History* (Oxford and New York 1996)
de Lange, Nicholas *Atlas of the Jewish World* (London and New York, 1984)
Elliott, JH (ed) *The Hispanic World* (London and New York 1991)
Fagan, Brian M T*he Journey from Eden: the Peopling of our World* (London and New York 1990)
Fagan, Brian M *Ancient North America* (London and New York 1995)
Fagan, Brian M *People of the Earth* (New York and London, 7th ed 1992)
Fage, JD and Oliver, R (eds) *The Cambridge History of Africa* (Cambridge and New York 1975–)
Fage, JD *An Atlas of African History* (London 1978)
Falkus, M and Gillingham J *Historical Atlas of Britain* (London and New York revised ed 1987)
Fiedel, SJ *Prehistory of the Americas* (Cambridge and New York, 2nd ed 1992)
Freeman-Grenville, GSP *Historical Atlas of the Middle East* (New York 1993)
Frye, RN *The Heritage of Persia* (London 2nd ed 1976)
Gamble, C *The Palaeolithic Settlement of Europe* (Cambridge 1986)
Gamble, C *Timewalkers: the Prehistory of Global Colonization* (Stroud 1993, Cambridge, Mass. 1994)
Gaur, A *A History of Writing* (London 1984, New York 1994)
Gilbert, Martin *The Atlas of Jewish History* (London and New York 5th ed 1996)
Green, MJ *The Celtic World* (London and New York 1995)
Grosser Historischer Weltatlas (3 vols (Munich 1981)
Hall, DGE *A History of South-east Asia* (London 4th ed 1981)
Hood, S *The Minoans* (London and New York 1973)
Johnson, Gordon, Bayly, C and Richards JF T*he New Cambridge History of India* (Cambridge 1987–)
Johnson, Gordon *Cultural Atlas of India* (London 1995, New York, 1996)
Kemp, BJ *Ancient Egypt* (London 1989, New York 1992)
Kinder, H and Hilgemann, W *Atlas of World History* (2 vols, Munich, London and New York 1974)
Kuhrt, A *The Ancient Near East* (2 vols, London and New York 1995)
Kulke, H and Rothermund, D *A History of India* (London 1990)
Langer, William L *An Encyclopedia of World History* (5th ed, London and New York 1973)
Levi, Peter *Cultural Atlas of the Greek World* (London and New York, 1984)

Ling, T *A History of Religion East and West* (London 1968)
Mallory, JP *In Search of the Indo-Europeans* (London 1989, New York 1991)
Moore, RI (ed) *The Hamlyn Historical Atlas* (London 1981)
Moseley, ME *The Incas and their Ancestors* (London and New York 1993)
Murray, Oswyn *Early Greece* (London 2nd ed 1993)
Phillipson, DW *African Archaeology* (Cambridge, 2nd ed 1993)
Roaf, Michael and Postgate, Nicholas *Cultural Atlas of Mesopotamia and the Ancient Near East* (London and New York, 1990)
Roberts, JM *The Hutchinson History of the World* (London 1976)
Rogerson, John *Atlas of the Bible* (London and New York 1985)
Scarre, Dr Chris *Past Worlds : The Times Atlas of Archaeology* (London and New York, 1988)
Schmidt, KJ *An Atlas and Survey of South Asian History* (New York and London 1995)
Schwartzberg, Joseph E (ed) *A Historical Atlas of South Asia* (Chicago and London, 2nd ed 1992)
Sharer, RJ *The Ancient Maya* (Stanford Ca 5th ed 1994)
Shepherd, William R. *Shepherd's Historical Atlas* (New York and London, 9th ed 1974)
Sinor, D (ed) *The Cambridge History of Early Inner Asia* (Cambridge 1990)
Smith, BD *The Emergence of Agriculture* (New York 1995)
Taylour, W *The Mycenaeans* (London and New York 2nd ed 1990)
The Times Atlas of the World (London and New York, 8th ed 1990)
Todd, M *The Early Germans* (Oxford and Cambridge, Mass. 1992)
Twitchett, D and Fairbank, J (eds) *The Cambridge History of China* (15 vols, Cambridge and New York 1978–91)
Vincent, Mary and Stradling, RA *Cultural Atlas of Spain and Portugal* (London 1994, New York 1995)
Walbank, FW *The Hellenistic World* (London 3rd ed 1992, Cambridge, Mass. 1993)
Watson, F *India, a Concise History* (London and New York 1993)
Whittle, A *Neolithic Europe: a Survey* (Cambridge and New York 1985)

Artwork
Artwork references have been assembled from a wide variety of sources. Any individual or institution who can demonstrate that copyright may have been infringed is invited to contact Andromeda Oxford Ltd.

Photographs
Introduction Telendos: Images Colour Library.